CW00496864

SCHOLASTIC

National Curriculum
MATHS

Teacher's

PLANNING & ASSESSMENT GUIDE

Years 3-4

NATIONAL CURRICULUM

TEXTBOOKS

Key Stage 2

Scholastic Education, an imprint of Scholastic Ltd
Book End, Range Road, Witney, Oxfordshire, OX29 0YD
Registered office: Westfield Road, Southam,
Warwickshire CV47 0RA
www.scholastic.co.uk

© 2016, Scholastic Ltd

1 2 3 4 5 6 7 8 9   6 7 8 9 0 1 2 3 4 5

British Library Cataloguing-in-Publication Data
A catalogue record for this book is available from the British Library.

ISBN 978-1407-16026-9

Printed and bound by Ashford Colour Press

All rights reserved. This book is sold subject to the condition that it shall not, by
way of trade or otherwise, be lent, hired out or otherwise circulated without the
publisher's prior consent in any form of binding or cover other than that in which
it is published and without a similar condition, including this condition, being
imposed upon the subsequent purchaser.

No part of this publication may be reproduced, stored in a retrieval system, or
transmitted, in any form or by any means, electronic, mechanical, photocopying,
recording or otherwise, other than for the purposes described in the content of
this product, without the prior permission of the publisher. This product remains
in copyright.

Due to the nature of the web we cannot guarantee the content or links of any
site mentioned. We strongly recommend that teachers check websites before
using them in the classroom.

Every effort has been made to trace copyright holders for the works reproduced
in this book, and the publishers apologise for any inadvertent omissions.

Extracts from National Curriculum for England, Maths Programme of Study ©
Crown Copyright. Reproduced under the terms of the Open Government Licence
(OGL). www.nationalarchives.gov.uk/doc/open-government-licence/version/3/

Author Paul Hollin
Editorial Rachel Morgan, Jenny Wilcox, Mary Nathan, Red Door Media
Cover and Series Design Neil Salt and Nicolle Thomas
Layout Neil Salt
CD-ROM Development Hannah Barnett, Phil Crothers and MWA
Technologies Private Ltd

Table of Contents Year 3

Table of Contents Year 4

About the Planning and Assessment Guides

Scholastic National Curriculum Mathematics scheme provides schools and teachers with a flexible scheme of work to meet all of your needs for the mathematics curriculum, allowing you to keep control of what you teach, and when, while saving precious teacher time.

The scheme consists of four components:
- Teacher's *Planning and Assessment Guide*
- Children's *Textbook*
- *100 Maths Lessons* resource books and CD-ROMs
- Children's *Maths Practice Book*

The main benefits of the programme include:
- Accessible content geared towards the demands of the National Curriculum.
- Flexibility to fit into the way you already teach using the award-winning *100 Maths Lessons* teacher's books.
- Detailed support in the *Textbooks* to build secure foundations and deep understanding of key concepts.
- A bank of well-structured exercises in the practice books linked to clear explanations, which parents can understand and use to help their children.

Using the Planning and Assessment Guide

This book provides guidance on how to introduce topics (including how quickly) and how to support and extend the content in the *Textbook*. It references the accompanying *100 Maths Lessons* and *Practice Books* so you can use this material to further support learning. Each teaching notes page uses the same heading structure:

- **Prior learning:** details what the children should already know prior to introducing this content.
- **Curriculum objectives and Success criteria:** provides information about which National Curriculum objectives the section covers and the specific success criteria which will come from it.
- **Learn:** relates to the 'Learn' heading in the *Textbook*, but it also goes beyond this and helps you to introduce the learning appropriately.
- **Talk maths:** relates the the 'Talk maths' heading in the *Textbook* but will often extend ideas for these activities to provide plenty of opportunity for speaking and listening.
- **Activities and Problems:** gives pointers for those activities in the *Textbook*, as well as giving ideas to extend or support the learning.
- *100 Maths Lessons* and *Practice Book* links: these detail related lessons and activities that you can use to enhance and further develop the teaching and learning of the subject area.

Planning and Assessment CD-ROM

The accompanying CD-ROM contains planning and assessment tools, the majority of these have been supplied as a word document so you can edit them to meet your needs. They can be used as effective tools for monitoring performance, identifying areas of weakness and communicating to parents.

Tracking progress

- **Maths progression overview:** gives an overview of the whole maths curriculum across Years 1–6.
- **Teacher tracking:** breaks down an individual year group into three stages of progress 'working towards', 'working at expected level' and 'working at greater depth'.
- **Child progress chart:** 'I can' statements related to the *Textbook*. The children tick to show whether they are 'not sure', are 'getting there' or 'have got' a concept.
- **I can statements:** a cut out format of the 'I can' statements from the child progress chart.

Planning and reporting templates

For templates – see the template menu on the CD-ROM.
- **Yearly, Termly and Weekly planning:** plan your teaching – templates and completed samples.
- **Termly report:** feed back to parents – templates and completed samples.

Other resources

- **Assessment framework for maths:** printable DfE Interim Teacher Assessment frameworks for mathematics
- **Curriculum links:** printable version of the curriculum links found on pages 8–11 of this book.
- **Glossary:** printable version of a child-friendly and age-appropriate mathematics glossary

Planning with Scholastic Maths

Although the series is arranged in line with the National Curriculum, teachers will need to plan a varied scheme of work for mathematics that provides opportunities to revisit objectives, in particular arithmetic, as well as allowing room for periodic assessment.

Most schools plan their mathematics curriculum with an emphasis on number and calculation, with thematic focuses planned on a weekly, fortnightly or termly basis, usually with flexibility to allow for extended or enriching topics, recapping difficult areas, repeated practice of key arithmetic skills, and focused assessments.

The table on pages 8–11 of this book provides the curriculum objectives with page references to the *Textbook*, *100 Maths Lessons* and *Practice Book* to assist your planning.

About the Textbooks

Using the Textbooks

The *Textbook* and *Planning and Assessment Guide* are arranged thematically and are completely in line with the National Curriculum, allowing teachers and Mathematics subject leaders to create long- and medium-term plans best suited to the school's needs. Each section of the *Textbook* presents the 'core' learning for that curriculum area, with the relevant pages in the *Planning and Assessment Guide* providing further advice and links to additional lessons and resources, in particular to *100 Maths Lessons* and *Maths Practice Book*.

Textbook structure

Each section has a similar structure (although single-page topics may not have Tips or Maths talk guidance).

- **Learn:** examples and facts specific to the objective in question.
- **Tips:** short and simple advice to aid understanding.
- **Talk maths:** focused activities to encourage verbal practice.
- **Activities:** a focused range of questions, with answers provided in the *Planning and Assessment Guide*.
- **Problems:** word problems requiring mathematics to be used in context. The problems are often pitched at two different levels enabling you to identify whether children can apply key mathematical concepts or skills.

Remember that the *Planning and Assessment Guide* provides advice and links for extending learning and practice in each of these areas.

Written methods for short multiplication

Learn

We know that multiplication is repeated addition.
$4 \times 7 = 7 + 7 + 7 + 7 = 28$
We have also looked at some mental methods for doing multiplications in your head.
$12 \times 20 = 12 \times 10 \times 2 = 120 \times 2 = 240$
Sometimes calculations are just too hard to do in your head.
1247×6
That's when it's time to use a **formal written method**.

We know that our number system uses these place-value columns:
1000s, 100s, 10s and 1s.
To make multiplication easier, we can use formal written methods using these columns.

When multiplying a larger number by a number less than 10, you must multiply each digit at the top by the single digit. If necessary, carry 1s, 10s or 100s, and then add them.

```
    2  3  5
 ×        4
 ─────────────
    9  4  0
    1  2
```

We call this short multiplication.

Notice how $4 \times 5 = 20$. We carry the two 10s and leave zero 1s in the 1s column. Also $4 \times 3 = 12$. We carry the one 100, then in the 10s column we add the two carried 10s to the two 10s and write 4 in this column. $4 \times 2 = 8$ but we need to add the carried 100 which makes 9, so we write 9 in the 100s column. So the answer is 940.

✓ Tips

- To carry out short multiplication, you still need to know your multiplication facts.
- And don't forget, you can estimate your answer. Use this to check that your formal written method gives you the size of answer you expect.
  For example, 124×6 will be a more than 720 but less than 780.
  ($6 \times 120 = 720$, $6 \times 130 = 780$)

Make sure you know your times tables facts!

Talk maths

Look at the short multiplications below and explain them aloud. Say how each stage was done.

```
a.      3  4        b.      4  6  2
   ×        4           ×         6
   ──────────           ─────────────
        1  3  6             2  7  7  2
           1                  3  1
```

Remember: you still have to multiply zeros, and anything times zero is... zero!

Activities

1. Copy and complete each of these short multiplications.

```
a.     3 8      b.    4 5 7     c.    3 4 2     d.    8 0 6
   ×      3         ×     2         ×     4         ×     5
   ───────         ───────         ───────         ───────
```

2. Multiply. Use a written method for short multiplication.
   a. 153×3 b. 267×2 c. 538×4 d. 1273×6

Problems

Brain-teaser
A school's tuck shop sells muesli bars for 7p each.
143 bars are sold. How much money is collected?

Brain-buster
The school tuck shop also sells cartons of juice for 20p each.
125 children buy a muesli bar and a carton of juice.
How much money is collected altogether?

26   Calculations

Calculations   27

Tracking progress

Assessment is always an ongoing process – formative assessments provide feedback to teacher and child for next steps; summative assessment provides snapshots of a child's current competence.

There is a self-assessment chart for children on the CD-ROM (Child progress chart). This is intended as a method of engaging children in considering their own achievement; it might also be referenced by teachers in making their own judgements. Each 'I can' statement is a generalisation for each section in the *Textbook*. These statements are also provided in a cut out and stick format.

The CD-ROM also provides a progression overview document – summarising the progress between year groups and a teacher tracking grid that allows you to track more detailed progress within a year group. The teacher tracking grid breaks each curriculum objective down into working towards the expected standard, working at the expected standard or working with greater depth. Each of these terms is explained below.

Working towards the expected standard

At this stage, children are able to access the objective at a simple level, or with some kind of support, whether from an adult, a peer or via some form of supportive resource. For example, children might be able to count in steps of two, but only using counting cubes or a number line. If questioned further they will not necessarily be able to explain the processes involved. Children requiring support to complete work may:

- correctly use skills with apparatus.
- solve simple problems.
- have difficulty correcting mistakes.
- talk about the concepts to some extent, with limited mathematical vocabulary.

Working at the expected standard

Children working at the expected level on a mathematical objective will be able to fulfil the essence of the objective independently. So, for counting in twos, they will be able to do this unsupported by person or resource, and will demonstrate a clear understanding of the process and their work. In talking about their work they will show an awareness of the mathematics involved, and may be able to apply it to solve problems in other contexts. Indications that children are working at the expected standard for a particular objective include:

- consistently apply skills correctly within the specified content.
- correctly use facts and procedures to solve straightforward problems.
- correct their own mistakes in work marked by others.
- provide straightforward explanations of their work and the concepts involved.

Working at greater depth

This category suggests that children have mastered the objective involved. They can recall facts easily, talk about them and use them in different contexts. Indicators that children are working at greater depth include:

- rapid application of the skills using different numbers.
- creative use of facts and procedures to solve unfamiliar, complex and multi-step problems.
- spot errors and self-correct them.
- reason about and clearly explain concepts, freely using correct mathematical terminology.

DFE interim guidance (2015) on Mathematics assessment is available on the CD-ROM.

Scholastic Maths and Mastery

There are many definitions of 'mastery' in maths. As well as judging how much a child has learned, it is important to assess how well they apply their learning. The National Curriculum includes the requirement for children to be able to apply their learning in different contexts, thereby deepening their knowledge, before moving onto new learning. The level to which they can make connections and apply their learning is one such definition of mastery.

Scholastic National Curriculum Mathematics offers many opportunities for children to demonstrate a skill or recall a number fact using the *100 Maths Lessons* content. To deepen or embed these skills the *Maths Practice Books* and *Textbooks* offer a range of well-structured practice exercises. Children can then go on to apply these skills using the range of problems in the *Textbooks* or the 'assess and review' content in *100 Maths Lessons*. The range of opportunities within the programme to embed or apply maths skills therefore should provide teachers with sufficient evidence to track how secure maths concepts are and whether they have truly been mastered by each child.

An individual report template has been provided on the CD-ROM to feed back to parents how well their child can apply their skills that they have learned. This might be done termly or at other times when children have attained a secure level of mastery in a particular area.

Curriculum objectives	Year 3 Textbook	100 Maths Lessons Year 3	Year 3 Practice Book
Number and place value			
Count from 0 in multiples of 4, 8, 50 and 100; find 10 or 100 more or less than a given number.	Pages: 6–7, 12–13, 14–15	Pages: 14–19, 90–95, 172–177	Pages: 6, 7, 8, 9, 12, 13
Recognise the place value of each digit in a 3-digit number (100s, 10s, 1s).	Pages: 10–11	Pages: 8–13, 90–95, 172–177	Pages: 10, 11
Compare and order numbers up to 1000.	Pages: 8–9	Pages: 8–13, 90–95, 172–177	Pages: 14, 15, 16
Identify, represent and estimate numbers using different representations.	Pages: 16–17	Pages: 90–95, 172–177	Pages: 18, 19, 20, 21
Read and write numbers up to 1000 in numerals and in words.	Pages: 8–9	Pages: 8–13, 90–95, 172–177	Pages: 14, 15, 16
Solve number problems and practical problems involving these ideas.	Pages: 16–17	Pages: 90–95, 172–177	Pages: 18, 19, 20, 21
Addition and subtraction			
Add and subtract numbers mentally, including: • a 3-digit number and 1s • a 3-digit number and 10s • a 3-digit number and 100s.	Pages: 18–19	Pages: 20–25, 49–54, 96–101, 184–189	Pages: 22, 23, 24, 25, 26, 27, 28, 30, 31
Add and subtract numbers with up to three digits, using formal written methods of columnar addition and subtraction.	Pages: 20–21, 22–23	Pages: 55–60, 131–137, 190–195, 213–219	Pages: 34, 35, 36
Estimate the answer to a calculation and use inverse operations to check answers.	Pages: 24–25	Pages: 55–60, 96–101, 131–137, 184–189, 213–219	Pages: 32, 33
Solve problems, including missing number problems, using number facts, place value, and more complex addition and subtraction.	Pages: 26–27	Pages: 20–25, 55–60, 96–101, 131–137, 184–189, 190–195, 213–219	Pages: 29, 38–39, 40, 41
Multiplication and division			
Recall and use multiplication and division facts for the 3, 4 and 8 multiplication tables.	Pages: 28–29	Pages: 26–31, 61–66, 102–106, 107–112	Pages: 42–43, 44–45, 46, 47, 50, 51, 64, 65
Write and calculate mathematical statements for multiplication and division using the multiplication tables that they know, including for 2-digit numbers times 1-digit numbers, using mental and progressing to formal written methods.	Pages: 30–31	Pages: 138–142, 143–147, 178–183, 220–225, 226–231	Pages: 52, 53, 54–55, 56, 57, 58–59, 60, 61, 62
Solve problems, including missing number problems, involving multiplication and division, including positive integer scaling problems and correspondence problems in which n objects are connected to m objects.	Pages: 32–33	Pages: 107–112, 143–147, 220–225, 226–231	Pages: 48–49, 63, 66–67, 68–69
Fractions			
Count up and down in tenths; recognise that tenths arise from dividing an object into 10 equal parts and in dividing 1-digit numbers or quantities by 10.	Pages: 34–35	Pages: 154–159, 232–237	Pages: 81, 82
Recognise, find and write fractions of a discrete set of objects: unit fractions and non-unit fractions with small denominators.	Pages: 36–37	Pages: 67–72, 154–159, 232–237	Pages: 70, 72, 75
Recognise and use fractions as numbers: unit fractions and non-unit fractions with small denominators.	Pages: 38–39	Pages: 67–72, 154–159, 232–237	Pages: 71, 73, 74
Recognise and show, using diagrams, equivalent fractions with small denominators.	Pages: 40–41	Pages: 154–159, 232–237	Pages: 76, 77, 78
Add and subtract fractions with the same denominator within one whole.	Pages: 44–45	Pages: 232–237	Pages: 80
Compare and order unit fractions, and fractions with the same denominators.	Pages: 42–43	Pages: 67–72, 154–159	Pages: 79
Solve problems that involve all of the above.	Pages: 46–47	Pages: 67–72, 154–159, 232–237	Pages: 74, 83–84, 85

Curriculum objectives	Year 3 Textbook	100 Maths Lessons Year 3	Year 3 Practice Book
Measurement			
Measure, compare, add and subtract: lengths (m/cm/mm); mass (kg/g); volume/capacity (l/ml).	Pages: 48–49, 50–51, 52–53, 68–69, 70–71, 72–73	Pages: 32–37, 148–153, 201–206	Pages: 86, 87, 88, 89, 90, 91, 92–93, 94, 95, 102, 103, 104
Measure the perimeter of simple 2D shapes.	Pages: 64–65	Pages: 32–37	Pages: 108
Add and subtract amounts of money to give change, using both £ and p in practical contexts.	Pages: 66–67	Pages: 113–118	Pages: 100–101
Tell and write the time from an analogue clock, including using Roman numerals from I to XII, and 12-hour and 24-hour clocks.	Pages: 54–55, 56–57, 58–59	Pages: 238–243	Pages: 96
Estimate and read time with increasing accuracy to the nearest minute; record and compare time in terms of seconds, minutes and hours; use vocabulary such as o'clock, am/pm, morning, afternoon, noon and midnight.	Pages: 60–61	Pages: 238–243	
Know the number of seconds in a minute and the number of days in each month, year and leap year.	Pages: 62–63	Pages: 238–243	Pages: 97, 98, 99, 104, 105
Compare durations of events.	Pages: 60–61, 62–63	Pages: 238–243	Pages: 97, 98, 99, 104, 105
Geometry			
Draw 2D shapes and make 3D shapes using modelling materials; recognise 3D shapes in different orientations and describe them.	Pages: 76–77, 78–79	Pages: 38–43, 119–124	Pages: 106, 107, 108, 109, 111, 114, 115, 116, 117
Recognise angles as a property of shape or a description of a turn.	Pages: 80–81	Pages: 119–124	Pages: 111, 112, 113
Identify right angles, recognise that two right angles make a half-turn, three make three quarters of a turn and four a complete turn; identify whether angles are greater than or less than a right angle.	Pages: 80–81	Pages: 119–124	Pages: 111, 112, 113
Identify horizontal and vertical lines and pairs of perpendicular and parallel lines.	Pages: 74–75	Pages: 196–200	Pages: 110
Statistics			
Interpret and present data using bar charts, pictograms and tables.	Pages: 82–83, 84–85	Pages: 79–84, 160–165, 244–248	Pages: 118, 119, 120, 121, 122, 123, 124, 125
Solve one-step and two-step questions using information presented in scaled bar charts and pictograms and tables.	Pages: 82–83, 84–85	Pages: 79–84, 160–165, 244–248	Pages: 118, 119, 120, 121, 122, 123, 124, 125

Curriculum objectives	Year 4 Textbook	100 Maths Lessons Year 4	Year 4 Practice Book
Number and place value			
Count in multiples of 6, 7, 9, 25 and 1000.	Pages: 10–11	Pages: 8–12, 172–177	Pages: 6–7, 8, 9, 24, 25
Find 1000 more or less than a given number.	Pages: 6–7	Pages: 8–12, 90–95, 172–177	Pages: 18
Count backwards through zero to include negative numbers.	Pages: 12–13	Pages: 172–177	Pages: 10
Recognise the place value of each digit in a 4-digit number (1000s, 100s, 10s and 1s).	Pages: 6–7	Pages: 8–12, 90–95, 172–177	Pages: 11, 12, 25
Order and compare numbers beyond 1000.	Pages: 6–7	Pages: 8–12, 90–95, 172–177	Pages: 13, 14
Identify, represent and estimate numbers using different representations.	Pages: 8–9	Pages: 8–12, 90–95, 172–177	Pages: 22, 23
Round any number to the nearest 10, 100 or 1000.	Pages: 8–9	Pages: 8–12, 90–95, 172–177	Pages: 19, 20, 21
Solve number and practical problems that involve all of the above and with increasingly large positive numbers.	Pages: 6–7, 8–9, 10–11, 12–13	Pages: 8–12, 90–95, 172–177	Pages: 6–7, 8, 9, 10, 11, 12, 13, 14, 15, 18, 19, 20, 21, 22, 23, 24, 25
Read Roman numerals to 100 (I to C) and know that over time, the numeral system changed to include the concept of zero and place value.	Pages: 14–15	Pages: 90–95	Pages: 16–17
Addition and subtraction			
Add and subtract numbers with up to four digits using the formal written methods of columnar addition and subtraction where appropriate.	Pages: 16–17, 18–19, 20–21	Pages: 13–18, 49–54, 96–101, 131–136, 137–141, 183–188, 213–218	Pages: 26, 27, 28, 29, 30, 31, 32, 33, 34, 35, 36, 37, 38, 39, 49
Estimate and use inverse operations to check answers to a calculation.		Pages: 13–18, 49–54, 96–101, 131–136, 137–141, 183–188	Pages: 40, 41
Solve addition and subtraction two-step problems in contexts, deciding which operations and methods to use and why.	Pages: 18–19	Pages: 49–54, 96–101, 137–141, 183–188	Pages: 32, 33, 36, 38, 39, 49
Multiplication and division			
Recall multiplication and division facts for multiplication tables up to 12 × 12.	Pages: 22–23	Pages: 19–24, 25–29, 55–60	Pages: 50, 51, 52, 53, 54, 55
Use place value, known and derived facts to multiply and divide mentally, including: multiplying by 0 and 1; dividing by 1; multiplying together three numbers.	Pages: 24–25, 28–29	Pages: 19–24, 25–29, 61–65, 107–112, 147–152, 189–193, 230–235	Pages: 56, 57, 58, 60, 61, 62–63, 64, 65, 66, 67, 68–69, 70, 71, 75
Recognise and use factor pairs and commutativity in mental calculations.	Pages: 24–25	Pages: 19–24, 25–29, 55–60	Pages: 59, 66, 67
Multiply 2-digit and 3-digit numbers by a 1-digit number using formal written layout.	Pages: 26–27	Pages: 55–60, 102–106, 147–152, 189–193, 230–235	Pages: 72–73, 74
Solve problems involving multiplying and adding, including using the distributive law to multiply 2-digit numbers by 1-digit, integer scaling problems and harder correspondence problems such as n objects are connected to m objects.	Pages: 24–25	Pages: 19–24, 25–29, 55–60	Pages: 56, 57, 58, 60, 61, 62, 63, 64, 65, 66, 67, 68, 69, 70, 71
Fractions and decimals			
Recognise and show, using diagrams, families of common equivalent fractions.	Pages: 30–31	Pages: 66–70, 113–117, 194–199	Pages: 76, 77, 80, 81
Count up and down in hundredths; recognise that hundredths arise when dividing an object by one hundred and dividing tenths by ten.	Pages: 34–35	Pages: 66–70, 113–117, 194–199	Pages: 86, 87
Solve problems involving increasingly harder fractions to calculate quantities, and fractions to divide quantities, including non-unit fractions where the answer is a whole number.		Pages: 66–70	Pages: 78
Add and subtract fractions with the same denominator.	Pages: 32–33	Pages: 194–199	Pages: 82, 83
Recognise and write decimal equivalents of any number of tenths or hundredths.	Pages: 36–37	Pages: 118–123, 194–199, 219–224	Pages: 79, 84, 85
Recognise and write decimal equivalents to ¼, ⅓, ¾.	Pages: 36–37	Pages: 118–123, 194–199, 219–224	Pages: 79, 84, 85

Curriculum objectives	Year 4 Textbook	100 Maths Lessons Year 4	Year 4 Practice Book
Fractions and decimals (continued)			
Find the effect of dividing a 1- or 2-digit number by 10 and 100, identifying the value of the digits in the answer as 1s, tenths and hundredths.	Pages: 38–39	Pages: 118–124, 219–224	Pages: 88–89
Round decimals with one decimal place to the nearest whole number.	Pages: 38–39	Pages: 118–124	Pages: 90
Compare numbers with the same number of decimal places up to two decimal places.	Pages: 38–39	Pages: 118–124	Pages: 91
Solve simple measure and money problems involving fractions and decimals to two decimal places.		Pages: 219–224	Pages: 90
Measurement			
Convert between different units of measure.	Pages: 40–41, 48–49, 50–51	Pages: 36–41, 159–164, 178–182, 200–205, 219–224	Pages: 46, 47, 92, 93, 96, 97, 98, 102
Measure and calculate the perimeter of a rectilinear figure (including squares) in centimetres and metres.	Pages: 52–53	Pages: 36–41, 200–205	Pages: 94, 95, 103
Find the area of rectilinear shapes by counting squares.	Pages: 54–55	Pages: 200–205	Pages: 94, 95
Estimate, compare and calculate different measures, including money in pounds and pence.	Pages: 46–47, 48–49, 50–51	Pages: 36–41, 96–101, 159–164, 178–182, 200–205	Pages: 42, 43, 44, 45, 46, 47, 48, 92, 93, 96, 97, 98, 101, 102
Read, write and convert time between analogue and digital 12- and 24-hour clocks.	Pages: 44–45	Pages: 77–82, 142–146	Pages: 99
Solve problems involving converting from hours to minutes; minutes to seconds; years to months; weeks to days.	Pages: 42–43	Pages: 77–82, 142–146	Pages: 100
Geometry			
Compare and classify geometric shapes, including quadrilaterals and triangles, based on their properties and sizes.	Pages: 57, 58–59	Pages: 71–76, 153–158, 236–241	Pages: 104, 105, 106, 107
Identify acute and obtuse angles and compare and order angles up to two right angles by size.	Pages: 56	Pages: 71–76, 153–158, 236–241	Pages: 108, 111
Identify lines of symmetry in 2D shapes presented in different orientations.	Pages: 60–61	Pages: 30–35, 236–241	Pages: 109, 110, 112, 113
Complete a simple symmetric figure with respect to a specific line of symmetry.	Pages: 60–61	Pages: 30–35	Pages: 112, 113
Describe positions on a 2D grid as coordinates in the first quadrant.	Pages: 62–63	Pages: 71–76, 153–158, 236–241	Pages: 114, 115, 116, 117
Describe movements between positions as translations of a given unit to the left/right and up/down.	Pages: 64–65	Pages: 153–158, 236–241	Pages: 119
Plot specified points and draw sides to complete a given polygon.	Pages: 62–63, 64–65	Pages: 71–76, 153–158, 236–241	Pages: 114, 115, 116, 117, 119
Statistics			
Interpret and present discrete and continuous data using appropriate graphical methods, including bar charts and time graphs.	Pages: 68–69, 70–71	Pages: 77–82, 159–164, 242–247	Pages: 120, 121, 125
Solve comparison, sum and difference problems using information presented in bar charts, pictograms, tables and other graphs.	Pages: 66–67, 68–69, 70–71	Pages: 77–82, 159–164, 242–247	Pages: 122, 123, 124, 125

Counting in multiples

Prior learning

- Can count in steps of 2, 3 and 5 from zero, and in 10s from any number, forward and backward.

Learn

- Draw a number line from 0 to 10 on the board. With the children, count from zero in steps of 1 and then 2, pointing out that the steps are the same size each time. Next, use a longer number line to count in steps of 5 and 10.

- Display a 100-square and look at the patterns that counting in steps of 2, 5 and 10 create.

- Move on to counting in 4s and 8s on a number line and then on a 100-square. Work with the children to consider the patterns involved, pointing out that every other multiple of 4 is also a multiple of 8.

- Separately, introduce counting in steps of 50 and 100 on a number line. Make the point that every

other multiple of 50 is also a multiple of 100. Moving back to the 100-square, can the children spot any similar relationships between multiples of 2, 5 and 10?

- *100 Maths Lessons Year 3, Autumn 1, Week 2* has a sequence of lessons on counting in steps, which includes use of interactive teaching resources on the CD-ROM.

Curriculum objectives

- To count from 0 in multiples of 4, 8, 50 and 100; find 10 or 100 more or less than a given number.

Success criteria

- I can count in steps of 4 and 8, and 50 and 100.

Counting in multiples

Learn

You can count in multiples of 5 and 10 on a number line.

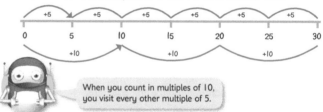

When you count in multiples of 10, you visit every other multiple of 5.

You can also count in multiples of 4 and 8 on a number line.

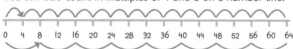

Look carefully at the two counts. What do you notice?

This number line shows how we count in multiples of 50 and 100.

Every other multiple of 4 is also a multiple of 8.

What do you notice about these two counts?

Every other multiple of 50 is also a multiple of 100.

✓ Tip

Hello! Here are some tips on multiples!

Double a multiple of 4 to find the multiple of 8.
$6 \times 4 = 24$ $6 \times 8 = 48$

Double a multiple of 50 to find the multiple of 100.
$4 \times 50 = 200$ $4 \times 100 = 400$

- Ask the children to work in small groups or pairs to practise counting in steps of different sizes. This can be made more fun by having them create chants, songs, try turn-taking going around the group, counting backwards, and so on.

- The questions in the textbook and the *Year 3 Practice Book* provide opportunities to count on from numbers other than zero. Children who are not ready for this might be provided with a number line and counting apparatus to support their learning.

- Challenge the children to apply their counting skills to other problems, such as considering packing items in pairs, 5s or 10s. Try basing problems around the number of children in the class, considering how many would be left over if they were grouped in 2s, 3s, 4s, and so on.

Talk maths

Read these counts out loud.

Count in 4s:	0	4	8	12	16	20	24	28	32	36	40
Count in 8s:	0	8	16	24	32	40	48	56	64	72	80
Count in 100s:	0	100	200	300	400	500	600	700	800	900	1000
Count in 50s:	0	50	100	150	200	250	300	350	400	450	500

Did you know?

Did you know that you can count in thousands in the same way?
0, 1000, 2000, 3000, 4000, 5000

Activities

Copy these counts and add the missing numbers.

1. 8, ___, 12, 20, ___, ___, ___
2. 16, 24, ___, ___, ___, 56, ___
3. 150, 200, 250, ___, ___, ___
4. 300, 400, ___, ___, ___, ___, 900
5. 1000, 900, 800, ___, ___, ___, ___

Problems

Brain-teaser
Sally writes all the multiples of 50, from 0 to 600. Which numbers does she write?

Brain-buster
Jon counts in 4s. Paul counts in 8s. They both start on 16 and they finish on 48. Which numbers do they both say?

Number and place value   7

100 Maths Lessons Year 3 links:

- Autumn 1, Week 2 (pages 14–19): count in steps of 4, 8, 50 and 100
- Spring 1, Week 1 (pages 90–95): count forwards and backwards from larger numbers
- Summer 1, Week 1 (pages 172–177): count in steps and investigate number patterns

Year 3 Practice Book links:

- (page 7): Counting in 8s
- (page 8): Counting in 50s
- (page 9): Counting in 10s and 100s

Numbers to 1000

Prior learning

- Can read and write numbers to at least 100 in numerals and words.

Learn

- Review the use of 10s and 1s for writing whole numbers. Using apparatus if desired, look at how we can write numbers up to 100 using only the digits 0–9. Remind the children of the importance of zero as a placeholder.
- Move on from 2-digit numbers to 3-digit numbers, focusing on the value that each digit represents according to its position. Move on to introduce the < and > signs, working with a range of numbers to consider their relative values. Demonstrate to the children how we read the numbers left to right to assess their value, both in themselves and relative to other numbers.
- *100 Maths Lessons Year 3, Autumn 1, Week 1* provides structured activities and focused resources to develop and consolidate this work.

Curriculum objectives

- To compare and order numbers up to 1000.
- To read and write numbers up to 1000 in numerals and in words.

Success criteria

- I can read, write, order and compare 3-digit numbers in numerals and words.

Numbers to 1000

Learn

tens	ones
7	2

Here is a 2-digit number.
The 7 represents 7 tens. The 2 represents 2 ones. This makes 72.

Look at this 3-digit number.
The first digit tells you how many hundreds.
The second digit tells you how many tens.
The third digit tells you how many ones.

hundreds   tens   ones

456

To compare two numbers, look at the hundreds digit in each number first.
Read this statement aloud. For the symbol > say *is bigger than*.

$$654 > 456 \text{ because } 6 > 4$$

If the hundreds digits are the same, look at the tens digits.
Read this statement aloud. For the symbol < say *is smaller than*.

$$325 < 381 \text{ because } 2 < 8$$

We can compare more than two numbers in the same way and put them in order. For example, $456 < 546$ and $546 < 645$, so $456 < 546 < 645$.

When you read numbers in words, remember to think about place value. If a number has no tens, or no ones, you need to write a 0.

We write two hundred and six as 206.

✓ Tip

Remember to check the hundreds digit first when comparing numbers. Then check the tens, then the ones. If you get mixed up with the > and < symbols just think of the symbol as the mouth of a crocodile – the crocodile always eats the bigger number!

Talk maths

- Using the numbers in the textbook as a starting point, challenge the children to arrange a set of numbers in increasing and decreasing order. As with all maths discussion work, ensure that key vocabulary is modelled, and check that children are using it correctly.

- This activity can be repeated using other numbers shown in numerals or in words. If children are to work with numbers written in words, point out the use of the hyphen (as in thirty-seven) and the use of 'and' (as in one hundred and three).

Activities

- The questions in the textbook and the activities in the *Year 3 Practice Book* provide practice and reinforcement. The links to *100 Maths Lessons Year 3* provide some more open-ended ideas for activities.

- Naturally, children will benefit from repeated, short activities to build familiarity with the concepts and spellings involved.

Problems

- The Brain-buster can be simplified or extended as desired by providing different sets of numbers. For children who are struggling, spend time practising with numbers lower than 100, and then move on to arranging numbers between 100 and 200, and so on.

Talk maths

Say these numbers in order. Start with the smallest.

312   516   499   844   484   488

Now read these numbers.

four hundred and thirteen

six hundred and forty-seven

nine hundred and ninety

- Which number has the smallest tens?
- Which number has the largest ones?
- Which number is closest to one thousand?

Activities

1. Write these numbers in digits.
   a. three hundred and sixty-five   b. two hundred and fifteen

2. Now write these numbers in words.
   a. 804   b. 970

3. Write these numbers in order, starting with the smallest.
   735   573   537   753   357

4. Copy these pairs of numbers and insert < or > to compare them.
   a. 321 243   b. 645 654   c. 720 702

Problems

Brain-buster
Sally makes four piles of swap cards. The first pile has 425 cards, the second pile has 245 cards, the third pile has 542 cards and the fourth pile has 524 cards. Write the number of cards in each pile in size order, starting with the smallest.

Number and place value   9

100 Maths Lessons Year 3 links:

- Autumn 1, Week 1 (pages 8–13): read, write and order 2- and 3-digit numbers
- Spring 1, Week 1 (pages 90–95): order 2- and 3-digit numbers
- Summer 1, Week 1 (pages 172–177): compare and order 2- and 3-digit numbers

Year 3 Practice Book links:

- (page 14): Number order
- (page 15): Numbers in digits and words
- (page 16): Number word match

Place value

Prior learning

- Can recognise the place value of each digit in a 2-digit number (10s, 1s).

Learn

- Present the children with a selection of 2-digit, and then 3-digit numbers. Work together to establish the value of each digit. For example, the value of 4 in 745 is 40. Point out the importance of zero as a place holder, and consider how numbers can be compared to each other as bigger, smaller or the same.

- Using number squares like that on page 10 of the textbook (there is an interactive number square on the CD-ROM for *100 Maths Lessons Year 3*), look at numbers between 201 and 300, 301 and 400, and so on. Work with the children to look at both rows and columns, noticing when the 10s digit remains the same and when it increases or decreases, and similarly for the 1s. Can the children identify patterns and differences? Demonstrate how 3-digit numbers can be partitioned into 100s, 10s and 1s.

- *100 Maths Lessons Year 3, Spring 1, Week 1* also has lessons that can support this work.

Curriculum objectives

- To recognise the place value of each digit in a 3-digit number (100s, 10s, 1s).

Success criteria

- I can say what each digit in a 3-digit number means.

Place value

Learn

hundreds	tens	ones
4	2	6

This number is made from 4 hundreds and 2 tens and 6 ones.

Here is a number square.

301	302	303	304	305	306	307	308	309	310
311	312	313	314	315	316	317	318	319	320
321	322	323	324	325	326	327	328	329	330
331	332	333	334	335	336	337	338	339	340
341	342	343	344	345	346	347	348	349	350
351	352	353	354	355	356	357	358	359	360
361	362	363	364	365	366	367	368	369	370
371	372	373	374	375	376	377	378	379	380
381	382	383	384	385	386	387	388	389	390
391	392	393	394	395	396	397	398	399	400

Look carefully at the numbers in the number square.

All the numbers in each column have the same ones digit.
Look at the third column. All the numbers have 3 as their ones digit.

All the numbers in each row have the same tens digit.
Look at the fifth row. All the numbers have 4 as their tens digit.

Find 356 in the number square. 356 has 3 hundreds and 5 tens and 6 ones. So 356 can be partitioned like this:
356 = 300 + 50 + 6
We can also partition 356 like this:
356 = 200 + 150 + 6

Can you think of another way to partition 356?

- Ask the children to work in pairs to partition a selection of 3-digit numbers into 100s, 10s and 1s. Challenge them to represent this as an addition. Ensure also that they consider how to partition numbers that have a zero in them, and perhaps practise writing each of these numbers in words.

Activities

- The questions in the textbook require the children to convert between words and numerals as well as understand partitioning. The *Year 3 Practice Book* activities listed provide good consolidation.
- Children who are struggling should have as much practice as possible in reading, ordering and comparing 2- and 3-digit numbers. They could use packs of 0–9 digit cards to make 2- and 3-digit numbers, and say the numbers they've made aloud.

Problems

- Note that the Brain-buster is a multi-step that involves addition and subtraction. Work through both with the children to model systematic approaches and the usefulness of neat layout.

Talk maths

Say these numbers aloud. What does each number represent? How could you partition them? Which number is the largest?

374   *365*   **408**   **273**

Activities

1. Write in digits the number with five hundreds and six tens and seven ones.

2. A number can be partitioned like this: 300 + 270 + 6. Write the number in digits.

3. A number can be partitioned like this: six hundred + two hundred and forty + sixteen. Write the number in digits.

4. Partition the number 379.

Problems

Brain-teaser
In a shop there are 300 red pens, 130 blue pens and six black pens. How many pens are there altogether?

Brain-buster
The shopkeeper also sells pencils. Yesterday he counted 200 black pencils, 250 green pencils and there were no red pencils. Then he sold 25 green pencils. How many pencils does the shopkeeper have now?

100 Maths Lessons Year 3 links:

- Autumn 1, Week 1 (pages 8–13): recognise the value of each digit in 3-digit numbers
- Spring 1, Week 1 (pages 90–95): partition 3-digit numbers into 100s, 10s and 1s
- Summer 1, Week 1 (pages 172–177): use the place value of numbers to solve problems

Year 3 Practice Book links:

- (page 10): Place value: 3-digit numbers
- (page 11): Place value patterns

Finding 10 or 100 more or less

Prior learning

- Can count in 10s forwards and backwards from any number.

- Write a selection of 1-, 2- and 3-digit numbers on the board and challenge the children to say the number that is one less or one more than each of those shown. For example, for 237, they should say 236.
- Demonstrate the finding 10 more or 10 less than a selection of 2-digit numbers, using equipment or a 100-square if desired. Eventually, move on to considering 10 more or 10 less than a selection of 3-digit numbers, where the 10s digit is 1–8. Consider how the 100s and 1s digits are unchanged.
- Return to this over a number of sessions, gradually introducing 3-digit numbers with 9 or zero in the 10s place – in other words, the 100s will change when finding 10 more or 10 less, respectively.
- Separately, repeat all of the above for adding and subtracting 100 from 3-digit numbers.

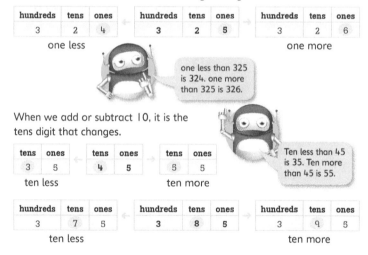

Curriculum objectives

- To count from 0 in multiples of 4, 8, 50 and 100; find 10 or 100 more or less than a given number.

Success criteria

- I can find 10 or 100 more or less than a 3-digit number.

- Provide groups of children with a selection of 3-digit numbers and ask them to challenge each other to answer one of these questions about each number: *What is 10 more? What is 10 less? What is 100 more? What is 100 less?* More confident learners might progress to adding and subtracting multiples of 10 or 100 to or from each number. Place value arrow cards for making numbers may provide good support for those struggling with the concepts involved.

Activities

- Note that questions 5 and 6 involve multiples of 10. Also, the *Year 3 Practice Book* provides good consolidation activities.

Problems

- Both problems involve money, and can be easily rewritten with different amounts to provide extended problem-solving practice.
- If desired, use similar problems to challenge children to add and subtract 11, 101 and 111.

Talk maths

Say aloud what is ten more than each number. Say aloud what is ten less than each number. Say aloud what is thirty more than each number. Say what is one hundred more or less than each number. How did you work it out?

777

503   **491**

665

Activities

Write the number that is:

1. ten more than 523.
2. ten less than 601.
3. one hundred more than 750.
4. one hundred less than 532.
5. eighty more than 246.
6. ninety less than 139.

Problems

Brain-teaser
Sang has £493 in his savings bank. He gives Kwan £100. How much money does Sang have now?

Brain-buster
Cai counts how much money she has. There is £507 in her savings account. She gives Hoa £100. Then she gives Hoa another £10. How much money does Cai have now?

100 Maths Lessons Year 3 links:

- Autumn 1, Week 2 (pages 14–19): find 1 or 10 or 100 more or less than 2- and 3-digit numbers
- Spring 1, Week 1 (pages 90–95): find 10 or 100 more or less than a given number

Year 3 Practice Book links:

- (page 12): 10 more or less
- (page 13): 100 more or less

Number patterns

Prior learning

- Can count in steps of 2, 3 and 5 from zero, and in 10s from any number, forward and backward.

Learn

- Using number lines and a 100-square as appropriate, review children's knowledge of counting in steps of 2, 5 and 10, progressing to steps of 3, 4 and 8, and finally to using steps of 50 and 100. For all of these sizes of steps, also practise counting backwards.

- Spend time looking at the patterns created on a 100-square by the different multiples.

- Using a 100-square, choose a random number to start at and count in 2s, 5s and 10s, noting that although the starting position is random, the pattern generated can be used to predict subsequent numbers in the pattern. Note also that the numbers in the sequence are not necessarily multiples of the number used for counting in steps.

- If appropriate, move on to patterns that come from counting back in steps.

- *100 Maths Lessons Year 3, Spring 1, Week 1* has activities and resources for developing children's awareness of number patterns.

Curriculum objectives

- To count from 0 in multiples of 4, 8, 50 and 100; find 10 or 100 more or less than a given number.

Success criteria

- I can identify a number pattern, continue the pattern and find missing numbers.

Number patterns

Learn

You should recognise this number pattern.

15   20   25   30

> What are the next three numbers in the pattern?

These are multiples of 5. Each number is five more than the previous number.

In this number pattern, the numbers get smaller.   28   24   20   16

These are multiples of 4. Each number is four less than the previous number.

Look at the number pattern on the hundred square.
Look at the shaded numbers. Each number is eight more than the previous number. So we can add 8 to find the next three numbers in the pattern.
$64 + 8 = 72, 72 + 8 = 80, 80 + 8 = 88$

1	2	3	4	5	6	7	8	9	10
11	12	13	14	15	16	17	18	19	20
21	22	23	24	25	26	27	28	29	30
31	32	33	34	35	36	37	38	39	40
41	42	43	44	45	46	47	48	49	50
51	52	53	54	55	56	57	58	59	60
61	62	63	64	65	66	67	68	69	70
71	72	73	74	75	76	77	78	79	80
81	82	83	84	85	86	87	88	89	90
91	92	93	94	95	96	97	98	99	100

You can use a number line to help you count on.
Look at this number pattern.

38   42   46   ★   ★   ★

Each number is four more than the previous number.

✓ Tip

Use whichever tool you find most helpful – a number square or a number line.
You can count along the rows or down the columns of a number square to look for number patterns.

- Ask the children to choose a number randomly from the 100-square on page 14 of the textbook. Discuss the patterns either side of it, starting with 2, 5 and 10, progressing to steps of 3, 4 and 8 as desired.

- To make this more challenging, provide each group with two packs of cards – one pack of random numbers between 1 and 100, the other with counting steps (for example 2, 3, 4, 5, 8, 10). Children take it in turns to turn a card over from each pile and state the subsequent pattern. Provide individual 100-squares for support as necessary.

Activities

- The textbook questions may be tricky for some children. If so, the *Year 3 Practice Book* activity is simpler, and there are support activities in *100 Maths Lessons Year 3, Spring 1, Week 1.*

Problems

- Ask the children who complete the problems to create their own, using similar wording to the book. Remind them that they must be sure of the answer before they can challenge anyone to try their problems.

- Extend this work further by creating problems based on money or other countable objects – farmyard animals, children in school, pencils in pots, and so on.

Talk maths

Read these number patterns aloud. What do you need to add to find the next number? Say the missing numbers.

45 50 55 60 65 ★ ★ ★
25 22 19 ★ ★ ★ 7 4

What do you notice about the numbers?

Find the mistake in this pattern. Say the correct pattern.
19 23 27 30 35 39
Explain to a partner how you found the mistake.

One number is missing from this pattern. Say the correct pattern.
100 104 108 116 120 124

Activities

1. Copy these patterns and write the next three numbers.
   a. 5, 45, 85, ___, ___, ___
   b. 150, 200, 250, ___, ___, ___

2. Find the mistakes in these patterns. Write them correctly.
   a. 11, 14, 17, 23, 26, 29
   b. 96, 90, 84, 80, 74, 68

Problems

Brain-teaser
Tom drew a number line, starting at 46. He counted on 3, and wrote the number. He did this five more times. What numbers did he write?

Brain-buster
David drew a number line and wrote 24 at the beginning of the line. Then he counted on 5 and wrote the number. He did that another ten times. Paul drew a number line and wrote 14 at the beginning. Then he counted on 10 and wrote that number. He did this another six times. Which numbers did both boys write on their number lines?

100 Maths Lessons Year 3 links:

- Autumn 1, Week 2 (pages 14–19): recognise counting patterns
- Spring 1, Week 1 (pages 90–95): investigate number patterns on a 100-square
- Summer 1, Week 1 (pages 172–177): create and investigate number patterns

Year 3 Practice Book links:

- (page 6): Counting in 3s, 4s and 5s

Solving number problems

Prior learning

- Can use place value and number facts to solve problems.

Learn

Learn

- Review all the counting and pattern skills developed so far, reminding children of the use of number lines, 100-squares and equipment they may have used. Explain that the main focus now is to use these skills in everyday situations.

- First, discuss the examples in the textbook. Then present the children with a range of simple money problems that involve subtracting £1, £10 or £100 from given prices. Move on to adding and subtracting multiples of £10 and £100 as appropriate, modelling suitable approaches to presenting work clearly and carefully.

- Over multiple sessions, try to cover the different multiples and skills covered so far: recognising place value, counting in multiples, using number patterns, and adding and subtracting 10 and 100.

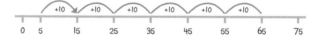

Solving number problems

Learn

You can use the skills you have learned so far to help you solve word problems.

This question asks you to count on. You can draw a number line to help you. Sam counts on from 5 in tens six times. What numbers does she say?

Look at this problem: Tim goes shopping. He wants to buy a new tablet computer. Which shop has the cheapest price?

First work out the price of the computer at each shop.

Buy Me Cheap: £455 − £100 = £355
Computer Express: £365 − £10 = £355
Geeks Rule: £440 − £100 = £340

Then compare the prices.

£340 < £355 so Geeks Rule is the cheapest.

Need help with number problems? No problem!

✓ Tip

Make sure you show your working with problems like these so that others can see how you thought through the problem. Don't panic when you see a lot of words! Read the question slowly and write down the calculations you need to do.

16   Number and place value

Curriculum objectives

- To solve number problems and practical problems involving counting place value.
- To identify, represent and estimate numbers using different representations.

Success criteria

- I can solve number problems using my number skills.

Talk maths

- After using the textbook examples as a starting point, ask the children to create and ask their own money problems. Provide each group with clear limits as to the amounts they can choose – such as adding and subtracting £10 or multiples of £10 from amounts between £100 and £200. The aim here is for children to relate the numbers to everyday contexts.

Activities

- The word problems provide a good starting point for further exercises, and the *Year 3 Practice Book* has ample practice material.
- If desired, *100 Maths Lessons Year 3, Spring 1, Week 1, Lesson 5* has activities and resources to develop children's use of place value in solving problems.

Problems

- Notice that the Brain-teaser problem is a two-step problem, involving subtraction and addition. It is important to model appropriate methods and layout for solving this correctly.

Talk maths

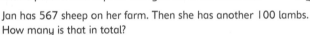

How would you solve these problems? Talk through them with a partner and explain how you know the answers.

Jan has 567 sheep on her farm. Then she has another 100 lambs. How many is that in total?

Paul has £157. His grandfather gives him another £10. Then Paul spends £100. How much money does he have now?

Activities

Answer these questions. Write down your working out. If there are units of measurement in the question, remember to write the units in your answer.

1. James measures some rope. It is 659cm long. He cuts off 100cm. How much rope does he have left?

2. There are 650 litres of water in a tank. 100 litres are poured out. Then 10 litres are added to the tank. How much water is in the tank now?

3. The sand in the blue sand timer runs through in 180 seconds. The sand in the red sand timer runs through 10 seconds slower than the blue sand timer. How long does the red sand timer take?

Problems

Brain-teaser
There are 640 children in the school. 100 of the children will leave in July. Another 10 children will come to the school in September. How many children will there be at the school in September?

Brain-buster
Dilshad writes the digits 579. He makes as many different numbers from these three digits as he can. What is the largest number he can make?

100 Maths Lessons Year 3 links:

- Spring 1, Week 1 (pages 90–95): use place value to solve money problems
- Summer 1, Week 1 (pages 172–177): use place value to solve number problems

Year 3 Practice Book links:

- (page 18): Rounding
- (page 19): Estimating and approximating
- (page 20): Multiples problem
- (page 21): Face value problems

Mental methods for addition and subtraction

Prior learning

- Can recall and use addition and subtraction facts to 20 fluently, and derive and use related facts up to 100.

Learn

- Recap the mental methods for addition and subtraction that the children have already encountered, either in the current year or in previous years.
- The textbook focuses on mental methods for adding 1s, 10s and 100s. (*100 Maths Lessons Year 3, Summer 1, Week 3* also focuses on this.)
- You should be able to cover all the required mental strategies for this age range by combining the activities in the textbook with the techniques covered in the links to *100 Maths Lessons Year 3*. The *Year 3 Practice Book* activities provide plenty of practice. It is recommended that you spread the different mental strategies over several sessions, revisiting them regularly in short, focused sessions. For the strategy in focus, model how to apply them to examples. Ideally, build up a permanent classroom display that shows examples for each.

Curriculum objectives

- To add and subtract numbers mentally, including:
  - a 3-digit number and 1s
  - a 3-digit number and 10s
  - a 3-digit number and 100s.

Success criteria

- I can use mental methods to add and subtract.

Mental methods for addition and subtraction

Learn

Sometimes it helps to break up the number you are adding or subtracting.

To add a 1-digit number to a 3-digit number, add enough ones to make the next ten, then add on the rest of the ones.

$$326 + 7 = 326 + 4 + 3 = 330 + 3 = 333$$

You can do the same to subtract. Subtract enough ones to leave 0 ones, then subtract the rest of the ones.

$$423 - 8 = 423 - 3 - 5 = 420 - 5 = 415$$

Or you could subtract 10 and then adjust the answer. For example, instead of subtracting 8, you could subtract 10 and then add 2.

$$423 - 8 = 423 - 10 + 2 = 413 + 2 = 415$$

To add tens to a 3-digit number, add the two tens digits together.

$$427 + 30 = 420 + 30 + 7 = 450 + 7 = 457$$

Or count on three tens from 427: 437, 447, 457

To subtract, take away the tens and then add the ones back.

$$527 - 30 = 520 - 30 + 7 = 400 + 120 - 30 + 7 = 400 + 90 + 7 = 497$$

Or count back three tens from 527: 517, 507, 497

To add hundreds to a 3-digit number, add the hundreds digits together.

$$438 + 300 = 400 + 300 + 38 = 700 + 38 = 738$$

Or count on three hundreds from 438: 538, 638, 738

To subtract, take away the hundreds and then add the tens and ones back.

$$927 - 400 = 900 - 400 + 27 = 500 + 27 = 527$$

Or count back four hundreds from 927: 827, 727, 627, 527

Talk maths

- Mental methods lend themselves well to oral work. The textbook demonstrates how certain calculations might be completed using mental methods. Provide the children with a selection of calculations that could be completed using one or more mental strategy. Challenge the children to complete each calculation and provide clear explanations of their method.

Activities

- The textbook questions can easily be extended to cover different strategies in isolation or combined together. The *Year 3 Practice Book* has a wide range of activities, including activities that challenge children to decide on the best method to use.

Problems

- Note that the Brain-buster is a two-step problem. If children are comfortable with solving this problem, provide them with money problems that have three or more steps.

Talk maths

Talk through these additions and subtractions with a partner. Make sure you understand them.

456 + 3	You know that 6 + 3 = 9 so 456 + 3 = 459.
527 − 3	You know that 7 − 3 = 4 so 527 − 3 = 524.
222 + 80	Add 20 and 80 to make 100. So 222 + 80 = 200 + 100 + 2 = 302.
516 − 60	Try this: 516 − 10 − 50 = 506 − 50 = 456.
451 + 300	Here just add the hundreds digits. So that makes 751.
621 − 400	Take away the 4 hundreds from 6 hundreds. This leaves 221.

This is slightly trickier.

Activities

Think about the best way for you to solve these mentally, then write the answers.

1. 392 + 5
2. 747 − 8
3. 391 + 40
4. 503 + 40
5. 321 + 200
6. 654 − 300

Problems

Brain-teaser
Peter has £652 in the bank. His grandfather gives him another £50. How much money does he have now?

Brain-buster
Megan has £205 to spend. She buys an MP3 player for £40 and an album for £6. How much money does Megan have now?

Calculations 19

Formal written addition methods

Prior learning

- Can mentally add 2-digit numbers.
- Can add three 1-digit numbers.

Learn

- Review children's understanding of number facts to 20 and how these can be used when adding multiples of 10. Move on to demonstrating how partitioning can be used to add two 2-digit numbers with no carrying 10s forward, such as 23 + 51. Progress to numbers that require a 10 to be carried forward, such as 48 + 35. Spend time considering how our number system allows this to work.

- Demonstrate two methods for adding two 3-digit numbers – partitioning and column addition – and consider the benefits and issues of them. Avoid examples that involve carrying 10s, intially.

- Note that the links to *100 Maths Lessons Year 3* has various units that focus on addition. *100 Maths Lessons Year 3, Summer 1, Week 4* deals specifically with columnar addition of numbers with up to three digits.

Curriculum objectives

- To add and subtract numbers with up to three digits, using formal written methods of columnar addition and subtraction.

Success criteria

- I can use formal written methods to add 2-digit and 3-digit numbers.

Formal written addition methods

Learn

You can add 2-digit numbers by adding the tens and ones separately.

Here is one way to work out 64 + 35.

60 + 4 + 30 + 5
= 90 + 9
= 99

This is a more formal method.

	60	+	4
+	30	+	5
	90	+	9

So 64 + 35 = 99

Here is another way.

	6	4
+	3	5
	9	9

Sometimes the ones total more than 10.

Here are two ways of working out 57 + 29.

	50	+	7
+	20	+	9
	70	+	16
		86	

	5	7
+	2	9
	8	6
		1

You can use the same methods to add 3-digit numbers.

Here are two ways of working out 135 + 287.

	100	+	30	+	5
+	200	+	80	+	7
	300	+	110	+	12
		410		+	12
			422		

	1	3	5
+	2	8	7
	4	2	2
		1	1

Carry 10s and 100s over by putting a small one under the line. Remember to add it on.

✓ Tip

Try all the different methods several times before you decide which you like best.

Set out your work carefully, using squared paper to help you if possible. This will help you to line up the hundreds, tens and ones.

Talk maths

- The textbook activity encourages the children to talk through the written methods shown for adding numbers. It is recommended that you move the children on to discuss a selection of calculations that show your school's preferred method.

Activities

- Ask the children to complete each calculation using your school's preferred method, providing further practice as desired. Encourage the children to check their answers by repeating the calculation with the numbers in the reverse vertical order. For example, check 24 + 49 with 49 + 24.
- Note that the links to *100 Maths Lessons Year 3* and the *Year 3 Practice Book* contain further practice materials.

Problems

- The Brain-teaser is a one-step problem, whereas the Brain-buster is multi-step. Both are easy to extend and adapt by adjusting the numbers. Note also that problem-solving using addition and subtraction is covered in detail in 'Solving addition and subtraction problems' on pages 32–33 of this book.

Talk maths

Here are three formal additions. Explain what is happening in each one.

26 + 38   156 + 47   564 + 297

		2	6
	+	3	8
		6	4
		1	

	1	5	6
+		4	7
		1	3
		9	0
	1	0	0
	2	0	3
		1	

	5	6	4
+	2	9	7
		1	1
	1	5	0
	7	0	0
	8	6	1

> Would you have used a different written method to work out these additions? Explain your choice to a partner.

Activities

Use a formal written method for each of these.

1. 56 + 47   2. 145 + 37   3. 468 + 259

Problems

Brain-teaser
There are 156 sweets in a jar. The shopkeeper pours into the jar another 48 sweets. How many sweets are there altogether?

Brain-buster
In one sweet jar there are 451 dolly mixtures. In another sweet jar there are 370 jelly babies. A child buys 30 dolly mixtures and 40 jelly babies. How many dolly mixtures and jelly babies are there now in total?

Calculations   21

100 Maths Lessons Year 3 links:

- Autumn 2, Week 2 (pages 55–60): addition using columns (not bridging multiples of 10)
- Spring 2, Week 1 (pages 131–137): add pairs of 2-digit numbers using columns (bridging multiples of 10)
- Summer 1, Week 4 (pages 190–195): columnar addition for numbers with up to three digits
- Summer 2, Week 1 (pages 213–219): addition using columns (bridging multiples of 10)

Year 3 Practice Book links:

- (page 34): Column addition
- (page 35): Column addition: 3-digit numbers

Formal written subtraction methods

Prior learning

- Can mentally subtract 2-digit numbers.

Learn

- Review children's understanding of subtraction facts between zero and 10, demonstrating how this can be used when subtracting multiples of 10. Model how to subtract one 2-digit number from another with no exchanging, such as 56 − 13, using both partitioning and column subtraction.

- Demonstrate column subtraction for 2-digit numbers where a 10 needs to be exchanged, such as 62 − 35. Spend time considering how our number system allows this to work. Move on to methods for adding two 3-digit numbers − both partitioning and column subtraction − and consider the benefits and issues of both methods. Initially, avoid any exchange of numbers.

- Note that the links to *100 Maths Lessons Year 3* have various units that focus on subtraction. *100 Maths Lessons Year 3, Summer 2, Week 1* deals specifically with columnar subtraction of numbers with up to three digits.

Curriculum objectives

- To add and subtract numbers with up to three digits, using formal written methods of columnar addition and subtraction.

Success criteria

- I can use formal written methods to subtract 2-digit and 3-digit numbers.

Formal written subtraction methods

Learn

You can use a formal written method to subtract, too.

$$
\begin{array}{r}
90 + 4 \\
- \ 30 + 3 \\
\hline
60 + 1
\end{array}
\qquad
\begin{array}{r}
9 \ 4 \\
- \ 3 \ 3 \\
\hline
6 \ 1
\end{array}
\qquad \text{So } 94 - 33 = 61
$$

If there are not enough ones you will need to partition the tens number.

Here are two ways of working out 85 − 37.

$$
\begin{array}{r}
80 + 5 \\
- \ 30 + 7 \\
\hline
70 + 15 \\
- \ 30 + 7 \\
\hline
40 + 8 \\
\hline
48
\end{array}
\qquad
\begin{array}{r}
\overset{70}{8\!\!\!/0} + \overset{1}{\ }5 \\
- \ 30 + 7 \\
\hline
40 + 8 \\
\hline
48
\end{array}
$$

You can use the same method to subtract a 2-digit number from a 3-digit number. Here is one way of working out 253 − 36.

$$
\begin{array}{r}
200 + 50 + 3 \ = \ 200 + 40 + 13 \\
- \qquad\ 30 + 6 \ = \ - \qquad\ 30 + 6 \\
\hline
200 + 10 + 7 \ = \ 217
\end{array}
$$

When you subtract a 3-digit number from a 3-digit number, sometimes you need to partition both the tens number and the hundreds number.

Here are two ways of working out 341 − 196.

$$
\begin{array}{r}
\overset{200}{3\!\!\!/00} + \overset{130}{4\!\!\!/0} + \overset{1}{\ 1} \\
- \ 100 + 90 + 6 \\
\hline
200 + 130 + 11 \\
- \ 100 + 90 + 6 \\
\hline
100 + 40 + 5 \\
\hline
145
\end{array}
\qquad
\begin{array}{r}
\overset{2}{3\!\!\!/} \ \overset{13}{4\!\!\!/} \ \overset{1}{1} \\
- \ 1 \ 9 \ 6 \\
\hline
1 \ 4 \ 5
\end{array}
$$

- Starting with the examples in the textbook, ask the children to work with a partner to discuss and explain each step of a subtraction shown as a columnar calculation. Ensure they use appropriate mathematical vocabulary.
This activity can be extended or supported as required by changing the size of the numbers involved.

Activities

- Encourage the children to complete each calculation using your school's preferred method, providing further practice as desired. A good way to get children to check their answers is to repeat the calculation, but this time subtract the answer.
For example, to check that $52 - 35 = 17$, we find $52 - 17 = 35$.

Problems

- Using the textbook problems as a starting point, provide the children with other problems to solve with columnar subtraction.

- Note also that children's reasoning skills can be effectively developed by presenting them with calculations presented as columnar subtractions, but with any one of the digits blanked out. They can then reason and discuss what the missing digit is.

Talk maths

Talk through these subtractions with a partner.
Explain each step.

In these examples you need to exchange a hundred for 10 tens, and then exchange one of those tens for 10 ones.

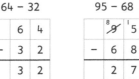

You need to exchange a ten for ones.

Activities

Use a formal written method for each of these.

1. $84 - 31$ 2. $237 - 59$ 3. $666 - 478$

Problems

Brain-teaser
A farmer counts how many eggs the chickens have laid. He counts 427. He sells 59 eggs. How many eggs are left?

Brain-buster
There are 728 eggs in their boxes. The farmer sells 150 on Monday, and 275 on Tuesday. How many eggs are left?

100 Maths Lessons Year 3 links:

- Autumn 2, Week 2 (pages 55–60): subtraction using columns (not bridging multiples of 10)

- Spring 2, Week 1 (pages 131–137): subtract pairs of 2-digit numbers (bridging multiples of 10)

- Summer 1, Week 4 (pages 190–195): columnar subtraction for numbers with up to three digits

- Summer 2, Week 1 (pages 213–219): subtraction using columns for numbers with up to three digits

Year 3 Practice Book links:

- (page 36): Column subtraction

Estimating and using inverses

Prior learning

- Can show that addition can be done in any order but subtraction of one number from another cannot.
- Can recognise and use the inverse relationship between addition and subtraction and use this to check calculations and solve missing number problems.

- Spend time using number facts to 20 to demonstrate the relationship between addition and subtraction. For example, 6 + 5 = 11 so 5 + 6 = 11, and also 11 − 5 = 6 and 11 − 6 = 5.

- Move on to examining this inverse relationship when adding and subtracting 2-digit numbers.
- Recap children's knowledge of your school's preferred technique for column addition and subtraction. Move on to demonstrating how to use their inverses for checking the addition and subtraction of 3-digit numbers.

- Using other calculations, consider approaches of estimating the total. Discuss the importance of this skill in helping us feel confident that our answer is correct.
- *100 Maths Lessons Year 3, Autumn 2, Week 2* has specific lessons focused on estimating skills. The children should be encouraged to estimate answers before completing any calculation – this is a good habit to develop.

Curriculum objectives

- To estimate the answer to a calculation and use inverse operations to check answers.

Success criteria

- I can estimate the answer to an addition or subtraction.
- I can check the answer to an addition or subtraction by using inverses.

Estimating and using inverses

Learn

Estimating

When you do a calculation, estimate the answer first so you can check your actual answer is about right. Look at the numbers and think of numbers that are close to them that are easier to work out. For example, for 64 + 12 you could estimate 60 + 10 = 70.

> This is a good estimate. The exact answer will be a bit larger than 70.

Using inverses

Addition is the inverse (or opposite) of subtraction. Subtraction is the inverse (or opposite) of addition.

This means we can use subtraction to check the answer to an addition or we can use addition to check the answer to a subtraction.

An estimate for 156 + 58 is 160 + 60 = 220.
Here is one way of working out 156 + 58.

	1	5	6
+		5	8
	2	1	4

Check with subtraction.

	^{1}2	^{10}1^{1}4
−		5	8
	1	5	6

We have 156, 58 and 214 in both calculations.

214 is just a bit smaller than 220 so our estimate helps us to check we are about right.

For subtraction, check with addition.

> Don't just guess – estimate, calculate, check!

✓ Tip

Your answer should be close to your estimate. If it's not, look and see if you made a mistake in your calculation.

Use the inverse to check your answer – if the numbers are not the same, do the calculation again.

- Arrange the children in groups and provide each with a selection of calculations like those in the book. Challenge them to work together to agree on estimates for each calculation, giving reasons for their chosen estimates. If desired, move on to carrying out each calculation and checking it with an appropriate inverse operation.

- Encourage the children to estimate the answer to each calculation, before they complete them. They should use inverse calculations to check their answers.

- Note that the *Year 3 Practice Book* provides further activities.

- Encourage the children to build the habits of estimating answers and using inverses for checking calculations when they solve problems too.

- In particular, they will need to think carefully about how to use estimation and checking methods when solving multi-step problems such as the Brain-buster.

Talk maths

Talk about these estimates with a partner. Which are good estimates? How do you know?

| 64 + 72 | Estimate about 130 | 75 + 38 | Estimate about 110 |

| 136 − 45 | Estimate about 100 | 169 − 130 | Estimate about 30 |

Don't forget: Estimate. Calculate. Check.

Activities

Estimate the answer to each calculation. Use the formal written method you like best. Use inverse calculations to check your answers.

1. 56 + 39   2. 92 − 44   3. 222 + 468

4. 143 − 76   5. 356 + 47   6. 596 − 217

Problems

Brain-teaser
A shop has 351 metres of blue ribbon. The shop assistant sells 94 metres of the ribbon. What length of ribbon is left?

Brain-buster
Some volunteers are going to plant 431 young trees in a wood. On the first day they plant 96 trees and on the second day they plant 29 trees. How many trees still need to be planted?

100 Maths Lessons Year 3 links:

- Autumn 2, Week 2 (pages 55–60): estimate answers to additions and subtractions with pairs of 2- or 3- digit numbers

- Spring 1, Week 2 (pages 96–101): use rounding to estimate answers and inverses to check calculations

- Spring 2, Week 1 (pages 131–137): estimate answers

- Summer 1, Week 3 (pages 184–189): use rounding to estimate answers and inverses to check calculations

- Summer 2, Week 1 (pages 213–219): estimate answers and check calculations

Year 3 Practice Book links:

- (page 32): Estimating answers
- (page 33): Check it

Solving addition and subtraction problems

Prior learning

- Can use addition and subtraction to solve problems.

Learn

- Spend time reviewing both mental and formal methods for addition and subtraction. Remind the children of the inverse relationship between addition and subtraction and encourage them continue to use initial estimates to gauge the accuracy of their answers.

- Using a selection of problems, work with the children to practise analysing each problem and deciding on the method needed to solve each one. Most of the

links to *100 Maths Lessons Year 3* given here have a final lesson based around problem-solving, using various methods for addition and subtraction.

- In working through problems, particularly in analysing them, try to model thought processes as much as possible by 'thinking aloud' and talking through strategies.

Talk maths

- Provide a selection of missing number problems and word problems on separate cards. Provide regular opportunities for the children to work in pairs to solve problems and to discuss the methods/strategies needed to solve them. (A nice extension to this is to provide children with an addition or subtraction, and ask them to come up with a problem based on it.)

Curriculum objectives

- To solve problems, including missing number problems, using number facts, place value, and more complex addition and subtraction.

Success criteria

- I can solve number problems using addition and subtraction.

Solving addition and subtraction problems

Learn

You can use the addition and subtraction methods you have learned so far to help you solve problems.

You can solve missing number problems like this by counting up.

$35 + \bigstar = 44$

> Can you think of another way to solve this problem?

Count on from 35: 35 and 5 is 40. Another 4 is 44.
5 + 4 = 9, so the missing number is 9.

This missing number problem has larger numbers.

$47 + \bigstar = 116$

You can still count on to solve it.

3 + 50 + 16 = 69, so the missing number is 69.

You can also solve the problem with a subtraction sentence.

$116 - 47 = 100 - 40 + 16 - 7 = 60 + 9 = 69$

> Don't let problems cause you problems! Take them one step at a time.

If you prefer, you can use a formal written method. This missing problem involves subtraction.

$237 - \bigstar = 156$

Count on from 156 to 237 to find the missing number.

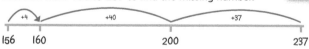

4 + 40 + 37 = 81, so the missing number is 81.
Or you can subtract 156 from 237 to find the missing number.

Activities

- The textbook focuses on missing number problems. These are important for developing children's reasoning skills – in particular, their understanding of the inverse relationship between addition and subtraction is essential for solving this type of problem correctly.

Problems

- Money problems provide excellent contexts for the children to apply their calculation skills. The links to *100 Maths Lessons Year 3* and the *Year 3 Practice Book* have further support and extension.

Talk maths

How would you solve these problems? Discuss with a partner what you know and what you need to work out. How many ways can you think of to find the answer?

Find the missing number.

$59 + \bigstar = 153$ $\bigstar - 92 = 200$

Jon has 256 marbles. He gives some to Mark. Now Jon has only 185 marbles. How many marbles does Mark have?

Can you write this as a missing number problem?

Activities

Copy and solve each missing number problem.

1. $94 + ? = 165$
2. $? + 89 = 200$
3. $? + 66 = 100$
4. $174 - ? = 36$
5. The difference between 156 and 251 is ?

Problems

Brain-teaser
Travis has £98 in his money box. He buys a guitar and now he has £65 in his money box. How much did the guitar cost?

Brain-buster
Lexi buys her mother a bunch of flowers for £33, a box of chocolates for £17 and a special card for £8. Now she has £74 left. How much money did Lexi have to begin with?

100 Maths Lessons Year 3 links:

- Autumn 1, Week 3 (pages 20–25): solve problems involving addition and subtraction of 1- and 2-digit numbers
- Autumn 2, Week 2 (pages 55–60): use columnar addition and subtraction to solve word problems
- Spring 1, Week 2 (pages 96–101): solve problems involving addition and subtraction of pairs of 2-digit numbers totalling 100 and and 3-digit numbers and 1s
- Spring 2, Week 1 (pages 131–137): use columnar addition and subtraction to solve missing number and word problems
- Summer 1, Week 3 (pages 184–189): solve problems involving addition and subtraction of 3-digit numbers and 1s, 10s and 100s
- Summer 1, Week 4 (pages 190–195): use columnar addition and subtraction to solve missing number and word problems
- Summer 2, Week 1 (pages 213–219): use columnar addition and subtraction to solve missing number and word problems using 2- and 3-digit numbers

Year 3 Practice Book links:

- (page 29): Add and subtract two 2-digit numbers
- (pages 38–39): Addition and subtraction word problems
- (page 40): More addition and subtraction
- (page 41): Sticker problems

3, 4 and 8 multiplication and division facts

Prior learning

- Can recall and use multiplication and division facts for the 2-, 5- and 10-times tables, including recognising odd and even numbers.

- Review the children's recall of the 2-, 5- and 10-times tables. Ensure that they can read a multiplication square correctly and appreciate that multiplication can be carried out in any order. If appropriate, discuss the relationship between multiplication and division facts. For example, knowing $2 \times 5 = 10$ means that you also know $10 \div 5 = 2$.

- Spend time, preferably in short bursts, introducing and practising each of the 3-, 4- and 8-times tables. Referring to a multiplication grid, remind the children that 4×8 also gives them 8×4, and so on.

- *100 Maths Lessons Year 3 Autumn 1, Week 4* contains relevant and useful lessons and some useful activities and worksheets.

Curriculum objectives

- To recall and use multiplication and division facts for the 3-, 4- and 8-times tables.

Success criteria

- I can use multiplication facts that I know to find related division facts.

3, 4 and 8 multiplication and division facts

Learn

You already know the multiplication facts for 2, 5 and 10. Look at the table below and check you remember them.

You need to learn the multiplication facts for 3, 4 and 8.

×	1	2	3	4	5	6	7	8	9	10	11	12
2	2	4	6	8	10	12	14	16	18	20	22	24
3	3	6	9	12	15	18	21	24	27	30	33	36
4	4	8	12	16	20	24	28	32	36	40	44	48
5	5	10	15	20	25	30	35	40	45	50	55	60
8	8	16	24	32	40	48	56	64	72	80	88	96
10	10	20	30	40	50	60	70	80	90	100	110	120

Remember, if you know $3 \times 4 = 12$, you also know $4 \times 3 = 12$.

You can use multiplication facts to find division facts.

If you know $4 \times 3 = 12$ and $3 \times 4 = 12$, you also know $12 \div 3 = 4$ and $12 \div 4 = 3$.

> ### ✓ Tip
>
> You can multiply numbers in any order.
>
> If you know a multiplication fact, you can work out a division fact.
>
> If you forget a multiplication fact, you can sometimes use doubling to help you. For example, to find 7×8, work out 7×4 and double the answer.

You know more facts than you think you do!

Talk maths

- Provide small groups with a multiplication grid for the 3-, 4- and 8-times tables and a selection of counters. Challenge them to pose quick-fire questions to each other, placing counters on the answers that they know on the grid. Use division too if desired.

Activities

- Use the textbook questions for a quick assessment of children's recall of multiplication facts. Move them on to activities and worksheets from the links to *100 Maths Lessons Year 3* and the *Year 3 Practice Book,* as appropriate. Notice that these include activities that involve doubling and halving – these will help the children's growing understanding of the 2-, 4- and 8-times tables.

Problems

- If the children answer the problems confidently, challenge them to create their own, reminding them that they must be able to explain the method and operation for finding their solutions.

Talk maths

Ask a friend to test you on your multiplication facts.

Use a multiplication table and circle the multiplication facts you know.

Can you think of ways to remember the ones you are not sure of?

Activities

Cover up the table with a piece of paper.

Write down the answers to these calculations using your memory.

1. 9×8 2. $44 \div 4$

3. $96 \div 8$ 4. 9×3

5. $36 \div 3$ 6. 4×12

Problems

Brain-teaser

Maia has 24 sweets to be shared between herself and three friends. How many sweets do they each get?

Brain-buster

There are 48 pencils to be shared out equally into pots. Each pot contains six pencils. How many pots are there?

100 Maths Lessons Year 3 links:

Year 3 Practice Book links:

Using mental and written methods for multiplication and division

Prior learning

- Can calculate mathematical statements for multiplication and division within the 2-, 5- and 10-times tables and write them using the multiplication (×), division (÷) and equals (=) signs.
- Can show that multiplication of two numbers can be done in any order but division of one number by another cannot.

Learn

- Refresh children's knowledge of all the times tables they should now know, using both a multiplication square as well as writing the calculations by hand, extending to divisions if appropriate.

- Move on to multiplying and dividing by 10 and 100, using simple examples.
- You should be aware that this section covers a great deal of ground, and should be spread over several weeks at various points in the school year, selecting methods as appropriate to children's needs and your school's preferred methods. The links to *100 Maths Lessons Year 3* and the *Year 3 Practice*

Book provide a wide range of structured lessons and activities to support this work throughout the year – many of which go further than the textbook does.
- Ensure that each method is introduced thoroughly before pointing out similarities and differences between methods. The extensive resources in *100 Maths Lessons Year 3* provide ample support and extension.

Curriculum objectives

- To write and calculate mathematical statements for multiplication and division using the multiplication tables that they know, including for 2-digit numbers times 1-digit numbers, using mental and progressing to formal written methods.

Success criteria

- I can use mental methods for multiplication and division.
- I can use written methods for multiplication and division.

Using mental and written methods for multiplication and division

Learn

You should now know multiplication table facts for the 2-, 3-, 4-, 5-, 8- and 10-times tables. Look at the multiplication table on page 88 if you are unsure.

You can use your multiplication tables to work out 2-digit by 1-digit multiplications.

Here are different ways of working out 16 × 4.

You can write a multiplication sentence:
16 × 4 = 10 × 4 + 6 × 4 = 40 + 24 = 64

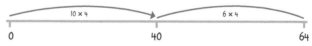

You can use the grid method.

×	4
10	40
6	24
Total	64

You can use a formal written method.

		1	6	
×			4	
		2	4	Multiply the ones.
		4	0	Multiply the tens.
		6	4	

You can also break a division down into sections. Here are two ways of working out 64 ÷ 4.

This is the division sentence method.
64 ÷ 4 = 40 ÷ 4 + 24 ÷ 4
       = 10 + 6
       = 16

This method is called chunking.

	6	4	
−	4	0	10 × 4
	2	4	
−	2	4	6 × 4
		0	16

So 64 ÷ 4 = 16

Talk maths

- For each method that you choose to present, encourage the children to explain what's happening at every stage.
- Work on written methods can be extended by presenting the children with multiplication and division problems that have a digit missing. Challenge the children to use both trial and error and reasoning skills to find the missing digit.

Activities

- Once the children have completed the questions in the textbook, provide them with more practice that involves as wide a number range as possible (within the limits of the times tables covered so far).

Problems

- Discuss the Brain-teaser and how the language used implies the operation needed. It is then up to the children to select their preferred method.
- The Brain-buster is a multi-step problem that requires multiplication and then subtraction.

100 Maths Lessons Year 3 links:

- Spring 2, Week 2 (pages 138–142): use arrays and for multiplication facts and to find remainders
- Spring 2, Week 3 (pages 143–147): multiply 1-digit numbers by multiples of 10
- Summer 1, Week 2 (pages 178–183): use partitioning to multiply or divide a 2-digit number by a 1-digit number
- Summer 2, Week 2 (pages 220–225): use doubling, grid multiplication and division by chunking
- Summer 2, Week 3 (pages 226–231): use short multiplication

Year 3 Practice Book links:

- (page 52): Multiply using teen numbers
- (page 53): Tens and units multiplication
- (pages 54–55): Short multiplication
- (page 56): Division hops
- (page 57): Division facts
- (pages 58–59): Short division
- (page 60): Multiply by 10 and 100
- (page 61): Multiplying and dividing by 10 and 100
- (page 62): Bigger and bigger

Talk maths

Look at the division below and talk through both methods aloud, saying how each stage was done. Which do you find easier?

$$54 \div 3$$

Division sentence method

$54 \div 3 = 30 \div 3 + 24 \div 3$
$= 10 + 8$
$= 18$

Chunking method

	5	4	
−	3	0	10×3
	2	4	
−	2	4	8×3
		0	18 So $54 \div 3 = 18$

Activities

Use a written method to solve these. Choose the method that you feel most confident with.

1. 23×3 2. $68 \div 4$ 3. $96 \div 3$ 4. $96 \div 4$

5. What is the product of 23 and 4?

Problems

Brain-teaser
Ben has 88cm of string. He wants to divide it equally into four lengths. How much will there be in each length of string?

Brain-buster
Sally buys three pens. Each pen costs 31p. How much change will Sally have from £1?

Solving multiplication and division problems

Prior learning

- Can solve problems involving multiplication and division, using materials, arrays, repeated addition, mental methods and multiplication and division facts.

Learn

- Work with the children to recall the multiplication facts they already know, using a multiplication square. (There is an interactive multiplication square on the CD-ROM for *100 Maths Lessons Year 3*.)
- Ensure that the children appreciate that each multiplication fact actually gives them four facts – two multiplication facts and two division.

- Over a number of sessions, work though a mixture of missing number problems and word problems. During whole-class work, use those that are relatively easy, partly to ensure that all children can follow the methods, but also to allow the focus to be on *application* and *process* rather than the complexity of the maths involved.
- The Tips on page 32 of the textbook give good hints on how to think through a problem.

Curriculum objectives

- To solve problems, including missing number problems, involving multiplication and division, including positive integer scaling problems and correspondence problems in which *n* objects are connected to *m* objects.

Success criteria

- I can solve multiplication and division problems.

Solving multiplication and division problems

Learn

You can use multiplication and division skills to solve problems.
Remember, if you know one fact, you also know three more facts.

| $5 \times 9 = 45$ | $9 \times 5 = 45$ | $45 \div 5 = 9$ | $45 \div 9 = 5$ |

Here is a missing number problem.
$\star \div 3 = 16$
Decide what you need to work out.
What number, divided by 3, gives 16?
The answer must be 3 times bigger than 16.
So you need to work out 16×3.

		1	6
×			3
		1	8
	3	0	
	4	8	

You can use a grid to help you answer some types of question.
Steve has four T-shirts and three pairs of jeans. How many different outfits can he make? The grid shows all the different possibilities.

	T-shirt 1	T-shirt 2	T-shirt 3	T-shirt 4
Jeans 1	✔	✔	✔	✔
Jeans 2	✔	✔	✔	✔
Jeans 3	✔	✔	✔	✔

Work out 4 × 3. What do you notice?

Steve has 12 possible outfits.

Use my tips to help you sort the numbers from the words!

✓ Tip

Look for the numbers in the question. What do you need to do with them?

If you are not sure what to multiply or divide, think about what size the numbers should be.

$\star \div 3 = 16$ Multiply or divide?

$\star$ must be bigger than 16. Three times bigger, in fact.
So $3 \times 16 = \star$.

- After the children have talked through the example in the textbook, provide pairs or groups with a range of other problems to be discussed. (More confident groups might be challenged to do all the maths mentally before agreeing on an answer.) The *Year 3 Practice Book* has a good selection of word problems.

- The missing number problems in the textbook should give a good indication of the children's confidence and ability to manipulate numbers. *100 Maths Lessons Year 3, Spring 1, Week 4* provides further structured activities focused on solving problems using multiplication facts. The other links to *100 Maths Lessons Year 3* move on to using written methods to solve problems.

- Bring shopping lists, catalogues and menus into the classroom, and organise sessions that involve working out how much multiple items would cost. The links to *100 Maths Lessons Year 3* have lessons and resources that can support this work.

Talk maths

Look at the problem below. Talk through the answers aloud. Explain where the numbers in the answers come from.

A cake for two people needs these ingredients.

How much flour, sugar, butter and egg would be needed to make a cake for six people?

100g of flour
100g of sugar
100g of butter
2 eggs

$6 \div 2 = 3$ so you need three times as much of each ingredient to make a cake for six people.

Multiply each ingredient by 3.
$100 \times 3 = 300g$ of flour, 300g of sugar, 300g of butter
$2 \times 3 = 6$ eggs

Activities

Find the missing numbers.

1. ★ × 8 = 104   2. ★ ÷ 4 = 15   3. 8 × ★ = 120   4. 52 ÷ ★ = 13

5. The product of 26 and 3 is ★.

Problems

Brain-buster

Tim buys 32 small cartons of juice, one for each guest at a party. He also buys 64 snack packs. Then he discovers that three times as many people will be coming to the party. How many more cartons of juice and snack packs does Tim need to buy?

100 Maths Lessons Year 3 links:

- Spring 1, Week 4 (pages 107–112): solve problems using known multiplication facts
- Spring 2, Week 3 (pages 143–147): solve problems involving rounding, multiplying by 10 and scaling
- Summer 2, Week 2 (pages 220–225): investigate a general statement using grid multiplication and division by chunking
- Summer 2, Week 3 (pages 226–231): solve a problem using multiplication facts

Year 3 Practice Book links:

- (pages 48–49): Table facts
- (page 63): Multiples of 10 calculations
- (pages 66–67): Multiplication and division word problems
- (pages 68–69): Division word problems

Tenths

Prior learning

- Can recognise, find, name and write fractions ⅓, ¼, ⅔ and ¾ of a length, shape, set of objects or quantity.

Learn

- If possible, bring a small selection of fruit into the class and demonstrate halving and quartering of different items. Emphasise that different-sized objects are still referred to as half or quarter, as fractions represent proportions. Consider how many of each fraction make up a whole, leading children to realise that two halves, four quarters, and so on, make up a whole. Discuss other things in real life that are presented as fractions, for example *half-time*, *quarter of an hour*.

- Line ten children up along the front of the class. Ask nine of them to each hold a piece of identically coloured paper. Give the tenth child a differently coloured piece. Work with the children to identify that one out of ten is (say) red, and nine out of ten are (say) blue. Remind the children that the whole group is *ten out of ten* or *one whole*.

- Spend time adjusting the proportions of blue to red, discussing the fractions (tenths) involved.

Curriculum objectives

- To count up and down in tenths; recognise that tenths arise from dividing an object into 10 equal parts and in dividing 1-digit numbers or quantities by 10.

Success criteria

- I can find tenths of objects and numbers.

Tenths

Learn

A fraction is made by dividing something into equal parts. This cake has been divided into quarters. Each slice is $\frac{1}{4}$ of the cake. If one slice is eaten then $\frac{3}{4}$ is left.

To find a tenth, divide squares or numbers by 10.

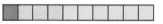

There are 10 squares in total.

1 out of 10 squares is red. $\frac{1}{10}$ is red.

3 out of 10 squares are blue. $\frac{3}{10}$ are blue.

6 out of 10 squares are green. $\frac{6}{10}$ are green.

10 out of 10 squares are coloured. $\frac{10}{10}$ is equivalent to (or the same as) one whole.

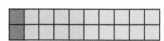

There are 20 squares in total.

$20 \div 10 = 2$. So two squares make $\frac{1}{10}$ of 20.

$\frac{1}{10}$ is red. $\frac{4}{10}$ are blue. $\frac{5}{10}$ are green.

Can you think of another fraction to describe the green squares?

✓ Tip

To find more than one tenth of a number, divide by 10 and then multiply.

$\frac{1}{10}$ of 20 is $20 \div 10 = 2$, so

$\frac{2}{10}$ of 20 is $2 \times 2 = 4$

$\frac{3}{10}$ of 20 is $2 \times 3 = 6$

$\frac{4}{10}$ of 20 is $2 \times 4 = 8$ and so on.

- The activity in the textbook focuses on calculating fractions of quantities. Children may need further practice at finding tenths of shapes before attempting this.

- If they are comfortable with calculating tenths, arrange the children in groups and provide them with a set of number cards (numbers that are multiples of 10) and a set of tenths fraction cards. Ask them to take turns to turn over one of each card and calculate the answer, supporting each other as appropriate. Can they create a word problem that uses their number and fraction?

Activities

- The textbook questions might be extended by providing 'missing number' type problems. For example, $\Box/10$ of 30 = 3 or $4/10$ of $\Box$ = 16.

- Note that the *Year 3 Practice Book* also provides more practice.

- Note that the links to *100 Maths Lessons Year 3* tend to have tenths embedded within activities focusing on other fractions too and may be better covered in subsequent sections.

Problems

- The Brain-buster moves on to adding tenths. *100 Maths Lessons Year 3, Summer 2, Week 4, Lesson 2* has specific work on adding tenths.

Talk maths

Look at these problems. Talk through the answers aloud.

How do you know that one tenth of 40 is 4?

How can you work out three tenths of 90?

Kelso had 60 apples but gave $\frac{2}{10}$ to her gran. Kelso's gran received 12 apples. Is this correct?

Activities

Copy and answer these questions.

1. $\frac{1}{10}$ of 30   2. $\frac{5}{10}$ of 100   3. $\frac{8}{10}$ of 50

4. $\frac{6}{10}$ of 30   5. $\frac{9}{10}$ of 20   6. $\frac{3}{10}$ of 40

Problems

Brain-teaser
Jon has 30 marbles. He gives Charlie $\frac{7}{10}$ of his marbles. How many marbles does Charlie receive?

Brain-buster
Daisy the cow produces 30 litres of milk a day. $\frac{1}{10}$ of this milk is kept for the calves to drink. The farmer's wife keeps $\frac{2}{10}$ for herself and $\frac{3}{10}$ is kept for making butter. The rest is turned into cheese. How much milk in litres is used for making cheese?

100 Maths Lessons Year 3 links:

- Spring 2, Week 5 (pages 154–159): count up and down in tenths, and find tenths of objects and quantities

- Summer 2, Week 4 (pages 232–237): count in tenths; find tenths; add tenths to 1

Year 3 Practice Book links:

- (page 81): Tenths
- (page 82): More on tenths

Fractions of objects

Prior learning

- Can recognise, find, name and write fractions $\frac{1}{3}$, $\frac{1}{4}$, $\frac{2}{4}$ and $\frac{3}{4}$ of a length, shape, set of objects or quantity.

Learn

- Refresh the children's knowledge of fraction notation, vocabulary and meaning. Draw different sets of dots on the board: 2, 3, 4, 5 and 10. Then work with the children to identify and circle different fractions of each: $\frac{1}{2}$, $\frac{1}{3}$, $\frac{1}{4}$, $\frac{1}{5}$ and $\frac{1}{10}$.
- Draw a 4 × 4 grid on the board and look at how this can be divided into halves and quarters, moving on to eighths if appropriate.
- In subsequent sessions, progress to different sets of objects. *100 Maths Lessons Year 3, Autumn 2, Week 4* provides further guidance and supportive activities.

Curriculum objectives

- To recognise, find and write fractions of a discrete set of objects: unit fractions and non-unit fractions with small denominators.

Success criteria

- I can find fractions of objects.

Fractions of objects

Learn

The top number (numerator) tells us how many of the equal parts there are. Here there is 1.

The bottom number (denominator) tells us how many equal parts there are in total. Here there are 5.

Numerator → $\frac{1}{5}$ ← Denominator

To find a fraction of a set of objects, divide the objects into equal groups. Here are 16 balls. To find $\frac{1}{2}$ divide the balls into two equal groups. There are eight balls in each group. $\frac{1}{2}$ of 16 is 8.

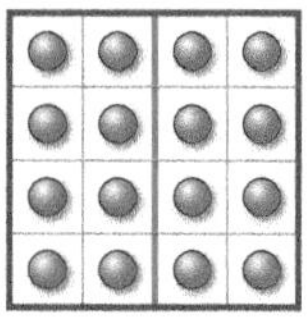

Here are the same 16 balls. To find $\frac{1}{4}$, divide the balls into four equal groups. There are four balls in each group. $\frac{1}{4}$ of 16 is 4.

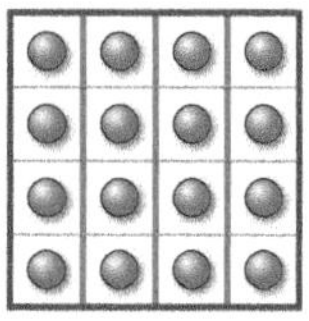

Here are the 16 balls again. To find $\frac{3}{4}$, divide the balls into four equal groups, then count the balls in three of the groups. $\frac{3}{4}$ of 16 is 12.

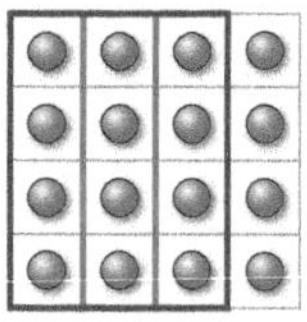

✓ Tip

Remember the denominator is down at the bottom.

- Arrange the children in small groups and give them some blank paper and plastic shapes of regular polygons. Ask them to draw around the shapes and divide them into different fractions, as shown in the textbook. (The denominator of each fraction for a shape will equal the number of sides of the shape.)

- More confident learners might be challenged to use different colours to demonstrate how two or more fractions with the same denominator can be added to create a whole.

Activities

- The textbook questions focus on calculating fractions of quantities, and suggest that children use squared paper to help them. Point out the link to times tables facts, for example 16 is 2 × 8 and 16 ÷ 8 = 2.

Problems

- The Brain-buster is quite complex and can be effectively supported using objects. Children who are finding this difficult can be given the *Year 3 Practice Book* activities for further practice.

Talk maths

Discuss aloud the fractions shown.

Explain how you know.

Activities

Copy and answer these questions. Use squared paper to help you.

1. $\frac{1}{8}$ of 16
2. $\frac{3}{5}$ of 45
3. $\frac{3}{4}$ of 36
4. $\frac{3}{4}$ of 12
5. $\frac{6}{8}$ of 80
6. $\frac{4}{5}$ of 60

Problems

Brain-teaser
Simon draws 24 squares, six squares along and four squares down. He shades in $\frac{3}{8}$ of the squares. How many squares does Simon shade in?

Brain-buster
Nina counts out 36 pennies. She puts nine pennies in a row, and repeats this three more times. Nina then takes away $\frac{5}{6}$ of the pennies. How many pennies are left?

100 Maths Lessons Year 3 links:

- Autumn 2, Week 4 (pages 67–72): find unit fractions of shapes and numbers
- Spring 2, Week 5 (pages 154–159): find unit fractions (including tenths) of shapes and numbers; identify and represent non-unit fractions
- Summer 2, Week 4 (pages 232–237): find tenths of numbers and quantities

Year 3 Practice Book links:

- (page 70): Fraction search
- (page 72): Wheel fractions
- (page 75): Fractions: number of parts

Fractions of numbers

Prior learning

- Can write simple fractions, for example, ½ of 6 = 3.

- Provide whole-class practice in finding unit fractions of whole numbers. Use objects to support work where necessary, but try to work with 'abstract' calculations as much as possible.

- Using sets of dots/objects, review children's knowledge of finding ½ and ¼, moving on to ⅔ and ¾, and one whole, pointing out that ²⁄₄ = ½, and ⁴⁄₄ = one whole.

- Work with the children to establish the procedure of finding the unit fraction first, and then multiplying by the numerator as required. For example, to find ¾ of 24, first find ¼ of 24, and then multiply the answer by 3.

- Over a number of sessions, introduce a variety of fractions and work with the children to find fractions of whole numbers, using diagrams and countable objects as necessary.

Curriculum objectives

- To recognise and use fractions as numbers: unit fractions and non-unit fractions with small denominators.

Success criteria

- I can find fractions of numbers.

Fractions of numbers

Learn

Fractions are numbers. For example, $\frac{1}{2}$ of 10 is 5.

To find a fraction of a number, divide by the denominator (bottom number).

$$\frac{1}{4} \text{ of } 12 = 12 \div 4 = 3$$

$$\frac{1}{3} \text{ of } 18 = 18 \div 3 = 6$$

$$\frac{1}{8} \text{ of } 16 = 16 \div 8 = 2$$

If the numerator (top number) of the fraction you are finding is not 1, first divide by the denominator, then multiply by the numerator.

$$\frac{1}{4} \text{ of } 12 = 3$$
$$\downarrow$$
$$\text{so } \frac{3}{4} \text{ of } 12 = 3 \times 3 = 9$$

$$\frac{1}{3} \text{ of } 18 = 6$$
$$\downarrow$$
$$\text{so } \frac{2}{3} \text{ of } 18 = 6 \times 2 = 12$$

$$\frac{1}{8} \text{ of } 16 = 2$$
$$\downarrow$$
$$\text{so } \frac{5}{8} \text{ of } 16 = 2 \times 5 = 10$$

Getting mixed up? I can help!

✓ Tip

Divide the number by the denominator first, then multiply by the numerator if that is greater than 1. Use your multiplication facts to help you.

Talk maths

- Create a selection of simple word problems similar to those in the activity in the textbook. Ask the children to talk through answers with each other, explaining their reasoning and checking that their partners also understand.

Activities

- Children who find the textbook work too challenging can complete the activities in the *Year 3 Practice Book* instead.
- *100 Maths Lessons Year 3, Autumn 2, Week 4, Lesson 5* provides paired work on fractions of money, which may be extended or simplified as desired.

Problems

- The children who are struggling should be reminded that grids of squares can be drawn (or indeed counting objects used) to help visualise the quantities and fractions involved.
- To challenge the children further, ask them to write their own word problem for each of the questions in Activities.

Talk maths

Look at the problems below and talk them through aloud, explaining each step in the answer.

There are 30 books on the shelf. The children take $\frac{2}{5}$ of the books. How many books did they take?

First find $\frac{1}{5}$ → $30 \div 5 = 6$ Use your answer to find $\frac{2}{5}$ → $6 \times 2 = 12$
The children took 12 books.

There are 32 children in a class. $\frac{7}{8}$ of the children bring a packed lunch. How many children is that?

$32 \div 8 = 4$ $4 \times 7 = 28$ 28 children take a packed lunch to school.

Activities

Copy and answer these questions. Write number sentences to show how you solved them.

1. $\frac{1}{3}$ of 27   2. $\frac{2}{3}$ of 30   3. $\frac{6}{10}$ of 100

4. $\frac{3}{5}$ of 25   5. $\frac{5}{8}$ of 72   6. $\frac{9}{10}$ of 100

Problems

Brain-teaser
Harry has £36 in the bank. He spends $\frac{3}{4}$ of his money. How much does Harry spend?

Brain-buster
There are 80 litres of petrol in the car tank. After a journey, $\frac{5}{8}$ of the petrol has been used. How many litres of petrol are left in the tank?

Fractions **39**

100 Maths Lessons Year 3 links:

- Autumn 2, Week 4 (pages 67–72): find unit fractions of shapes and numbers
- Spring 2, Week 5 (pages 154–159): find unit fractions (including tenths) of shapes and numbers; identify and represent non-unit fractions
- Summer 2, Week 4 (pages 232–237): find tenths of numbers and quantities

Year 3 Practice Book links:

- (page 71): Fractions of numbers
- (page 73): Non-unit fractions
- (page 74): Fraction measures (1)

Equivalent fractions

Prior learning

- Can write simple fractions, for example, ½ of 6 = 3.

Learn

- If possible, bring a large bar of chocolate into the children and use it to demonstrate the use of halves and quarters to demonstrate equivalence. If appropriate, move on to examining sixths for equivalence with thirds and halves.

- Display a selection of fraction walls like those in the textbook. If possible, keep these on permanent display. Over regular, short sessions, challenge the children to find equivalences, from simple challenges such as fractions equivalent to one half, to fractions equivalent to three quarters, two thirds, and so on.

- *100 Maths Lessons Year 3, Spring 2, Week 5, Lesson 3* provides further lesson ideas and activities, and the accompanying CD-ROM contains an interactive resource for equivalent fractions.

- Children struggling with these concepts might be given coloured strips of paper that are all the same length. They can spend time folding these strips up to create different fractions and then stick them together to make their own fraction walls.

Curriculum objectives

- To recognise and show, using diagrams, equivalent fractions with small denominators.

Success criteria

- I can find and recognise equivalent fractions.

Equivalent fractions

Learn

$\frac{1}{2}$ is equivalent to (or the same as) $\frac{2}{4}$. Look at these two rectangles.

$\frac{1}{2}$ of one rectangle is the same as $\frac{2}{4}$ of the other rectangle.

This fraction wall shows how halves, quarters and eighths are related.

Two $\frac{1}{2}$ s are the same as one whole.

$\frac{1}{2}$ is equivalent to $\frac{2}{4}$ and $\frac{4}{8}$.

Here is a fraction wall for halves, fifths and tenths.

$\frac{5}{10}$ are equivalent to $\frac{1}{2}$.

$\frac{2}{5}$ are equivalent to $\frac{4}{10}$.

What other equivalent fractions can you see in the wall?

Now look at this fraction wall for halves, thirds, sixths and ninths.

$\frac{2}{6}$ are equivalent to $\frac{1}{3}$.

$\frac{3}{9}$ are also equivalent to $\frac{1}{3}$.

$\frac{1}{2}$ is equivalent to $\frac{3}{6}$.

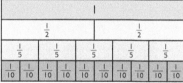

✓ Tip

Look at the fraction walls above to help you see the fraction families.

- Give the children time to discuss each pair of fractions in the activity on page 41 of the textbook, encouraging them to notice the relationship between the numerators and the denominators. For example, looking at ⅓ and ⅖, they can see that the numerator and denominator in ⅖ are doubles of those in ⅓ (2 is double 1 and 6 is double 3).

Activities

- The children should be encouraged to create small, one-off fraction walls for each question in turn. The children can also continue to represent fractions using coloured cubes or shading squared paper.

Problems

- Both problems require more than one step – to find equivalence and then perform a calculation. If necessary, the children could draw diagrams to help them to solve the problems: a simplified circle for the pizza and a rectangle divided into tenths for the garden.

Talk maths

Here are some pairs of equivalent fractions.

$\frac{1}{3}$ and $\frac{2}{6}$ $\frac{3}{4}$ and $\frac{6}{8}$ $\frac{1}{2}$ and $\frac{3}{6}$ $\frac{3}{5}$ and $\frac{6}{10}$

$\frac{1}{4}$ and $\frac{2}{8}$ $\frac{2}{3}$ and $\frac{6}{9}$ $\frac{2}{5}$ and $\frac{4}{10}$ $\frac{4}{5}$ and $\frac{8}{10}$

What do you notice about the numbers in each pair?

Your 2- and 3-times tables might help.

Activities

Use the fraction walls to answer these questions.

1. How many sixths are equivalent to $\frac{1}{3}$?

2. How many tenths are equivalent to $\frac{1}{2}$?

3. How many quarters are equivalent to $\frac{6}{8}$?

4. How many ninths are equivalent to $\frac{2}{3}$?

5. How many sixths make a whole?

6. How many sixths are equivalent to $\frac{1}{2}$?

Problems

Brain-teaser
Jamie cuts a pizza into eight equal slices. He takes half of the pizza to eat. Susie takes a quarter of the pizza. How many slices of the pizza are left?

Brain-buster
Tom decides to divide a flowerbed into ten equal sections. He plants $\frac{1}{5}$ of the sections with flowers. In half of the sections he puts flowerpots. In two sections he puts garden gnomes. What fraction of the garden is left?

100 Maths Lessons Year 3 links:

- Spring 2, Week 5 (pages 154–159): use diagrams to show equivalent fractions
- Summer 2, Week 4 (pages 232–237): recognise and represent equivalent fractions

Year 3 Practice Book links:

- (page 76): Equivalent fractions: numbers
- (page 77): Equivalent fractions: shapes
- (page 78): Fraction match

Comparing and ordering fractions

Prior learning

- Can recognise, find, name and write fractions ⅓, ¼, ⅔ and ¾ of a length, shape, set of objects or quantity.

Learn

- Display a large fraction wall, and review children's understanding of equivalent fractions.
- Next, display four equal circles on the whiteboard and divide them respectively into halves, thirds, quarters and fifths. Work with the children to create mathematical statements, starting with *one half is more than one third*, progressing to more complex statements such as *one quarter is more than one fifth but is less than one third*. It may help to exemplify this further by rubbing out all of each circle except the unit fractions shown.
- Keeping the unit fractions displayed (as sectors of circles with their fractions written inside), draw a large number line for 0 to 1 below them.
- Work with the children to write ½, ⅓, ¼ and ⅕ in their correct positions on the line.

Comparing and ordering fractions

Learn

Look at the denominator of the fraction first. This tells you the total number of parts.

The numerator, the top number, tells you how many of the parts are being used.

This bar of chocolate has been divided into 12 equal parts.

So $\frac{1}{4}$ of the chocolate is three pieces. And $\frac{3}{4}$ of the. chocolate is 3 x 3 or nine pieces.

You can use a fraction number line to help you to compare and order fractions. This number line shows eighths.

$$0 \quad \frac{1}{8} \quad \frac{2}{8} \quad \frac{3}{8} \quad \frac{4}{8} \quad \frac{5}{8} \quad \frac{6}{8} \quad \frac{7}{8} \quad 1$$

Look at the numerators. What do you notice?

Look at the fractions on this number line. They are all unit fractions – the numerators are all 1. As the unit fractions get bigger, the denominator gets smaller.

Where would $\frac{1}{6}$ go on the number line? What about $\frac{1}{8}$?

$$0 \qquad \frac{1}{5}\,\frac{1}{4}\,\frac{1}{3} \quad \frac{1}{2} \qquad\qquad 1$$

Look at $\frac{1}{3}$ and $\frac{1}{2}$. Denominator 3 divides 1 into 3 parts. Denominator 2 divides 1 into 2 parts. So is larger than $\frac{1}{2}$ than $\frac{1}{3}$.

✓ Tip

Use a fraction wall such as this to compare and order fractions.

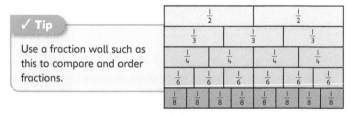

Curriculum objectives

- To compare and order unit fractions, and fractions with the same denominators.

Success criteria

- I can compare and order simple fractions.

Talk maths

- Ask the children to come up with a method or rule for showing how they can easily compare fractions. They should find this fairly straightforward for unit fractions, where the larger the denominator is, then the smaller the value of the fraction. More confident learners might be challenged to compare larger fractions, such as ⅔ and ¾. This is again quite straightforward if the children use diagrams. Some might start to discover that if they change the fractions to equivalents that share the same denominator, then they can easily compare the fractions.

Activities

- The textbook questions are relatively straightforward. Learning can be extended with the *Year 3 Practice Book* activity, and *100 Maths Lessons Year 3, Spring 2, Week 5, Lesson 4* provides further activities.

Problems

- For both problems, insist that the children explain their answers either in words or using diagrams. Further practice in problem solving with fractions is provided in the following sections.

Talk maths

Compare $\frac{1}{3}$ and $\frac{1}{4}$ and find out which fraction is bigger.

Compare $\frac{1}{8}$ and $\frac{1}{10}$ and find out which fraction is the smallest.
How do you know?

Activities

1. Order these fractions. Begin with the smallest. $\frac{1}{2}, \frac{1}{6}, \frac{1}{5}, \frac{1}{3}$

2. Order these fractions. Begin with the smallest. $\frac{3}{8}, \frac{2}{8}, \frac{7}{8}, \frac{5}{8}$

3. Put these fractions in order. Begin with the smallest. $\frac{7}{10}, \frac{5}{10}, \frac{9}{10}, \frac{1}{10}$

 You can draw a fraction number line to help you.

Problems

Brain-teaser
Sam cuts a cake. His little sister Emily asks him whether $\frac{1}{3}$ or $\frac{1}{2}$ of the cake would be bigger. What is the correct answer to tell Emily?

Brain-buster
Grandad offers Sam some pocket money. He can choose to have $\frac{1}{3}$ of £15 or $\frac{1}{5}$ of £20. Which offer gives Sam more pocket money?

100 Maths Lessons Year 3 links:

- Autumn 2, Week 4 (pages 67–72): compare and order unit fractions using models and number lines
- Spring 2, Week 5 (pages 154–159): compare and order unit fractions, and fractions with the same denominator

Year 3 Practice Book links:

- (page 79): Ordering fractions

Adding and subtracting fractions with the same denominator

Prior learning

- Can recognise, find, name and write fractions ⅓, ¼, ²⁄₄ and ¾ of a length, shape, set of objects or quantity.

Learn

- Present the children with a large, drawn circle divided into eighths with ⅛ written in each sector. Spend time considering what ⅛, ²⁄₈, ³⁄₈ and so on looks like, and then draw a number line showing 0 to 1 and mark ⅛, ²⁄₈ and so on along the line.

- Using the eighths number line, demonstrate how it is possible to count along the number line in fractions, just as it is with whole numbers. Starting at zero, demonstrate that ⅛ + ²⁄₈ = ³⁄₈, and so on.

- Repeat this for a range of fractions (page 44 of the textbook contains number lines for sevenths), stressing the importance of all fractions sharing the same denominator when adding.

- Then move on to considering subtractions using number lines. Starting with one whole is the best approach, for example 1 − ³⁄₈ = ⁵⁄₈. Reinforce this using objects or drawn shapes/grids as necessary.

- *100 Maths Lessons Year 3, Summer 2, Week 4* provides structured lessons and resources to support teaching.

Curriculum objectives

- To add and subtract fractions with the same denominator within one whole.

Success criteria

- I can add and subtract fractions with the same denominator.

Adding and subtracting fractions with the same denominator

Learn

All these fractions belong to the same family.
The fractions have 8 as their denominator.

$$\frac{1}{8} \quad \frac{2}{8} \quad \frac{3}{8} \quad \frac{4}{8} \quad \frac{5}{8} \quad \frac{6}{8} \quad \frac{7}{8} \quad \frac{8}{8}$$

We can add and subtract fractions that have the same denominator.

You can use a fraction number line to count on or back.

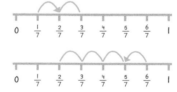

$$\frac{1}{7} + \frac{2}{7} = \frac{3}{7}$$

$$\frac{6}{7} - \frac{4}{7} = \frac{2}{7}$$

Remember, you only add the numerators.

Or you can just add or subtract the numerators, or top numbers.

$$\frac{1}{7} + \frac{2}{7} = \frac{1+2}{7} = \frac{3}{7}$$

$$\frac{6}{7} - \frac{4}{7} = \frac{6-4}{7} = \frac{2}{7}$$

When the numerator and denominator are the same, the fraction equals one.

> **✓ Tip**
>
> Sometimes two fractions make a whole one.
>
> $\frac{3}{7} + \frac{4}{7} = \frac{3+4}{7} = \frac{7}{7} = 1$

- Arrange the children in pairs and ask them to list of six fraction pairs that add up to one, such as ⅓ + ⅔ = 1. If appropriate, remind the children that one whole means that the numerator is equal to the denominator – ten out of ten parts is one whole, and so on.

- Once they are comfortable with mentally adding fractions, such as the textbook examples, challenge them to use their fraction pairs to create subtraction calculations.

Activities

- The textbook questions should not provide too many difficulties. Children who struggle should try the *Year 3 Practice Book* activity listed.

- A suitable extension to this work is to provide additions of three or more simple fractions, challenging more confident learners to consider what to do if the fractions total more than one whole.

Problems

- Once children have completed the Brain-teaser and the Brain-buster, provide them with other sum and difference problems, as well as two- and three-step real-life problems. Those who are up to the challenge could try adding fractions with different denominators by finding equivalent fractions.

Talk maths

Talk about pairs of fractions that equal one. Share at least two examples.

Talk about how you would solve these these sums. Would you use a number line or a different method? Explain why you say that.

$\frac{2}{8} + \frac{4}{8}$ $\frac{4}{8} - \frac{2}{8}$ $\frac{6}{9} + \frac{2}{9}$ $\frac{7}{9} - \frac{3}{9}$

Activities

Copy and complete these calculations. Try to work mentally. You can draw fraction number lines to help you if necessary.

1. $\frac{4}{8} + \frac{3}{8}$ 2. $\frac{9}{10} - \frac{3}{10}$ 3. $\frac{6}{7} - \frac{3}{7}$

4. $\frac{4}{6} + \frac{2}{6}$ 5. $\frac{3}{5} - \frac{2}{5}$ 6. $\frac{5}{6} - \frac{4}{6}$

Problems

Brain-teaser
Tim eats $\frac{5}{10}$ of a bar of chocolate and Lorna eats $\frac{4}{10}$. How much do they eat all together.

Brain-buster
Jamie, Susie and Penny have a pizza cut into 12 slices. Jamie eats $\frac{6}{12}$ of the pizza. Susie eats $\frac{3}{12}$ of the pizza. How much is left for Penny to have?

100 Maths Lessons Year 3 links:

- Summer 2, Week 4 (pages 232–237): add and subtract fractions with the same denominator

Year 3 Practice Book links:

- (page 80): Adding and subtracting fractions

Solving fraction problems

Prior learning

- Can compare and order fractions.
- Can count in tenths.
- Can add and subtract simple fractions.

Learn

- Using diagrams, number lines and objects, review all aspects of fractions that children should be familiar with to date. Model vocabulary, notation, identifying equivalences, ordering, adding and subtracting.

- In separate sessions, introduce missing-fraction problems and word problems. Missing-fraction problems are particularly important as they require reasoning to solve them, which is only possible when the concepts are correctly understood. Work with the children to consider a wide range of such problems similar to the example $\frac{6}{8} - \square = \frac{1}{8}$ on page 46 of the textbook. Use 'thinking aloud' to model thought processes and mathematical techniques. Diagrams and number lines may be useful to demonstrate counting on and back.

- Similarly, word problems such as that on page 46 of the textbook require analysis to consider what is being asked for. The children should also use estimation to check whether their answer seems correct. Model all of this, again 'thinking aloud', and work with the children on a range of further problems. *100 Maths Lessons Year 3, Spring 2, Week 5, Lesson 5* focuses on word problems and has accompanying resources.

Curriculum objectives

- To solve problems that involve fractions.

Success criteria

- I can solve fraction problems.

Solving fraction problems

Learn

To add or subtract fractions, check the denominators are the same, then add or subtract the numerators. You can solve problems with fractions. Remember the strategies you used to solve problems with whole numbers.

Here is a missing number problem. $\quad \frac{6}{8} - \bigstar = \frac{1}{8}$

Decide what you need to work out. What number do you need to subtract from $\frac{6}{8}$ to get to $\frac{1}{8}$?

Count back in eighths from $\frac{6}{8}$ to $\frac{1}{8}$: $\frac{5}{8}, \frac{4}{8}, \frac{3}{8}, \frac{2}{8}, \frac{1}{8}$ is five eighths.

$\frac{6}{8} - \frac{5}{8} = \frac{1}{8}$, so the missing number is $\frac{5}{8}$.

Or you can work out $\frac{6}{8} - \frac{1}{8} = \frac{6-1}{8} = \frac{5}{8}$.

 You can draw a fraction number line to help you.

Here is a word problem.

Freya eats $\frac{2}{5}$ of a bar of chocolate. How much of the chocolate is left?

You can write this as a missing number problem. $\frac{2}{5} + \bigstar = \frac{5}{5}$ or 1

Decide what you need to work out. What number do you need to add to $\frac{2}{5}$ to get to 1?

Count on in fifths from $\frac{2}{5}$ to 1: $\frac{3}{5}, \frac{4}{5}, \frac{5}{5}$.

$\frac{2}{5} + \frac{3}{5} = 1$, so there is $\frac{3}{5}$ of the bar of chocolate left.

Or you can work out: $1 - \frac{2}{5} = \frac{5}{5} - \frac{2}{5} = \frac{5-2}{5} = \frac{3}{5}$

 My tips can help make fractions fun!

 ✓ Tip

Read the question carefully, then write a number sentence. When adding or subtracting fractions, make sure the denominators are the same.

46   Fractions

Talk maths

- Provide children with missing-fraction problems and word problems (such as those in activities in the *Year 3 Practice Book*). Encourage them to work with partners to discuss and explain solutions to each. Although this is a talking activity, allow them to use diagrams, mathematical methods, number lines, equipment and so on – the important thing is to encourage the children's discussion and explanation of their thoughts.

Activities

- The questions can be used as a basis for other missing-fraction problems. These should cover as wide a range of fractions as possible from thirds to tenths. More confident learners might be challenged to start considering equivalences to solve problems such as ½ + ☐ = ¾.

Problems

- Children who complete the problems might be set a particularly challenging task: ask them to write problems based on the missing-fraction questions in Activities. They could also build on the *Year 3 Practice Book* activities focusing measures using practical equipment to create different problems involving fractions of quantities.

Talk maths

Which method do you prefer?

Look at the problems below and talk them through aloud.

$\frac{3}{10} + \star = \frac{7}{10}$ Count on: $\frac{4}{10}, \frac{5}{10}, \frac{6}{10}, \frac{7}{10}$. The missing number is $\frac{4}{10}$.

Subtract: $\frac{7}{10} - \frac{3}{10} = \frac{3-7}{10} = \frac{4}{10}$. The missing number is $\frac{4}{10}$.

There is $\frac{7}{8}$ of a chocolate cake left. Joe eats some of the cake. Now there is $\frac{5}{8}$ left. What fraction of the cake did Joe eat?

$\frac{7}{8} - \star = \frac{5}{8}$. Count back: $\frac{6}{8}, \frac{5}{8}$. Joe ate $\frac{2}{8}$ of the cake.

Subtract: $\frac{7}{8} - \frac{5}{8} = \frac{7-5}{8} = \frac{2}{8}$ → Joe ate $\frac{2}{8}$ of the cake.

Activities

1. Find the missing number. $\star + \frac{4}{7} = \frac{5}{7}$

2. What is the difference between $\frac{2}{7}$ and $\frac{5}{7}$?

3. Find the missing number. $\star - \frac{3}{9} = \frac{2}{9}$

4. What is the sum of $\frac{5}{12}$ and $\frac{4}{12}$?

Use the method that suits you best.

Problems

Brain-teaser
There are ten cakes on the tray. Five of the cakes are put into a box. What fraction of the cakes is left?

Brain-buster
There are 12 bottles of juice on the counter. The first customer buys $\frac{3}{12}$ of the juice. The second customer buys $\frac{5}{12}$ of the juice. What fraction of the bottles of juice is left?

---

100 Maths Lessons Year 3 links:

- Autumn 2, Week 4 (pages 67–72): solve simple fraction problems

- Spring 2, Week 5 (pages 154–159): solve problems involving fractions

- Summer 2, Week 4 (pages 232–237): solve problems involving fractions and addition and subtraction

Year 3 Practice Book links:

- (page 74): Fraction measures (1)

- (pages 83–84): Fraction word problems

- (page 85): Fraction measures (2)

Measuring and comparing lengths

Prior learning

- Can choose and use appropriate standard units to estimate and measure length and height.
- Can compare and order lengths using >, < and =.

Learn

- Review the children's knowledge of length and measurement, focusing on key vocabulary of length and height such as long/short, longer/shorter, tall/short, double/half, and so on.
- Review the units of measurement, eliciting simple examples of items measured in millimetres, centimetres and metres, as well as considering the equipment used for measuring each.

- Demonstrate the correct use of a ruler for measuring in millimetres and centimetres. If possible, use a digital ruler for ease of visibility. Review the process of estimating before measuring, and then considering the accuracy of the estimate. Next, using a metre rule, consider the difficulties of measuring larger objects (for example the width of the classroom) and how such measurements could be made accurately.

- *100 Maths Lessons Year 3, Autumn 1, Week 5, Lessons 1–3* support this work, including using measuring tapes and rulers.

Curriculum objectives

- To measure, compare, add and subtract: lengths (m/cm/mm); mass (kg/g); volume/capacity (l/ml).

~~Success criteria~~

- I can measure and compare different lengths.

Measuring and comparing lengths

Learn

To write lengths, we use these units of measurement:

metres (m)   millimetres (mm)   centimetres (cm)

When recording a length, always write the units of measurement. You can use the shortened form of m, cm or mm.

1m = 100cm

You will need a ruler that is marked in cm and mm.
To measure a line, place 0cm on your ruler pointing to the end of the line.

This line is 6cm long.

Before you measure a line, estimate how long you think it is. Compare your estimate and measurement to see how accurate you were.

This line is longer than 7cm and shorter than 8cm.

Find the mark on the ruler for $7\frac{1}{2}$cm or 7cm 5mm. This is halfway between 7cm and 8cm.

Count on in millimetres from there to where the line ends. The line is 7.8cm long, or 7cm 8mm.

There are 10mm in 1cm.

Comparing lengths
We can compare two lines like this.
A 7cm 8mm line is shorter than a 9cm 3mm line.

7cm 8mm < 9cm 3mm

Or we could say that a 9cm 3mm line is longer than a 7cm 8mm line.

9cm 3mm > 7cm 8mm

- Arrange the children in pairs or groups and provide a wide range of items for them to measure. Ask them to follow the instructions on page 48 of the textbook. Ensure that the children understand the procedure for estimating and then accurately measuring an item. Allow time for them to practise and hone their skills, encouraging them to describe what they're doing to their partners or group. The activity can be concluded by asking the children to arrange the items in ascending or descending order of length.

- If desired, this activity can be repeated for measuring in metres, focusing on the lengths of different spaces within the school, ideally using a trundle wheel.

Activities

- When the children have completed these questions, they could try the activities in the *Year 3 Practice Book* for support.

- Note that the second question moves on to adding lengths. This may need additional support, as well as a secure understanding of how to add two millimetre lengths. Encourage the children to use rulers and to draw the actual lengths.

Problems

- Both problems are tricky. The Brain-teaser requires the subtraction of centimetres and millimetres, which could be supported by drawing the actual lengths.

Talk maths

Look at your pencil. How long do you think it is?

Now measure it carefully. Don't forget to count any millimetres too! Did you make a reasonable estimate?

Now do the same for your book. Estimate its length first, then measure.

Now do the same for its width. Estimate then measure.

Now compare your estimates and measures.

Practise this with other things around you. You will find that your estimates become more accurate.

Activities

1. Draw these lines as accurately as you can.
   a. $8\frac{1}{2}$ cm
   b. 9cm 6mm

2. Write the answers for these. Show your working out.
   a. What is the total length of two lines measuring 8cm 4mm and 9cm 5mm?
   b. How much longer is $7\frac{1}{2}$ cm than 7cm 4mm?

Problems

Brain-teaser
Mr Smith asks Paul to draw a line that is 10cm 4mm long. Paul draws a line that is 9cm 8mm long. What is the difference in the two lengths?

Brain-buster
Jon has a 35m length of rope. He cuts off 17m. Then he cuts the remaining piece of rope into two equal pieces. How long are each of the two equal pieces of rope?

100 Maths Lessons Year 3 links:

- Autumn 1, Week 5 (pages 32–37): measure and compare length, using millimetres, centimetres and metres

Year 3 Practice Book links:

- (page 86): Using a ruler
- (page 87): 10 centimetres
- (page 88): Measuring equipment
- (page 95): Reading scales (choose appropriate questions)
- (page 102): Problems with length
- (page 103): Which unit of length?

Measuring and comparing mass

- Can choose and use appropriate standard units to estimate and measure mass.
- Can compare and order masses using >, < and =.

Learn

- Review the basic units of mass. Look at a range of weighing scales and discuss how they are used to measure mass. Balance scales are good for helping the children to see the equivalence of units of weight and objects; dial scales are good for reading and comparing numeric values.

- If possible, display images of items along with their weights, both in grams and kilograms, to develop children's appreciation of the relative size of the units involved.

- Focusing on the use of dial scales, work with the children to demonstrate correct procedures for reading them accurately. The main difficulty for children is reading 'in-between' values, forcing them to interpret the scales. As well as using easier scales, additional work on counting in steps between 10s and 100s may be beneficial.

- *100 Maths Lessons Year 3, Spring 2, Week 4* provides further advice and resources. Note that the later lessons move on to adding and subtracting weights, and are referenced in the section on adding and subtracting mass.

Curriculum objectives

- To measure, compare, add and subtract: lengths (m/cm/mm); mass (kg/g); volume/capacity (l/ml).

Success criteria

- I can measure and compare different masses.

Measuring and comparing mass

Learn

Mass is measured in kilograms (kg) and grams (g).

> 1 kg = 1000g

Look at the dial. It is measuring in hundreds.

Count around the dial in hundreds. 0g, 100g, 200g... and so on to 1000g. 1000g is the same as 1 kg.

The arrow points to 300g. So the mass is 300g.

Now look at this dial.

This time the count is in 200s. 0g, 200g, 400g... to 1 kg.

The arrow is midway between 600g and 800g, so the mass is 700g.

We can compare the two masses like this.

The 300g mass is lighter than the 700g mass.

300g < 700g

Use my tips to help you read scales accurately!

✓ Tip

Check the numbers on the dial.

Remember, the arrow may point in between two numbers.

Always write the units of measurement with your answer: kilograms or kg, grams or g.

Talk maths

- Children should have opportunities to work with various scales, unit weights and masses. The textbook work can be adapted by providing children with actual scales to explore and discuss with each other. Interpreting readings between divisions on the scales can be taken as far as children are comfortable with. Throughout any practical work ensure that children always estimate masses before measuring them.

Activities

- This section can be used as a starting point for comparing masses of two objects. Some children might move on to calculating the difference between different masses.
- Note that the *Year 3 Practice Book* has a range of resources for supporting this work.

Problems

- Both problems are quite straightforward. Both can be easily adapted to provide further practice, though note that there is also a section on adding and subtracting masses. The main thing is that children develop an understanding of the size of grams and kilograms, as well as a secure ability to estimate weights and read scales.

Talk maths

This dial counts up in 500s. Read the labels on the scale aloud. Can you say them in grams? 0g, 500g...

The arrow is pointing halfway between 500g and 1kg.

So the mass is 750g.

Discuss with a partner how you could work that out.

Tell them what the reading halfway between 1kg and $1\frac{1}{2}$kg would be.

What about the reading halfway between $1\frac{1}{2}$kg and 2kg?

Activities

1. Write the reading on each dial in grams.

2. Use < or > to show which is heavier, the mass of c or the mass of d.

Problems

Brain-teaser

Martha is making bread. She needs 400g of flour. She pours the flour out onto the scale pan. The reading on the dial is 500g. How much flour does Martha need to take off the pan?

Brain-buster

Alfie weighs some tins. The first one weighs 340g, the second one weighs 350g and the third one weighs 330g. What is the difference in mass between the lightest and the heaviest tin?

Measurement **51**

100 Maths Lessons Year 3 links:

- Spring 2, Week 4 (pages 148–153): measure and compare mass, using grams and kilograms

Year 3 Practice Book links:

- (page 89): Weighing things
- (page 90): How heavy?
- (page 91): Balance the mass
- (page 95): Reading scales (choose appropriate questions)

Measuring and comparing volume and capacity

Prior learning

- Can choose and use appropriate standard units to estimate and measure capacity and volume.
- Can compare and order capacities and volumes using >, < and =.

Learn

- Review the basic units of capacity. Look at a range of measuring equipment and discuss how they are used to measure capacity.
- If possible, display images of items along with their capacities (both in millilitres and litres) to develop children's appreciation of the relative sizes of the units involved.

- Spend time working with a range of capacity-measuring equipment, focusing on accurate reading of the scales. Estimate and measure the capacity of a range of containers, from a few millilitres up to more than 1 litre. Discuss how measuring equipment might be used to measure capacities that are bigger than the measuring equipment, such as a bowl of water or bathtub.

- Move on to comparing capacities, both in terms of 'more than' and 'less than', as well as introducing multiples, such as: *How many 200ml glasses would a 1-litre bottle of milk fill?* Children often find this easier to calculate than using abstract quantities.
- *100 Maths Lessons Year 3, Summer 1, Week 6* has structured lessons, including an interactive measuring jug on the CD-ROM.

Curriculum objectives

- To measure, compare, add and subtract: lengths (m/cm/mm); mass (kg/g); volume/capacity (l/ml).

Success criteria

- I can measure and compare different capacities and volumes.

Measuring and comparing volume and capacity

Learn

Volume and capacity are measured in litres (l) or millilitres (ml).

    1 litre = 1000 millilitres

Here is a measuring jug.
Look carefully at the scale.

The scale goes up in 100ml.
0, 100, 200, 300... and so on to 1 litre.

The capacity of the jug is 1 litre.

1 litre is the same as 1000ml.

The water level is at 300ml. So the volume of the water is 300ml.

Here is another measuring jug.

The water in the jug comes to halfway between 500ml and 600ml.

So the volume of the water is 550ml.

You can compare two amounts of water.

The water in jug A comes to halfway between 400ml and 500ml. This is 450ml.

The water in jug B comes to halfway between 600ml and 800ml. This is 700ml.

450ml < 700ml so there is more water in jug B.

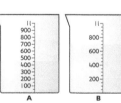

> ✓ **Tip**
>
> Check the scale on the jug carefully.
>
> Always write the units of measurement with your answer: litre or l, millilitre or ml.

Talk maths

- In groups or pairs, probably as a carousel activity, provide children with two different measuring jugs – ideally both the capacities and the scales will be different. Ask the children to explore how the same amounts can appear different according to the shape of the container. Ideally, children will also move on to estimating and measuring the capacities of a range of containers, small and large.

Activities

- The textbook has five questions that follow on from each other. It is suggested that this is worked through with the class. Then you could provide several sets of similar sequences using different quantities.

- Further practice is provided in the *Year 3 Practice Book* resources. Also provide the children with other opportunities to use suitable equipment for measuring capacity.

Problems

- The Brain-buster is tricky. It is a division and remainder problem, though it can be solved by using diagrams and repeated addition or subtraction. The children could also use equipment to find the solution. Further problems can easily be generated by simply adjusting the capacity of the glasses.

Talk maths

Here are two measuring jugs.

Jug A measures in 50ml. The scale goes 0ml, 50ml, 100ml, 150ml, 200ml.

Jug B measures in 20ml. The scale goes up in 20ml steps.

Which jug has more water in it?

If you used jug B to fill jug A, how many times would you need to fill it?

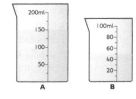

Activities

1. What is the capacity of the jug?

2. What is the volume of the water in the jug?

3. Another 200ml is poured into the jug. What is the volume of the water now?

4. Next, 400ml is poured out of the jug. How much water is left in the jug?

5. How much more water do you now need to fill the jug to the 1 litre mark?

Problems

Brain-buster

A Juicy Juice bottle contains 1 litre of juice. The glasses on the table each hold 300ml. How many glasses can be filled? How much juice is left in the bottle?

Measurement **53**

100 Maths Lessons Year 3 links:

- Summer 1, Week 6 (pages 201–206): measure and compare capacity and volume, using millilitres and litres

Year 3 Practice Book links:

- (pages 92–93): Measuring capacity
- (page 94): Measuring jugs
- (page 95): Reading scales (choose appropriate questions)

Telling the time with analogue clocks

- Can tell and write the time to five minutes, including quarter past/to the hour.
- Can recall the number of minutes in an hour and the number of hours in a day.

Learn

- Spend time looking at 12-hour clock faces. Point out that time has units that are unlike those for other measures, for example 60 seconds = 1 minute, 60 minutes = 1 hour. Finally, review times that children are already familiar with, such as 'o'clock', 'quarter to', 'quarter past', 'five past', 'ten to' and 'half past'.
- Consider the difference between the minute hand and the hour hand, looking at how far each hand moves during one minute and during one hour. Over repeated sessions, practise counting in minutes, in steps of both one minute and five minutes.
- Discuss the vocabulary of 'minutes past' and 'minutes to', reminding the children that the numbers on the 12-hour clock stand for the hours. To work out the minutes past the hour, they have to remember the 5-times table fact for a particular number. For example, when the minute hand is at 4, the number of minutes is 4 × 5 = 20 minutes past.

- Note that am and pm, and the representation of times digitally (for example, 08:15), are discussed in 'Telling the time with a 24-hour clock' on pages 64–65 of this book. The *Year 3 Practice Book* activity 'Telling the time' uses times written digitally.
- Several interactive clocks are available on the CD-ROM for *100 Maths Lessons Year 3*.

Curriculum objectives

- To tell and write the time from an analogue clock, including using Roman numerals from I to XII, and 12-hour and 24-hour clocks.

Success criteria

- I can tell and write the time from an analogue clock.

Telling the time with analogue clocks

Learn

There are 24 hours in a day.
Clock faces show 12 hours.
They are usually numbered 1 to 12.
There are 60 minutes in each hour.
On a clock, there are 5 minutes between each number.

Make sure you can tell the time to the nearest minute.

The minute hand is in the first half of the clock.
Count on from the 3 (15 minutes past) until you reach the minute hand: 16, 17, 18, 19.

The hour hand is just past the 7.

The clock shows 19 minutes past 7.

The minute hand is in the second half of the clock.
Count on anticlockwise from the 8 (20 minutes to) until you reach the minute hand: 21, 22, 23.

The hour hand is coming up to 11.

The clock shows 23 minutes to 11.

> **✓ Tip**
>
> Remember, if the minute hand is in the first 30 minutes, the time is 'past' the hour. If the minute hand is in the second 30 minutes, the time is 'to' the next hour.
>
> For minutes past the hour, start at 12 and count in fives for each number on the clock until you reach the minute hand. Then count on in ones for any more minutes.
>
> For minutes to the next hour, start at 12 and count anticlockwise in fives for each number on the clock until you reach the minute hand. Then count on in ones for any extra minutes.

- Display a selection of key times of the day as written statements. These might be children's favourite times, as in the textbook activity, but they could also be significant times of the school day or other times of day. (Be sure to mention 'noon' and 'midnight'.) Provide pairs or groups with a teaching clock, and ask them to create each time on the clock. This can progress to considering additional expressions, such as: *five minutes after school ends*, *ten minutes before playtime* and so on.

Activities

- Use the activities in the textbook as a starting point for representing times on clock faces. Continue practising this as much as necessary and extending to more complex statements (such as 'half an hour later') as desired. The *Year 3 Practice Book* provides questions on analogue clocks.

- You could use blank clock-face stamps to enter clock faces quickly into the children's exercise books, or to create pages of clock faces that can be photocopied, cut out and stuck in their books.

Problems

- The problems are both straightforward, particularly if supported with teaching clocks. Challenge the children to pose similar questions by calculating the duration, or times between, different events of the day.

Talk maths

What is your favourite time of day?

Draw the time on a clock face.

Tell someone about your favourite time of day.

Activities

1. **Draw hands on clock faces to show these times.**

   a. 19 minutes past 7

   b. 24 minutes to 8

   c. 17 minutes to 1

2. **Write the time for these clocks.**

   a.   b.

Problems

Brain-teaser

Tim thinks the time is 24 minutes to five. Barry thinks the time is 24 minutes past four. The clock shows the minute hand at just past the 7. Who is telling the correct time?

Brain-buster

At the end of the lesson the time is a quarter to 11. Playtime lasts until five minutes past 11. How long is playtime?

Measurement 55

Year 3 Practice Book links:

- (page 96): Telling the time (choose the questions about clocks with numbers on the faces)

Telling the time with Roman numerals

Prior learning

- Can tell and write the time to five minutes, including quarter past/to the hour.
- Can recall the number of minutes in an hour and the number of hours in a day.

Learn

- Remind the children how to use a 12-hour clock to read hours and minutes. Explain that there are 60 minutes in one hour, and that the numbers on a clock face are arranged in five-minute intervals (12 × 5 = 60). Count around the clock faces in hours, and then in minutes.
- Show the children a real 12-hour clock face with Roman numerals (or use pictures – Big Ben has Roman numerals). Compare it to an ordinary clock face. In discussion, elicit what number each Roman numeral represents. Remove the clock and create a chart for the numbers 1–12

Curriculum objectives

- To tell and write the time from an analogue clock, including using Roman numerals from I to XII, and 12-hour and 24-hour clocks.

Success criteria

- I can tell and write the time from an analogue clock that uses Roman numerals.

as shown on page 56 of the textbook. Spend time explaining the rules that the numerals follow, focusing on how the letters for 1, 5 and 10 are also used to represent other numbers.

- *100 Maths Lessons Year 3, Summer 2, Week 5, Lessons 1–3* combine work on telling the time with reading Roman numerals. (Note that times in these lessons are presented digitally, for example 7:35.)

- Note that am and pm, and the representation of times digitally (for example, 08:15), are discussed in 'Telling the time with a 24-hour clock' on pages 64–65 of this book. The *Year 3 Practice Book* activity 'Telling the time' uses times written digitally.

- Several interactive clocks are available on the CD-ROM for *100 Maths Lessons Year 3*.

Telling the time with Roman numerals

Learn

There are 24 hours in a day. Clock faces show 12 hours.
There are 60 minutes in each hour.
On a clock, there are 5 minutes between each number.

Clocks do not always have the numerals we use in maths. This clock uses Roman numerals. You can tell the time in the same way with these numerals.

Here are some Roman numerals.

I	V	X
1	5	10

All the other numerals on the clock are made from these.

I	II	III	IV	V	VI	VII	VIII	IX	X	XI	XII
1	2	3	4	5	6	7	8	9	10	11	12

Look at IV. This shows 1 less than 5.
VI shows 1 more than 5.
VII shows 2 more than 5.
VIII shows 3 more than 5.
IX shows 1 less than 10.
XI is 1 more than 10.
XII is 2 more than 10.

Did you know?

A famous clock with Roman numerals is Big Ben.

Roman numerals are tricky, but my tips will help!

✓ Tip

Sometimes clocks with Roman numerals use IIII for IV.

There's a simple rule with Roman numerals. Any I before V or X means the number is I less than 5 or 10. Any I after V means it is 1 more than 5. The same works with X.

- Provide children with a model of a clock face with Roman numerals (paper will do), and ask them to challenge each other to tell and show a range of times. Start with o'clock times, progressing to times with minutes past the hour, and then minutes to the hour.

- Children who are progressing well might be encouraged to start assimilating this knowledge by using Roman numeral clocks to answer questions about time. For example: *How long is it until noon?*

Activities

- Use the *Year 3 Practice Book* link to provide further practice.

- Extend children's learning by providing a list of times and have them show these times by drawing the hands on blank clock faces with Roman numerals.

Problems

- Both problems are straightforward. Further practice can be easily provided by rewriting the problems for different times. This can progress to calculating differences between times shown in Roman numerals.

Talk maths

Look at these clocks with Roman numerals and read the time on them.

Activities

1. **How many minutes past the hour?**

2. **How many minutes to the hour?**

3. **Draw hands on clock faces to show these times.**

   a. Quarter past 6   b. 27 minutes to 9   c. 27 minutes past 9

Problems

Brain-teaser
Sam's watch has Roman numerals. The hour hand points to just past V and the minute hand points to II. What is the time?

Brain-buster
The Roman numeral clock minute hand points to one minute past VI. The hour hand is past VIII. What is the time?

100 Maths Lessons Year 3 links:

- Summer 2, Week 5 (pages 238–243): tell the time on 12-hour analogue clocks with Roman numerals

Year 3 Practice Book links:

- (page 96): Telling the time (choose the questions about clocks with Roman numerals on the faces)

Telling the time with a 24-hour clock

- Can tell and write the time to five minutes, including quarter past/to the hour.
- Can recall the number of minutes in an hour and the number of hours in a day.

Learn

- Work with the children to recap the key features of how we measure time: 24 hours in a day, 60 minutes in one hour, 60 seconds in one minute. Remind them that we split the day up into two lots of 12 hours, calling these 'am' (ante meridian) and 'pm' (post meridian), relating to the movement of the Earth in relation to the sun, with 'noon' and 'midnight' being the transition points between the two. Note

also that 'morning', 'afternoon', 'evening' and 'night' are slightly more ambiguous terms.

- Using a selection of clocks (there are several interactive clocks on the CD-ROM for *100 Maths Lessons Year 3*), introduce the children to the concept of the 24-hour clock. Work together to compile a 'conversion' chart for 12- and 24-hour times. Ideally, this should be displayed permanently.

- Spend time ensuring that everyone understands the terminology involved: using a colon or full stop to separate hours from minutes, using am and pm only with 12-hour times.

- Present a selection of times digitally, using 12-hour times only (for example 06:20) and show their clock equivalents alongside.

Curriculum objectives

- To tell and write the time from an analogue clock, including using Roman numerals from I to XII, and 12-hour and 24-hour clocks.

Success criteria

- I can tell and write the time using 24-hour clocks.

Telling the time with a 24-hour clock

Learn

There are 24 hours in each day. Midnight is 12 o'clock at night. Noon is 12 o'clock in the day.

This clock shows the hours from midnight to noon, then the hours from noon to midnight. Count around the clock: 1, 2, 3..., 12, 13, 14..., 22, 23, 0.

Digital clocks and watches usually tell the time using the 24-hour clock. On a digital clock:
- 02:30 means half past two in the morning.
- 14:30 means half past two in the afternoon.
- 00:15 means a quarter past midnight.

When we write times in digits, we count on for minutes past the hour, all the way to 59. So 15:34 means 34 minutes past three in the afternoon, or 26 minutes to four in the afternoon.

For 12-hour time, we use am and pm:
- 12:27am means 27 minutes past 12 in the morning (or past midnight).
- 12:27pm means 27 minutes past 12 in the afternoon.

Did you know?

Ante meridian (am) means 'before noon'. *Post meridian* (pm) means 'after noon'.

Subtract 12 from the 24-hour time to find the 12-hour time.

✓ Tip

On an ordinary clock you cannot tell if the time is am or pm.

On a digital watch set to 24-hour clock time you can tell whether it is morning or afternoon. am times start with the digits 00–11, pm times start with the digits 12–23.

Remember to use 'am' or 'pm' when writing 12-hour times.

Talk maths

- Using the textbook activity as a starting point, ask the children to work in pairs or groups to read and write as many 24-hour clock times as possible. They could arrange the times in sets of three and create short sequences of events for each set of times. The times might be only a few minutes apart, or many hours, with children encouraged to think about their lives and what could happen in such time spans.

Activities

- The textbook questions are straightforward. *100 Maths Lessons Year 3, Summer 2, Week 5* has further lessons activities and resources to consolidate learning.

Problems

- Children who successfully complete both problems might move on to the activity outlined in *100 Maths Lessons Year 3, Summer 2, Week 5, Lesson 5*, involving reading train timetables. More confident learners should be provided with a selection of timetables (or use the internet to find some) to plan a range of multi-stage journeys.

Talk maths

Read the time on these clocks.

Are they am times, pm times, or can't you tell?
Make up a story about what you might be doing at these three times of day.

Activities

1. Write these times in 24-hour clock time.

   a. Half past six in the morning

   b. 8:45pm

   c. 27 minutes to four in the afternoon

   d. 10 minutes to three in the afternoon

   e. 12:07am

   f. Quarter past four in the morning.

Problems

Brain-teaser
Khalid sets the alarm on his digital clock to ring at 23 minutes to seven in the morning. What time does the clock show when it rings?

Brain-buster
Peter reads the time on his Roman numeral clock as the hour hand points to beyond X and the minute hand to two minutes past VIII. It is evening. Write the time in 24-hour clock time.

Measurement **59**

100 Maths Lessons Year 3 links:

- Summer 2, Week 5 (pages 238–243): read 12- and 24-hour time on a digital clock and understand the link to an analogue clock

Using the vocabulary of time

- Can compare and sequence intervals of time.
- Can recall the number of minutes in an hour and the number of hours in a day.

Curriculum objectives

- To estimate and read time with increasing accuracy to the nearest minute; record and compare time in terms of seconds, minutes and hours; use vocabulary such as o'clock, am/pm, morning, afternoon, noon and midnight.
- To compare durations of events.

Success criteria

- I can use the vocabulary of time.
- I can compare time in terms of seconds, minutes and hours.

Learn

- Review a range of time vocabulary, for example 'yesterday', 'tomorrow', 'in a while', and so on. Ideally, use these a short story or set of sentences. Talk about how these words show us when things happened.
- Also review the correct spelling, and use of capital letters, for the days of the week and months of the year. If appropriate, also cover leap years.
- Using the word box on page 60 of the textbook as a starting point, spend time creating sentences about different times during the day. Consider the length of events and compare them, working towards simple mental calculations with time. For example, compare the length of a mathematics lesson to lunchtime, or the average time it takes to write a signature to the time it takes to write out the 5-times table. Model and emphasise time vocabulary at all times.

Using the vocabulary of time

Learn

Here is some of the vocabulary of time that we use often in everyday life.

> morning afternoon noon midnight
> am pm day hour minute second

Here are some sentences that use some of these words.

Molly ran a race. She took 15 seconds to reach the finish line.

This morning it took me 2 minutes to really clean my teeth thoroughly.

The journey to London took 3 hours by train.

We can order these events by how long each one took.
15 seconds is the shortest time. 3 hours is the longest time.
So, 15 seconds < 2 minutes < 3 hours. This is from the shortest to the longest time.
And 3 hours > 2 minutes > 15 seconds. This is from the longest to the shortest time.

Some digital watches show time in hours, minutes and seconds like this one.
It shows an evening time.
The time is 8:15pm and 14 seconds.

Sometimes we need to calculate with time.
Timothy writes his name eight times in 72 seconds.
How long does he take to write his name once? 72 ÷ 8 = 9
So Timothy takes nine seconds to write his name once.

✓ Tip

Always check the units of time that you are working with.

If you are timing an event, it may be in seconds, minutes or even hours.

- The textbook activity can be extended to talking about months, duration of events and times between events. Ideally, each group would be provided with a 'diary planner' sheet for daily events and a monthly calendar for other events.

- If children are confident answering these questions, ask them to create a storyboard of a typical school day, showing the times for the commencement of each event, from getting up to returning to bed 12 or so hours later.

- Once the children have worked through both problems, ask them to make up similar questions for a partner to answer. They must know the answers to every question they ask!

Talk maths

Here are some sentences that use the vocabulary of time.
Read each one and look for words to do with time.

> I get up in the morning at 7:30am.

> I go to bed at 8:30pm.

> I am sound asleep by midnight.

> I have my school dinner at noon.

Now think of your own sentences about time. Try to use all the words in the box on the opposite page.

Activities

1. Copy these sentences and add the missing time word.

   a. In the ___ I have my breakfast at 8:00.

   b. I come home from school in the ___ at 4:00.

   c. At school we have our lunch at ___, which is when the afternoon starts.

2. a. Which takes longer, 35 seconds or half a minute?

   b. Which is the shorter time, one day or 23 hours and 59 minutes?

Problems

Brain-teaser
Which is shorter, 1 minute and 15 seconds or 70 seconds?

Brain-buster
Georgiana writes her name six times. This takes her 48 seconds. How many seconds does it take her to write her name just once?

Measurement   61

100 Maths Lessons
Year 3 links:

- Summer 2, Week 5 (pages 238–243): use the vocabulary of time; compare durations of events

Numbers and time

Prior learning

- Can compare and sequence intervals of time.
- Can recall the number of minutes in an hour and the number of hours in a day.

- Recap the relationships between different units of time: seconds, minutes, hours, days, weeks. Display a large electronic calendar and examine how months are laid out in a calendar, and show how weekly events can be added and adjusted, as well as monthly and annual events. Throughout, model vocabulary and correct spellings.

- In separate sessions, focus on revising longer time units (days, weeks, months) and shorter time units (hours, minutes, seconds). Children need to be proficient in both vocabulary and relationships. Wherever possible, create displays or cue cards that children can have to hand to support their independent work.

- *100 Maths Lessons Year 3, Summer 2, Week 5* provides various lessons and resources to support this work.

Curriculum objectives

- To know the number of seconds in a minute and the number of days in each month, year and leap year.
- To compare durations of events.

Success criteria

- I can calculate the duration of different events and make comparisons.
- I can say how many days there are in each month, year and leap year.

Numbers and time

Learn

There are seven days in a week: Monday, Tuesday, Wednesday, Thursday, Friday, Saturday and Sunday.

There are 60 seconds in one minute.
There are 60 minutes in one hour.
There are 24 hours in one day.
There are 365 days in one year.
In a leap year there are 366 days.
There is a leap year every fourth year.
A leap year number is exactly divisible by 4.

You need to learn these time facts.

Use this poem to help you remember the number of days in the months of the year.

> Thirty days has September,
> April, June, and November.
> All the rest have 31,
> Except for February all alone,
> It has 28 each year,
> but 29 each leap year.

Did you know?

There are 3600 seconds in an hour and 86,400 seconds in one day!

Here are the months and their days set out in a table.

Jan	Feb	Mar	Apr	May	Jun	Jul	Aug	Sep	Oct	Nov	Dec
31	28 or 29	31	30	31	30	31	31	30	31	30	31

✓ Tip

To work out if it is a leap year look at the last two numbers in the year. If it divides exactly by 4 it is a leap year. So, for 2016, look at just the 16. As 16 does divide by 4, 2016 is a leap year.

62   Measurement

- Arrange the children in small groups and provide them with calendars, diaries and clocks. Using the examples in the textbook as starting points, challenge the groups to pose and solve a range of time problems. Encourage them to include both longer times (days, weeks, months) and shorter times (hours, minutes, seconds).

Activities

- The questions can easily be adapted by adjusting the numbers to create new problems. In addition, children should be encouraged to create their own problems to try out on each other, ensuring that they know the correct answer before challenging anyone.
- A small extension task could be to ask each child to find out the exact date and time of their birth. More confident learners can then do all sorts of calculations from this, such as: *How long have you been alive? Exactly how much older/younger are you than another child?*

Problems

- Once children have completed the problems move them on to the *Year 3 Practice Book* problems, which also focus on calculating durations in minutes.
- If further extension is required, create a database of all the children's dates of birth (including the actual times of birth if possible). This data can be used to create differentiated problems, from age difference in weeks and days to hours lived, time until next birthday, and so on.

Talk maths

Look at these problems and talk them through aloud.
Explain each step in the answers.
How many days are there from 15th March to the end of the month (not including the 15th)?
There are 31 days in March. 31 − 15 = 16 days

Tom times himself doing his homework. He starts at 4:35pm and finishes at 5:12pm. How long does he take?
Count around the clock from 4:35. 35 to 40, 50, 60 is 25 minutes.
5:00 to 5:12 is 12 minutes. 25 + 12 = 37 minutes
So Tom's homework takes 37 minutes.

Activities

1. **Write your working as well as the answers for these questions.**

   a. How long is it from 2nd December to the end of the month (not including the 2nd)?

   b. How long is it from 6:30pm to 7:45pm?

   c. How many minutes are there in 3 hours?

   d. How long is 90 seconds in minutes and seconds?

Problems

Brain-teaser
Janie runs to school in 6 minutes 15 seconds. Peter runs to school in 6 minutes 27 seconds. How much long does Peter take than Janie?

Brain-buster
Kiri decides to make a cake. It takes her 6 minutes to find the ingredients, 2 minutes to weigh the ingredients and 10 minutes to mix the ingredients. The cake takes 35 minutes to bake. How many minutes is that in total?

Measurement 63

100 Maths Lessons Year 3 links:

- Summer 2, Week 5 (pages 238–243): use units of time; calculate time intervals

Year 3 Practice Book links:

- (page 97): TV times
- (page 98): Units of time
- (page 99): Months
- (page 104): Measures word problems (choose appropriate problems)
- (page 105): Time problems

Finding the perimeter of 2D shapes

Prior learning

- Can identify and describe the properties of 2D shapes.
- Can use a ruler to accurately measure straight lines.

Learn

- Explain that the perimeter of a shape is the distance around its edge. A nice visualisation is to imagine that you are an ant walking around a small shape, or you yourself are walking around a large shape. Using the textbook examples on page 64

as a starting point, demonstrate how to add side lengths together to find the perimeter. It is useful to cover irregular shapes at this point – if anything this makes the concept more obvious.

- Next, return to the regular shapes listed at the top of page 64 in the textbook – triangle, square, rectangle, pentagon, hexagon and circle. Draw examples of these shapes on the board and write side lengths on them

as appropriate. Work with the children to calculate the perimeter of each shape. Ask: *What is difficult about finding the perimeter of a circle?* Consider how it might be found.

- *100 Maths Lessons Year 3, Autumn 1, Week 5, Lessons 4 and 5 focus on the perimeter of 2D shapes.*

Curriculum objectives

- To measure the perimeter of simple 2D shapes.

Success criteria

- I can find the perimeter of 2D shapes.

Finding the perimeter of 2D shapes

Learn

2D shapes include triangles, squares, rectangles, pentagons, hexagons and circles.

> To find the perimeter we measure each side, then we add them together.

Perimeter is the distance all the way around a 2D shape.

The perimeter of this rectangle is 3cm + 2cm + 3cm + 2cm = 10cm

```
        3cm
2cm  [        ]  2cm
        3cm
```

You can find the perimeter of any 2D shape in the same way.

The perimeter of the square is 1.5cm + 1.5cm + 1.5cm + 1.5cm = 6cm

```
    1.5cm
1.5cm [   ] 1.5cm
    1.5cm
```

> The perimeter is the distance an ant would walk if it went all the way around the shape.

Here is an irregular hexagon.
The perimeter of the hexagon is
16m + 16m + 5m + 5m + 5m + 5m
= 32m + 20m
= 52m

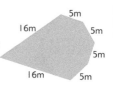

> This time there are six sides to add.

✓ Tip

Make sure the units of all the lengths are the same before you add.

You can add centimetres to centimetres, metres to metres and millimetres to millimetres. Trace around the shape with your finger to make sure you include all the sides.

Talk maths

- Provide children with a range of shapes and ask them to explain to each other how they would find the perimeter of each. Some children might notice the link to multiplication for regular shapes, and more confident learners can be challenged to find the perimeter of composite shapes formed by joining two regular shapes together.

Activities

- The textbook questions are easy enough to adapt to create more questions if desired by adjusting either/both sizes and units of length.
- The *Year 3 Practice Book* activity 'Measuring 2D shapes' challenges children to create shapes from a limited number of facts and then to find the perimeters.

Problems

- Once children have completed the problems, challenge them to measure and calculate the perimeters of a range of items in the classroom or school. They can tabulate these, listing length, width and perimeter for each one, and ensuring the correct units are used.

Talk maths

Explain to a friend how to find the perimeter of these shapes.

- The green shape.
- All four sides of a square measure 7cm. Find the perimeter.
- A triangle has two sides that measure 6cm each and one side that measures 10cm. Find the perimeter.

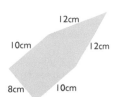

12cm

10cm   12cm

8cm   10cm

Activities

1. **Measure and find the perimeters of these shapes.**

    a.   b.   c.

2. **Find the perimeter of these shapes.**

    a. A garden with six sides all 10m in length.

    b. A triangle with sides measuring 7cm, 8cm and 13cm.

Problems

Brain-teaser
Riley cuts out a regular hexagon from paper. Each side of the hexagon measures 8cm. What is the perimeter of the hexagon?

Brain-buster
A computer tablet is a rectangle shape. It is 19cm along its width and 25cm in length. What is its perimeter?

Measurement   **65**

100 Maths Lessons Year 3 links:

- Autumn 1, Week 5 (pages 32–37): find the perimeter of simple 2D shapes

Year 3 Practice Book links:

- (page 108): Measuring 2D shapes

Money

Prior learning

- Can find different combinations of coins that equal the same amounts of money.
- Can solve simple problems in a practical context involving addition and subtraction of money of the same unit, including giving change.

Learn

- Look at the coins used in daily life (there is an interactive resource on the CD-ROM with *100 Maths Lessons Year 3*). Discuss the value of each coin, listing items that each might buy. As appropriate, discuss the value of each coin in relation to the others, creating statements such as two 10p coins equals one 20p coin.
- Similarly, look at and discuss the notes used in daily life.
- Over several sessions, look at the relationships between pounds and pence, converting between the two. Explain how to read money presented in decimal form and consider mental and formal methods for adding and subtracting a range of amounts.
- *100 Maths Lessons Year 3, Spring 1, Week 5* provides a structured sequence of lessons and resources to support this work.

Curriculum objectives

- To add and subtract amounts of money to give change, using both £ and p in practical contexts.

Success criteria

- I can add and subtract amounts of money and find change.

Money

Learn

Here are our coins.

We also have £5, £10, £20 and £50 notes.

If you are given an amount in pence, you can write it in pounds and pence by seeing how many lots of 100p there are. For example,

546p = 500p + 46p   500p = £5

So 546p is £5 and 46p. We write this as £5.46.

You can find the difference between amounts of money by counting up. This is useful for finding change. For example,

Polly buys a comic for 87p and pays with a £1 coin. Count on from 87p to £1 to find her change.

Can you count on from 87p to £1 in your head?

```
        +3p              +10p
   87p        90p                      £1
```

Change = 3p + 10p = 13p

Or you can write a subtraction sentence: £1 − 87p = 100p − 87p = 13p

Here is one way of working out £3.45 plus £2.67.

£3.45 = 345p, £2.67 = 267p

	3	4	5
+	2	6	7
		1	2
	1	0	0
	5	0	0
	6	1	2

612p = £6.12

✓ **Tip**

To find the sum of several amounts of money, change them all to pence first then add them together. Change them back to pounds and pence at the end.

Talk maths

- Using the textbook example as a starting point, provide groups of children with a selection of everyday objects with price tags attached. Challenge them to decide on the coins and notes they would need to hand over to pay for each item, and to calculate the change they would receive. Adjust the price tags to support or extend groups as appropriate.

Activities

- The textbook questions can be extended or simplified as desired, with support available in the links to *100 Maths Lessons Year 3*.
- Further support and practice might be provided by making sets of plastic coins available. The children could count in multiples of 5p, 10p, 20p and so on, to consolidate their understanding of both the numbers and the relationships of the coins.

Problems

- The Brain-teaser should be straightforward for most children. The Brain-buster is a two-step problem, requiring conversion between pence and pounds as well as subtraction. You may need to work with the children to carefully demonstrate good practice in laying out and presenting each step of solving this type of problem. (*100 Maths Lessons Year 3, Spring 1, Week 5, Lesson 5* will help with this work.)

Talk maths

Look at the problems below and talk them through aloud.
Do you prefer to count on using a number line, or in your head? Why?

I have £5. I want to buy this DVD.
How much change will I get?

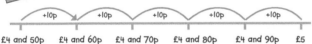

| £4 and 50p | £4 and 60p | £4 and 70p | £4 and 80p | £4 and 90p | £5 |

Count on: £4 and 50p, then 60, 70, 80, 90, £5
That is a count of 50p. The change is 50p.

> Talk about buying different items with different prices.

Activities

1. **Show your working out.**
   a. Find 65p + 47p. Answer in £ and p.
   b. Find £1 − 38p.
   c. Find the sum of £3.32 and £4.89.
   d. How much more is £2.34 than £1.67?

Problems

Brain-teaser
Shani buys a drink of squash for 85p.
How much change does she get from £5?

Brain-buster
Dan spends 75p on a drink, 37p on a biscuit and 46p on an apple.
How much change does Dan get from £5?

100 Maths Lessons Year 3 links:

- Spring 1, Week 5 (pages 113–118): add and subtract money

Year 3 Practice Book links:

- (pages 100–101): Money calculations

Adding and subtracting lengths

- Can estimate and measure lengths in metres and centimetres.
- Can use mental and written methods for addition and subtraction.

Learn

- Revise how to use large and small rulers, and recap the relationship between metres, centimetres and millimetres. Point out that 1m = 1000mm. Revise the meaning of each measure, examining units of length, considering and comparing the lengths of a selection of items.

- Note that 'Measuring and comparing lengths' on pages 54–55 of this book provides guidance and advice on this.
- Over several sessions, work with the children to consider how lengths can be added and subtracted. Demonstrate the importance of using the same units when calculating, and discuss how to convert lengths to all use the same unit. This will involve selecting mental

and written methods, with an additional emphasis on checking and converting units if necessary.

- *100 Maths Lessons Year 3, Autumn 1, Week 5, Lessons 4 and 5* cover addition of lengths in the context of perimeter, which children may already be familiar with.

Curriculum objectives

- To measure, compare, add and subtract: lengths (m/cm/mm); mass (kg/g); volume/capacity (l/ml).

Success criteria

- I can add and subtract lengths.

Adding and subtracting lengths

Learn

Lengths are measured in metres (m), centimetres (cm) and millimetres (mm).

$$1m = 100cm \qquad 1cm = 10mm$$

When working with lengths, always check the units of measurement. Add or subtract the same units.

To find the total of 3m 30cm and 2m 80cm, change the metres to centimetres.
330cm + 280cm

$$= 300 + 30 + 200 + 80$$
$$= 300 + 200 + 30 + 80$$
$$= 500 + 110$$
$$= 610cm \text{ or } 6m \ 10cm$$

To find the difference between two lengths, subtract the shorter length from the longer.

My pencil used to be 19cm long. Now it is 15cm long. How much of my pencil has gone ?

We must find the difference between 19cm and 15cm.
19cm – 15cm is 4cm, so the pencil is 4cm shorter than it used to be.

This subtraction problem has mixed units. Work out 5m 60cm – 3m 46cm.

First change the units to centimetres.
5m 60cm is 560cm and 3m 46cm is 346cm.

Here is one way of doing the subtraction.

	5	$^5\cancel{6}$	$^{1}0$
–	3	4	6
	2	1	4

The answer is 214cm or 2m 14cm.

> ### ✓ Tip
>
> Remember that 10mm is the same as 1cm.
>
> And 100cm is the same as 1m.
>
> When you add or subtract lengths, make sure the units of measurement are the same.

- Decide whether they want the children to use both of the methods demonstrated in the textbook, or to focus on just one. With this decided, challenge the children to work in pairs and discuss their strategies to a range of addition and subtraction calculations, presenting numbers in appropriate units as desired to differentiate work.

- It is important that children have the opportunity to explain their thinking to ensure that there are no misconceptions or errors.

Activities

- The questions in the textbook can be modified to create further practice calculations as desired. Children who need support should focus on adding and subtracting simple lengths below 30cm, so that they can use rulers to confirm their answers. More confident learners might be presented with problems that involve lengths in different units, thus requiring an initial step of conversion.

Problems

- The Brain-buster involves perimeter. Further practice can be presented using the activities in the *Year 3 Practice Book*, as well as by revising perimeters of 2D shapes. Extension work can be provided using simple plans and maps (from classroom to local area) and challenging children to calculate a range of distances between several places.

Talk maths

Talk through the problem below. Which method do you prefer?

What is 15cm 9mm add 24cm 7mm?

Method 1: Convert both lengths to millimetres first.
15cm 9mm = 159mm   24cm 7mm = 247mm
159mm + 247mm = 406mm or 40cm 6mm

Method 2: Add the centimetres and millimetres separately.
15cm + 24cm = 39cm   9mm + 7mm = 16mm
Convert the millimetres length to centimetres and millimetres.
16mm = 1cm 6mm
Then add it to 39cm. 39cm + 1cm 6mm = 40cm 6mm

Now try adding different lengths with your preferred method.

Activities

1. **Find the answers.**

   a. Work out 64cm − 35cm.

   b. Work out 156m + 247m.

   c. Find the sum of 6cm 2mm and 3cm 9mm.

   d. What is the difference between 2cm 4mm and 5cm 6mm?

Problems

Brain-teaser
Freddie's mum measures him each birthday. When he was seven his height was 1 metre 25 centimetres. When he was eight he was 1 metre 33 centimetres. How much has he grown in one year?

Brain-buster
The perimeter of a rectangular garden is 90m. The width of the garden is 12m. What are the measurements of each side of the garden?

Measurement **69**

100 Maths Lessons Year 3 links:

- Autumn 1, Week 5 (pages 32–37): add and subtract lengths

Year 3 Practice Book links:

- (page 104): Measures word problems (choose appropriate problems)

Adding and subtracting mass

Prior learning

- Can estimate and measure masses in kilograms and grams.
- Can use mental and written methods for addition and subtraction.

Learn

- Recap the relationship between kilograms and grams. Point out that 1kg = 1000g. Revise the meaning of each measure, examining units of weight, considering and ordering the masses of a selection of items.
- Note that 'Measuring and comparing mass' on pages 56–57 of this book provides guidance and advice on this.
- Over several sessions, work with the children to consider how masses can be added and subtracted. Demonstrate the importance of using the same units when calculating, and discuss how to convert masses to all use the same unit. This will involve selecting mental and written methods, with an additional emphasis on checking and converting units if necessary.
- *100 Maths Lessons Year 3, Spring 2, Week 4, Lessons 4 and 5 provides structured lessons which progress to adding and subtracting masses.*

Curriculum objectives

- To measure, compare, add and subtract: lengths (m/cm/ mm); mass (kg/g); volume/ capacity (l/ml).

Success criteria

- I can add and subtract mass.

Adding and subtracting mass

Learn

Mass is measured in kilograms (kg) and grams (g).

1kg is the same as 1000g.

So $\frac{1}{2}$kg is 500g, $\frac{1}{4}$kg is 250g and $\frac{3}{4}$kg is 750g.

Use your favourite method to add masses in grams.

Here is one way of working out the total mass of these fruits

	1	2	9
	1	2	1
		7	6
+		7	5
	4	0	1
		2	2

75g   129g   76g   121g

So the total mass is 401g.

Here is one way of working out the difference in mass between the heaviest and lightest of the four fruits above.

The orange is heaviest at 129g.

The apple is lightest at 75g.

Count on from 75 to 129: 75 to 100 is 25, and 100 to 129 is 29.

25 + 29 is 54.

So the difference in mass between the orange and apple is 54g.

To find the difference between masses subtract the smaller from the larger one.

✓ Tip

Be sure to show your working. This helps others to follow your thinking.

You can draw a number line to help you to add or subtract masses.

- Ideally, the example in the textbook should be recreated in the classroom, placing an identical pair of scales side by side and having a selection of objects available. Children can then work in pairs to compare masses. The items can then be ordered and compared, moving on to calculating combined masses and the difference between masses.

- A further challenge might be to ask children to find the combined mass of all objects available for weighing.

Activities

- The questions in the textbook can be modified to create further practice calculations as desired. Children who need support should focus on adding and subtracting simple masses below 100g, ideally using actual weights to confirm their answers. More confident learners might be presented with problems that include masses in different units, thus requiring an initial step of conversion.

Problems

- The Brain-buster requires several steps. *100 Maths Lessons Year 3, Spring 2, Week 4, Lessons 4 and 5* provide a range of context-based problems.

- To develop work further, bring some accurate digital scales into the classroom. Challenge the children to weigh heavier objects (including themselves if appropriate), and compare larger weights that are presented in both kilograms and grams.

Talk maths

Look at the scales below. Discuss with a partner which mass is smaller, then write a sentence to compare the two masses.

A B

Can you complete this sentence? ... is the smaller mass.

Explain the method you would use to:
- total the two masses
- find the difference between the two masses.

Activities

1. **Copy these questions and find the answers.**
   a. 95g + 45g
   b. 136g − 97g
   c. 74g − 58g
   d. What is the difference between 120g and 167g?

Problems

Brain-teaser
Two children are going on a helicopter ride and have to be weighed beforehand. One child weighs 59kg. The other child weighs 52kg. How much is that in total?

Brain-buster
Sara mixes together 100g of flour, 100g of sugar and 100g of butter. Then she adds three eggs, each of which weighs 56g. How much do the ingredients weigh in total?

100 Maths Lessons Year 3 links:

- Spring 2, Week 4 (pages 148–153): add and subtract masses

Year 3 Practice Book links:

- (page 104): Measures word problems (choose appropriate problems)

Adding and subtracting volume and capacity

Prior learning

- Can estimate and measure capacity in litres and millilitres.
- Can use mental and written methods for addition and subtraction.

Learn

- Using large and small measuring equipment, examine the relationship between litres and millilitres. Point out that 1 litre = 1000 millilitres. Revise the meaning of each unit, considering and ordering the capacity of a selection of items.

- Note that 'Measuring and comparing volume and capacity' on pages 58–59 of this book provides guidance and advice on this.

- Over several sessions, work with the children to consider how different capacities or volumes can be added and subtracted. Demonstrate the importance of using the same units when calculating, and discuss how to convert capacities or volumes to all use the same unit. This will involve selecting mental and written methods, with an additional emphasis on checking and converting units if necessary.

- *100 Maths Lessons Year 3, Summer 1, Week 6, Lesson 5* progresses to adding and subtracting capacity via practical problems, with an interactive measuring jug available on the CD-ROM that accompanies *100 Maths Lessons Year 3*.

Curriculum objectives

- To measure, compare, add and subtract: lengths (m/cm/mm); mass (kg/g); volume/capacity (l/ml).

Success criteria

- I can add and subtract volumes and capacities.

Adding and subtracting volume and capacity

Learn

Capacity and volume are measured in litres (l) and millilitres (ml).

1 litre is the same as 1000ml. So $\frac{1}{2}$ litre is 500ml, $\frac{1}{4}$ litre is 250ml and $\frac{3}{4}$ litre is 750ml.

Use your favourite methods to add and subtract volumes.

Read the scale on this jug carefully.

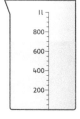

Capacity is how much a container can hold. This measuring jug has a capacity of 1000ml. It has a volume of 700ml in it.

It contains 700ml of water.

Another 200ml of water is added to the jug.
Add 200ml to 700ml to find the new volume of water.
700ml + 200ml = 900ml

450ml is poured away.
Subtract 450ml from 900ml to find the new volume of water.
900ml − 450ml = 450ml

✓ Tip

Be sure to show your working. This helps others to follow your thinking.

You can draw a number line to help you to add or subtract millilitres or litres.

I'll add some tips to help you add and subtract!

Talk maths

- The activity in the textbook shows the link between practical problems and mental methods. The activity can be developed without the need for equipment by providing groups with a selection of capacities (in millilitres) on flashcards. The children can take it in turns to pick a card at random and subtract the amount shown from 1 litre, or take two cards and find their total capacity. This can be extended by providing amounts that total more than 1 litre, as well as amounts that combine units, such as 2l 300ml and 1l 300ml, which can be added and subtracted as desired

Activities

- The questions in the textbook can be modified to create further practice calculations as desired. Children who need support should focus on adding and subtracting simple capacities below 100ml, ideally using actual capacities to confirm their answers.
- More confident learners might be presented with problems that include capacities or volumes in different units, thus requiring an initial step of conversion.

Problems

- To develop this work further, provide a wet area in the classroom. Challenge the children to measure the capacity of a range of containers, calculating differences and total capacities as appropriate.

Talk maths

Look at this problem and talk it through aloud with a partner.

There is 1 litre or 1000 millilitres of water in the jug. 450ml is poured out. How much is left in the jug?

Use a number line to work out 1000ml − 450ml.

500 + 50 = 550   So 550ml is left.

Work with a partner to add and subtract different volumes of water.

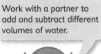

Activities

1. Copy and answer these questions.
   a. 65ml + 92ml
   b. 135ml − 45ml
   c. What is the sum of 230ml and 330ml?
   d. What is the difference between 950ml and 760ml?

Problems

Brain-teaser
A car has 80 litres of fuel in the tank at the start of a journey. At the end of the journey there is 32 litres of fuel left. How much fuel was used?

Brain-buster
A full litre jug is used to fill three 125ml cups. How much water is left in the jug?

100 Maths Lessons Year 3 links:

- Summer 1, Week 6 (pages 201–206): add and subtract capacities

Year 3 Practice Book links:

- (page 104): Measures word problems (choose appropriate problems)

Lines

Prior learning

- Can draw and measure straight lines using a ruler.
- Can identify a range of 2D shapes.

Learn

- Draw a selection of regular polygons on the board, and work with the children to elicit facts about them, including differences. List any vocabulary and clarify definitions as necessary.
- Take time to discuss the main difference of a circle: it has no straight lines, only curved, so much of the following vocabulary will not apply to it.

- Using a fresh set of shapes, focus on the key vocabulary of lines. Through discussion, identify and label all instances of vertical, horizontal, perpendicular and parallel lines on the 2D shapes on the board.
- *100 Maths Lessons Year 3, Summer 1, Week 5* provides a sequence of lessons incorporating investigation of lines alongside drawing 2D shapes.

Curriculum objectives

- To identify horizontal and vertical lines and pairs of perpendicular and parallel lines.

Success criteria

- I can identify horizontal, vertical, perpendicular and parallel lines.

Lines

Learn

Squares and rectangles have four right angles. Triangles can have one right angle but most types of triangle have no right angles.

Here is some vocabulary for lines.

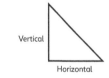

Perpendicular lines meet at a right angle.

Horizontal   Vertical   Perpendicular   Parallel

Look at this shape. It has one vertical line and one horizontal line.
The vertical and horizontal lines make a right-angle. They are perpendicular.
The shape is a right-angled triangle.

Vertical
Horizontal

Here's another shape. It has two vertical lines. They are parallel. It has two horizontal lines. They are also parallel. The vertical and horizontal lines are perpendicular. They make four right angles. The shape is a rectangle.

Horizontal
Vertical   Vertical
Horizontal

✓ Tip

Horizontal lines go across the page – like the *horizon*.

Vertical lines go up – people with *vertigo* don't like going up high.

Parallel lines run alongside each other – like train tracks.

Perpendicular lines make a right angle.

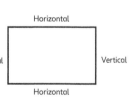

Use my tips to help your remember lots about lines!

74   Geometry

Talk maths

- The textbook activity on page 75 is very useful for consolidating the new vocabulary of lines. Allow the children to work in pairs drawing simple shapes to start with. As their competence grows, encourage them to create more precise shapes, introducing exact dimensions, as well as pairs of shapes and abstract designs. To conclude, work with the whole class to review and model these processes.

Activities

- The textbook questions should be straightforward, as should the *Year 3 Practice Book* activity. Following the lessons and activities in *100 Maths Lessons Year 3, Summer 1, Week 5* will allow children to use their new knowledge in context, also reinforcing their understanding of 2D shapes.

Problems

- As an additional problem, set the children the task of creating a line drawing of the front elevation of a house. Explain that the house must have a pointed roof. All lines must be vertical, horizontal, and/or perpendicular (the roof will need to be a right angle), and their finished drawing must contain at least three rectangles, one right-angled triangle, and four squares.

Talk maths

Read this description aloud. Draw what you read.

This shape has three sides. One side is horizontal. None of the sides are the same length. You should have drawn a scalene triangle.

Draw shapes and describe them to a partner (without showing them).

Use some of these words: horizontal, vertical, parallel, perpendicular.

Do their drawings match yours?

Activities

1. Are these lines parallel or perpendicular?

   a.   b. ————————
                 ————————

2. Draw a vertical line.   3. Draw a horizontal line.

4. Copy this shape.

   a. Label the horizontal lines **H**.
      Label the vertical lines **V**.

   b. Are any of the lines perpendicular?
      Write **P** where they meet.

   c. How many pairs of parallel lines does it have?

Problems

Brain-buster
Beth draws a shape with eight sides. The opposite sides are parallel to each other and all the sides are the same length. What does she draw?

Geometry **75**

100 Maths Lessons Year 3 links:

- Summer 1, Week 5 (pages 196–200): identify horizontal, vertical, parallel, perpendicular and curved lines

Year 3 Practice Book links:

- (page 110): Lines

Drawing 2D shapes

Prior learning

- Can identify and describe the properties of 2D shapes, including the number of sides and line symmetry in a vertical line.

Learn

- Ask the children to identify and spell the names of common 2D shapes. Sketch them on the board, and spend time discussing their properties and naming the parts. Find out what the children already know about angle names and sizes, but focus on the relationships between side lengths for each shape.

- Review the work on lines from the previous unit, covering key vocabulary and identifying instances of when and where children have seen such lines.

- Model good techniques for drawing squares and rectangles. Although the textbook demonstrates the use of a set square, using squared paper and a ruler is acceptable. Using protractors is not necessary at this stage.

- Both of the links to *100 Maths Lessons Year 3* provide suggestions for lessons to develop children's competence in understanding 2D shapes, combining skills in drawing, measuring, identifying shapes and classifying by properties, and recognising right angles and symmetry.

Curriculum objectives

- To draw 2D shapes and make 3D shapes using modelling materials; recognise 3D shapes in different orientations and describe them.

Success criteria

- I can draw 2D shapes that are quite accurate.

Drawing 2D shapes

Learn

Some shapes have special lines. These can be parallel, horizontal, vertical or perpendicular.

> Look back at page 74 to remind yourself what these words mean.

To draw 2D shapes, you will need squared paper, a pencil, a ruler and a set square.

Follow these steps to draw a rectangle with sides of 8cm and 4cm.

1. First use a set square to draw a right angle.
2. Then use a ruler to measure the length of the lines accurately.

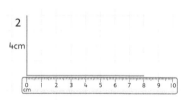

3. Use the set square to draw a second right angle.

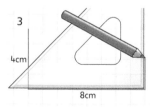
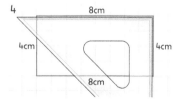

- Use a ruler to measure the length of the line accurately.
- Then join the top two corners to make a rectangle.

4. Use your set square to check the top two corners are right angles.

Talk maths

- Arrange the children in groups and provide them with a set of cards showing named shapes, with dimensions. Ask them to take turns to pick up a card and describe the shape to the rest of the group, with each member of the group drawing their own shape as it is described to them. All of the group should then compare their work and discuss errors and accuracies as appropriate.

Activities

- Ensure that the children have access to all appropriate equipment. Although the textbook describes the use of a set square, if the children are using squared paper all they will need is a pencil and ruler. The *Year 3 Practice Book* has a wide range of activities to support and extend this work, including investigating simple symmetry and reflections.

Problems

- Both problems are straightforward. To provide other problems, challenge the children to start thinking about shapes in real life which they could draw. This can be tricky if scale is to be avoided, so try considering patterns using repeating shapes, progressing to shapes within shapes if appropriate.

Talk maths

Follow the steps on page 76 to draw a rectangle measuring 7cm by 6cm. Discuss with a partner what you are doing.

Try drawing some other shapes accurately.

Activities

1. Draw these shapes on squared paper.

   a. A square with sides 7cm.

   b. A rectangle with sides 6cm and 10cm.

   c. An irregular pentagon. It must have one right angle and one side of 5cm.

   d. A right-angled triangle. The two perpendicular lines must be 6cm long.

Problems

Brain-teaser
Draw a shape with four sides each 5cm and four right angles. Use a set square and ruler.

What shape have you drawn?

Brain-buster
A shape has four right angles and four sides, measuring 6cm, 6cm, 8cm and 8cm.
The shape has two pairs of parallel sides.

What is the shape?

Use a set square and ruler to draw the shape.

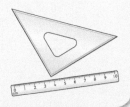

Geometry **77**

100 Maths Lessons Year 3 links:

- Autumn 1, Week 6 (pages 38–43): recognise, describe and draw 2D shapes
- Spring 1, Week 6 (pages 119–124): recognise right angles in 2D shapes

Year 3 Practice Book links:

- (page 106): Sorting 2D shapes
- (page 107): Drawing 2D shapes
- (page 108): Measuring 2D shapes
- (page 111): Is it a right angle?
- (page 114): Is it symmetrical?
- (page 115): Reflecting shapes
- (page 116): What's my shape?
- (page 117): Shape pictures

3D shapes

Prior learning

- Can identify and describe the properties of 3D shapes, including the number of edges, vertices and faces.

Learn

- Display a range of 3D shapes, real or illustrated, and discuss their properties with the class. Model and spell out key vocabulary: 'vertex' (and 'vertices'), 'edge' and 'face'. Spend time looking at the properties of each shape, in particular identifying 2D shapes on faces, parallel and perpendicular edges.
- Display the shapes shown on page 78 of the textbook and create blank versions of the charts on the board. Work with the children to complete each chart, ideally displaying the completed charts permanently.

- *100 Maths Lessons Year 3, Autumn 1, Week 6* has further guidance on helping children become familiar with the properties of these shapes.
- Children who require further support might work with construction equipment to create cubes and cuboids. Using modelling clay can be helpful too, though accuracy is obviously difficult.

Talk maths

- Write descriptions for common 3D shape on cards. (Use the example in the activity on page 79 of the textbook.) Ask the children work in pairs or groups to identify each shape, if possible trying to sketch it once they have identified it from the description.

Curriculum objectives

- To draw 2D shapes and make 3D shapes using modelling materials; recognise 3D shapes in different orientations and describe them.

Success criteria

- I can recognise and name 3D shapes and make models of them.

3D shapes

Learn

3D shapes are solid.

3D shapes have faces that are 2D shapes.

A vertex is where straight edges on a shape come together.

More than one vertex are called vertices.

Make sure you can name all of these 3D shapes.

| Cube | Cuboid | Triangular prism | Cone | Square-based pyramid | Sphere |

Look at the pictures of the shapes (or make them using modelling clay) and count the faces, vertices and edges. Did you count them all?

We can describe 3D shapes using their properties.
The faces of these shapes are all flat.

3D shape	Number of faces	Number of vertices	Number of edges
Cube	6	8	12
Cuboid	6	8	12
Triangular prism	5	6	9
Square-based pyramid	5	5	8

These shapes have curves.

3D shape	Number of faces	Number of vertices	Number of edges
Cone	2	0	1
Sphere	1	0	0

- The textbook questions can be extended to cover all the 3D shapes that the children have encountered. Children might write their own questions too. Create a nice display by placing 3D shapes inside small, identical boxes. Children can then write single-sentence clues to place on the lid of each box. These can be varied each day until all possible clues (that is, shape facts) have been used up.

- Note that the *Year 3 Practice Book* activity '3D shape tree' contains a tree diagram for sorting 3D shapes.

Problems

- Once children have completed the problem, challenge them to write their own, ensuring they use correct vocabulary at all times.

Talk maths

Read this description of a 3D solid. What is it?
- I have six square faces.
- I have 12 vertices.
- I have eight edges.

Did you need all the clues, or was the first one enough?
Describe a different 3D solid to a friend.
How many clues do you need to give them before they can guess what it is?

Activities

Cover up the charts on the opposite page with a piece of paper. Answer these questions using your memory.

1. Name these shapes.

 a.   b.   c.

2. How many vertices does a triangular prism have?

3. How many faces does a square-based pyramid have?

Problems

Brain-teaser
I have four triangular faces. These come to a vertex.
My base is square-shaped. What am I?

Geometry **79**

100 Maths Lessons Year 3 links:

- Autumn 1, Week 6 (pages 38–43): recognise, describe and make 3D shapes

Year 3 Practice Book links:

- (page 109): 3D shape tree

Angles

Prior learning

- Can use mathematical language to describe position, direction and movement, including movement in a straight line and distinguish between rotation as a turn and in terms of right angles for quarter, half and three-quarter turns (clockwise and anticlockwise).

Learn

- Review children's knowledge of angles, by drawing on the board to demonstrate how two straight lines meet at a point to form an angle. Show how that angle can change as a form of rotation as one line moves, though still joined at the point to the other line.

- If possible, take the children to a large space and issue instructions for them to turn their body through quarter turns (right angles), looking at the effect of two and four quarter turns in particular. Back in the classroom, show how these quarter turns combine to make half and whole turns, drawing these as on page 80 of the textbook. A nice reinforcement is to give each child a square of paper and have them number the corners 1–4. Next, ask them to cut off each corner and join them together, showing that four right angles make one complete turn.

- Look at 2D shapes that the children are familiar with, and discuss and compare the angles in these. Ask the children to identify the right angles in different shapes, and also to identify angles that are less than or more than a right angle. Move on to introducing acute and obtuse angles, defining both in relation to one and two right angles.

- *100 Maths Lessons Year 3, Spring 1, Week 6* provides focused lessons and resources to support the teaching of these concepts.

Curriculum objectives

- To recognise angles as a property of shape or a description of a turn.
- To identify right angles, recognise that two right angles make a half turn, three make three quarters of a turn and four a complete turn; identify whether angles are greater than or less than a right angle.

Success criteria

- I can recognise that angles are a property of shape or a description of a turn.
- I can identify right angles, make and recognise right-angled turns.
- I can identify whether angles are greater or less than a right angle.

Angles

Learn

The point where two lines meet is called a vertex.

The space between the two lines is the angle.

The angle shows how much one line has turned on its vertex from the other.

A right angle is a quarter turn.

Two right angles make a straight line, or a half turn.

Three right angles make three quarters of a turn.

An acute angle is less than a right angle.

An obtuse angle is more than a right angle and less than two right angles.

✓ Tip

Practise recognising angles. Look at some 2D shapes and decide what sort of angles they have.

The corner of a piece of paper is (usually!) a right angle. You can use this to check whether an angle is smaller (acute) or larger (obtuse) than a right angle.

Don't get in a tangle with angles! Here are some tips to help you.

Talk maths

- The textbook activity extends the previous suggestion to follow instructions to turn in quarter turns. Have children work in pairs to challenge each other to turn different numbers of quarter or half turns, extending learning by focusing on clockwise or anticlockwise. A further extension is to have children guide each other through mazes made from chairs and tables in the classroom or hall (or drawn on paper), issuing instructions such as: *Move forward x paces, do one-quarter turn left.*

Activities

- To consolidate the textbook activities, provide the children with card strips or construction equipment and have them make each of the angles shown. The *Year 3 Practice Book* provides ample further practice.

Problems

- The problem is straightforward, and can be extended by asking the children to draw a selection of shapes with a given number of acute or obtuse angles in them, taking an investigative approach. For example: *Is it possible to draw a triangle with two obtuse angles? Is it possible to draw a quadrilateral with four acute angles?*

Talk maths

Ask your partner to read these instructions aloud for you to follow.
- Stand up.
- Turn a quarter turn to the right.
- You have turned through one right angle.
- Now turn another quarter turn to the right.
- You have turned through two right angles.
- Turn again to the right for a quarter turn.
- That is three quarters of a full turn and is three right angles in total.
- Turn once more a quarter turn to the right.
- That is a full turn now. You have turned through four right angles.

Now try turning left.

Activities

1. Name these angles. Are they acute, obtuse or right angles?

   a.   b.   c.

2. How many right angles make
   a. a half turn?   b. three quarters of a turn?

Problems

Brain-teaser
Here is a 2D shape. Copy it and label each angle with the correct letter.
A = acute   O = obtuse   R = right angle
How many right angles are there?

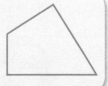

Geometry 81

100 Maths Lessons Year 3 links:

- Spring 1, Week 6 (pages 119–124): recognise right angles in 2D shapes; identify angles that are greater than or less than a right angle

Year 3 Practice Book links:

- (page 111): Is it a right angle?
- (page 112): Right-angled turns
- (page 113): Acute, obtuse or right?

Tables and pictograms

Prior learning

- Can interpret and construct simple pictograms, tally charts, block diagrams and simple tables.
- Can ask and answer simple questions by counting the number of objects in each category and sorting the categories by quantity.
- Can ask and answer questions about totalling and comparing categorical data.

Learn

- Review children's knowledge of pictograms and tables. If possible, create a simple pictogram that uses one symbol per item, such as one following a quick pet survey with the class. (The CD-ROM with *100 Maths Lessons Year 3* has a useful graphing tool that can help generate this rapidly.)

Curriculum objectives

- To interpret and present data using bar charts, pictograms and tables.
- To solve one-step and two-step questions using information presented in scaled bar charts and pictograms and tables.

Success criteria

- I can interpret and present data using tables and pictograms.
- I can solve one-step and two-step problems using information from tables and pictograms.

- Represent the data as a table and as a simple pictogram. Discuss the pros and cons of each representation with the class. Revise the uses of these charts for asking and answering simple questions about the data.
- Show the pictogram on page 82 of the textbook, and demonstrate to the children how to work out how many dogs of each type have been entered for the dog show. (In this pictogram, one head represents two dogs.) Work with the children to create a table that shows the correct dog numbers.
- *100 Maths Lessons Year 3, Autumn 2, Week 6* provides a structured set of lessons for extended work on this area.

Tables and pictograms

Learn

In a pictogram, each picture represents one or more items.
Look at this pictogram.

Dogs entered for a local dog show   = 2 dogs

Irish setter	🐶 🐶 🐶 🐶 🐶 🐶 🐶 🐶
Labrador	🐶 🐶 🐶 🐶 🐶 🐶 🐶 🐶 🐶 🐶 🐶 🐶
Boxer	🐶 🐶 🐶 🐶 🐶 🐶 🐶 🐶 🐶
Great Dane	🐶 🐶
Border collie	🐶 🐶 🐶 🐶 🐶 🐶 🐶 🐶 🐶 🐶 🐶 🐶 🐶 🐶
Corgi	🐶 🐶 🐶 🐶 🐶 🐶 🐶 🐶
Bloodhound	🐶 🐶 🐶

- The title tells you what the data is about.
- This pictogram shows the number of dogs of different breeds that were entered in a local dog show.
- Look at the key. This tells you that one picture represents two dogs.
- Count in 2s to find the number of each breed of dog.

Look at the pictures for Irish setter.
There are 2, 4, 6, 8, 10, 12, 14 and then a half picture.
Half a picture represents one dog. So there are 15 Irish setters.

Use my tips to help you get the picture!

> **✓ Tip**
>
> If you are asked to collect your own data, use tallies. Count the tallies when you have collected all the data.
>
> When making a pictogram make sure that the pictures are spaced evenly so that they can be compared easily across the pictogram.
>
> Always read the key so you know what each picture represents.

- The activity in the textbook requires the children to devise and answer appropriate questions based on the dog pictogram on page 82 of the textbook. Ensure that they are asking comparative questions, not just about the number of each dog entered for the dog show. Naturally, this activity can be repeated for any pictogram, including those generated if you work through the lessons from *100 Maths Lessons Year 3*.

- Children who work though this section might take things further by creating their own questions about cat breeds. Additional work on pictograms can be done using the activities 'Pictograms' and 'Weather chart' in the *Year 3 Practice Book*.

- The Brain-teaser is straightforward once the wording has been understood. The phrasing of increasingly complex questions is the best way to develop children's thinking further, such as: *Thirteen more cats are entered: eight of these are Siamese and five are ragdolls. Say three facts about how the data changes.*

Talk maths

Look at these questions about the pictogram shown on the page opposite. Explain the answers to a partner.

Which breed of dogs has the least number entered?

How many more Irish setters are there than corgis?

Make up some questions of your own about the pictogram.

If you get stuck, look at the key again.

Activities

The table shows the number of cats of different breeds that were entered in a local cat show.

1. **Use the data to make a pictogram. Give it a title. Choose a picture to represent two cats.**

   Then answer the questions.

   a. How many cats are there if you total the munchkin, Russian blue and British shorthair cats?

   b. Which breed has the least number of cats?

   c. Which breed has the greatest number of cats?

Cat breed	Numbers
Siamese	15
Ragdoll	18
Russian blue	11
British shorthair	20
Persian	13
Munchkin	10

Problems

Brain-teaser
How many more Siamese need to be entered so that there is the same number as the British shorthair cats?

100 Maths Lessons Year 3 links:

- Autumn 2, Week 6 (pages 79–84): read and interpret information in pictograms and tables

- Spring 2, Week 6 (pages 160–165): interpret and present data in pictograms and tables

Year 3 Practice Book links:

- (page 118): Frequency tables
- (page 119): Pictograms
- (page 123): Weather chart
- (page 124): Statistics problems (1)

Tables and bar charts

Prior learning

- Can interpret and construct simple block diagrams and tables.
- Can ask and answer simple questions by counting the number of objects in each category and sorting the categories by quantity.
- Can ask and answer questions about totalling and comparing categorical data.

- Using appropriate bar charts, work with the children to demonstrate how they are constructed and then interpreted. Compare them to pictograms and tables and consider ways they are both easier and more challenging to use. Note that the bar chart on page 84 of the textbook has a scale on the vertical axis that increases in 4s.

- It is suggested that you plan for two separate sets of lessons, ideally in different terms, to cover and then extend this work. *100 Maths Lessons Year 3, Spring 2, Week 6* and *Summer 2, Week 6* both have comprehensive lesson sequences with supporting resources.

Learn

- Review pictograms, demonstrating how a pictogram can become a bar chart by changing individual icons to blocks that join to make the individual bars. (The interactive graphing tool on the CD-ROM with *100 Maths Lessons Year 3* may be helpful here.)

Curriculum objectives

- To interpret and present data using bar charts, pictograms and tables.
- To solve one-step and two-step questions using information presented in scaled bar charts and pictograms and tables.

Success criteria

- I can interpret and present data using tables and bar charts.
- I can solve one-step and two-step questions using information from tables and bar charts.

Tables and bar charts

Learn

Bar charts are made in a similar way to pictograms, except the individual pictures become blocks.

Look at the scale on the bar chart below. Each marker represents 4°C.

The temperature in February is 16°C.

The top of the bar for January is just below 16, so the temperature in January is 15°C.

The top of the bar for April is halfway between 20 and 24, so the temperature in April is 22°C.

This bar chart shows the average temperature each month in Orlando, USA

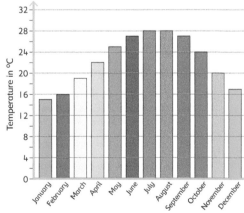

✓ Tip

Use squared paper when making bar charts. This helps you to be accurate in the size of the bar.

- Provide groups of children with a selection of bar charts (differentiated if required). You could use those in the textbook, the resources from *100 Maths Lessons Year 3* and page 120 of the *Year 3 Practice Book*. Ask the children to analyse them and discuss what they show. This is recommended rather than having children generate their own charts just yet – it tends to be more productive.

- Notice when children are asking more complex questions that require deduction rather than straight readings of information, and share this with the class.

Activities

- The textbook activity is tricky. Children will probably need a scale which increases in 2s. Less confident learners could try the *Year 3 Practice Book* activities first.

- Learning can be further extended with some of the activities from *100 Maths Lessons Year 3, Summer 2, Week 6*.

Problems

- The Brain-buster requires the children to interpret one graph by using information from another. This is well worth working on with the whole class. Ask them to pose other questions that might also be answered by comparing information from both charts.

Talk maths

Look at these questions about the bar chart on the opposite page. Discuss them with a partner.

Can you create some other questions about data in the chart?

- Which are the hottest months?
- What is the difference in temperature between January and July?

Activities

The table shows the average sea temperatures each month in Orlando.

Jan	23°C	May	26°C	Sep	29°C
Feb	23°C	Jun	28°C	Oct	27°C
Mar	23°C	Jul	29°C	Nov	26°C
Apr	25°C	Aug	29°C	Dec	24°C

1. Use squared paper to draw a bar chart for these temperatures. Give it a title. Then answer the questions.

   a. What is the sea temperature in October?

   b. By how much does the sea temperature rise between March and April?

   c. What is the difference between the hottest sea temperature and the coldest sea temperature?

Problems

Brain-buster
Look at both bar charts. Jamie loves swimming. He doesn't like the sea temperature to be above 25°C. He likes the land temperature to be at least 20°C. In which month would you suggest he goes to Orlando?

100 Maths Lessons Year 3 links:

- Spring 2, Week 6 (pages 160–165): read and use bar charts, pictograms and tables
- Summer 2, Week 6 (pages 244–248): present and interpret data on bar charts

Year 3 Practice Book links:

- (page 120): Bar charts
- (page 121): Make a bar chart
- (page 122): Finding out
- (page 125): Statistics problems (2)

Numbers to 9999

Prior learning

- Can recognise the place value of each digit in a 3-digit number (100s, 10s, 1s).
- Can read, write, compare and order numbers up to 1000.

Learn

- Spend time revising the number system, reminding the children how we use only ten digits to represent any number. Stress the importance of zero. Discuss the place value of digits in 3-digit numbers and move on to examining 4-digit numbers. Model good use of the language of place value and show a range of numbers written in numerals and words.

- Use a digital or physical abacus (interlocking cubes will also do) to represent numbers, challenging the children to interpret the values of different combinations of beads. Then progress to considering 1000 more and 1000 less, noting how only beads on the 1000s spike are affected.

- The links to *100 Maths Lessons Year 4* provide lessons and resources to consolidate learning in this area.

Curriculum objectives

- To order and compare numbers beyond 1000.
- To recognise the place value of each digit in a 4-digit number (1000s, 100s, 10s and 1s).
- To find 1000 more or less than a given number.
- To solve number and practical problems that involve all of the above and with increasingly large positive numbers.

Success criteria

- I can read, write, order and compare numbers with up to four digits.
- I can find 1000 more or less than a 4-digit number.

Numbers up to 9999

Learn

Our number system uses 100s, 10s and 1s.
265 in words is two hundred and sixty-five.

100s	10s	1s
2	6	5

The **place value** of the digit 2 is 100s. The digit 2 represents 200.
The **place value** of the digit 6 is 10s. The digit 6 represents 60.
The **place value** of the digit 5 is 1s. The digit 5 represents 5.

The value of a digit depends on which column it is in.

This number is five thousand, seven hundred and nine.

1000s	100s	10s	1s
5	7	0	9

Zeros are important. They help to show the place value of all the digits.

We can write numbers in words or using numerals.

- six thousand, four hundred and eighty-five → 6485
- three thousand, nine hundred and one → 3901
- two thousand and seven → 2007

Did you know?

A thousand is ten hundreds.

✓ Tips

- When you're asked to write a number, write the place values above the digits if you're stuck. Say this number. 8704
  Write the place values above the digits.

1000s	100s	10s	1s
8	7	0	4

The number is eight thousand, seven hundred and four.

6   Number and place value

Talk maths

- Provide groups of children with digit cards and/or an abacus, and ask them to create ten different 4-digit numbers. They should then work together to write these numbers in words as well as in numerals. They could progress to arranging them in order from smallest to largest, and vice versa.

Activities

- The questions in the textbook can easily be expanded upon by suggesting different numbers to be written in words or digits, arranged in order, and so on. Use the links to the *Year 4 Practice Book* to support and extend learning to consider partitioning as well as finding numbers that are 10 and 100 more or less than a given number.

Problems

- Both problems should be achievable, even though the Brain-buster goes beyond 10,000. Children could also arrange the villages in ascending or descending order, as well as finding the number that is 10, 100 or 1000 more or less than each population.

Talk maths

What are the biggest and smallest numbers you can make?

| 0 | 1 | 2 | 3 | 4 | 5 | 6 | 7 | 8 | 9 |

Write the digits 0 to 9 on some pieces of card or paper. Use them to make ten different 4-digit numbers. Write them down, and then read them aloud.

Activities

1. Write these numbers in words.
   a. 7380   b. 2069

2. Write these numbers in digits.
   a. six thousand, eight hundred and forty-one
   b. five thousand and two

3. Arrange these numbers in order, from smallest to largest.

   | 1612 | 5000 | 725 | 8 | 250 | 3875 | 92 | 9999 |

4. Copy and complete this chart.

1000 more	3350				
Number	2350	1243	4789	7000	8999
1000 less	1350				

Problems

Five villages count their populations.

	Blinkton	Dipton	Mumsford	Pilbery	Wester
	4307	974	3824	1092	1003

Brain-teaser
a. Which village has the smallest population?
b. Which village has the largest population?

Brain-buster
The number of people living in all the villages, added together, is 11,200. Write this in words.

---

100 Maths Lessons Year 4 links:

- Autumn 1, Week 1 (pages 8–12): read, write, order and compare 3- and 4-digit numbers

- Spring 1, Week 1 (pages 90–95): read, write, order and compare 4-digit numbers; find 1000 more or less than a 4-digit number

- Summer 1, Week 1 (pages 172–177): read, write, order and compare 4-digit numbers

Year 4 Practice Book links:

- (page 11): 4-digit place value

- (page 12): Partitioning 4-digit numbers

- (page 13): Ordering numbers

- (page 14): Ordering amounts (choose appropriate questions)

- (page 15): Numbers in numerals and words

- (page 18): 10, 100 and 1000 more or less

- (page 25): Place-value test (choose appropriate questions)

Estimating and rounding

Prior learning

- Can identify and represent numbers up to 10,000.
- Can estimate numbers up to 1000.

Learn

- Using number lines up to 20, recap how numbers are rounded to the nearest 10, stressing how 5 and 15 round up.
- Develop this to look at numbers 0–100, then 0–1000, and finally 0–10,000, considering how to round numbers to the nearest 10, 100 and 1000.
- After working though each level of rounding, demonstrate and practise how to use rounding to estimate calculations (for example, 52 + 37 is roughly 50 + 40 = 90). Allow plenty of time for practice as larger numbers are introduced.
- *100 Maths Lessons Year 4, Autumn 1, Week 1, Lesson 4* focuses on this, and has an accompanying photocopiable resource.

Curriculum objectives

- To round any number to the nearest 10, 100 or 1000.
- To identify, represent and estimate numbers using different representations.
- To solve number and practical problems that involve all of the above and with increasingly large positive numbers.

Success criteria

- I can identify, represent and estimate numbers.
- I can round any number to the nearest 10, 100 or 1000.

Estimating and rounding

Learn

We sometimes have to round numbers. This can help us to estimate amounts and calculations more easily.

To round a number to the nearest 10 we look at its position on the number line. We then look for the nearest 10.

- 12 rounds down to 10.
- 18 rounds up to 20.
- 15 is halfway, but we always round it up.

We can also round large numbers to the nearest 100 or 1000.

432 rounds down to 400.

450 and 473 both round up to 500.

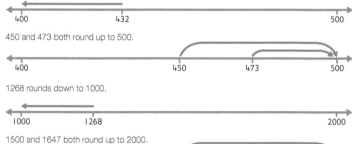

1268 rounds down to 1000.

1500 and 1647 both round up to 2000.

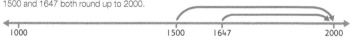

✓ Tips

- Think carefully about what you want to round to: 10s, 100s or 1000s.
  - 6852 rounds to the nearest 10 as 6850.
  - 6852 rounds to the nearest 100 as 6900.
  - 6852 rounds to the nearest 1000 as 7000.

We can round numbers to give a quick estimate. This is useful for seeing if your answers are about right. So, for 372 + 221, a quick estimate is 400 + 200 = 600.

8 Number and place value

- The textbook activity can be extended and further differentiated by providing each group with appropriate sets of numbers on cards. Challenge each group to round the numbers to the nearest 10, 100 and 1000, as appropriate.

- The questions in the textbook start with rounding and move on to estimation. Encourage more confident learners to move on to estimating and calculating mentally. The *Year 4 Practice Book* has several useful activities for this topic.

- *100 Maths Lessons Year 4, Summer 1, Week 1, Lesson 5* has an activity that nicely extends the problems in the textbook. This can be developed further using appropriate real-life data.

Talk maths

What is 45 rounded to the nearest 10?

Write down six different numbers between 0 and 9999. For example:

45	94	143	2530	5265	9250

Work with a partner and challenge each other to round the numbers.

What is 2530 rounded to the nearest 1000?

Activities

1. Copy the table and then round each number to the nearest 10, 100 and 1000.

	To the nearest 10	To the nearest 100	To the nearest 1000
a. 77			
b. 583			
c. 1232			
d. 3765			

2. Estimate to the nearest 10. Round each number before you add.
   a. 43 + 36   b. 25 + 36   c. 82 + 37

3. Estimate to the nearest 100. Round each number before you add.
   a. 423 + 186   b. 75 + 215   c. 452 + 821

4. Estimate to the nearest 1000. Round each number before you add.
   a. 4233 + 1836   b. 825 + 3336   c. 7852 + 3500

Problems

Blinkton	Dipton	Mumsford	Pilbery	Wester
4307	974	3824	1092	1003

Brain-teaser
Look at these different village populations.
Which villages have populations that are 4000, when rounded to the nearest 1000?

Brain-buster
Estimate the total number of people living in all five villages to the nearest 1000.

Number and place value 9

100 Maths Lessons Year 4 links:

- Autumn 1, Week 1 (pages 8–12): round 2-, 3- and 4-digit numbers to the nearest 10 or 100

- Spring 1, Week 1 (pages 90–95): round 4-digit numbers to the nearest 10, 100 or 1000

- Summer 1, Week 1 (pages 172–177): round 4-digit numbers to the nearest 10, 100 or 1000

Year 4 Practice Book links:

- (page 19): Rounding to the nearest 10

- (page 20): Rounding to the nearest 100 and 1000

- (page 21): Rounding to the nearest 10, 100 or 1000

- (page 22): Estimating and approximating

- (page 23): Close enough?

Counting in steps

Prior learning

- Can count from zero in multiples of 4, 8, 50 and 100.
- Can find 10 or 100 more or less than a given number.

Curriculum objectives

- To count in multiples of 6, 7, 9, 25 and 1000.
- To solve number and practical problems that involve all of the above and with increasingly large positive numbers.

Success criteria

- I can count in steps of 6, 7, 9, 25 and 1000.

Learn

- Display a large 100-square and work with the children to count in steps of 4 and 5 from zero (which the children should visualise as just next to the 1 and outside the 100-square). Note the patterns for each count. Point out that sometimes the patterns overlap at particular numbers and explain that these numbers are multiples of 4 and 5. (You could use this to demonstrate that 4 × 5 is the same as 5 × 4, and that both numbers are factors of 20.)

- In short bursts over multiple sessions, practise counting in steps of 6, 7 and 9, always starting at zero. If possible, keep a 100-square on permanent display with each pattern shown in a different colour.

- Over time, extend this to counting in steps of 10, 25, 100 and 1000.

Counting in steps

Learn

When we count in steps, we add or subtract the same number each time.

In this 100-square all the multiples of 4 have been shaded.

Can you count in steps of 5?

Which numbers are multiples of 4 **and** 5?

1	2	3	4	5	6	7	8	9	10
11	12	13	14	15	16	17	18	19	20
21	22	23	24	25	26	27	28	29	30
31	32	33	34	35	36	37	38	39	40
41	42	43	44	45	46	47	48	49	50
51	52	53	54	55	56	57	58	59	60
61	62	63	64	65	66	67	68	69	70
71	72	73	74	75	76	77	78	79	80
81	82	83	84	85	86	87	88	89	90
91	92	93	94	95	96	97	98	99	100

Use the 100-square above to count in steps of 6, 7 and 9.

0	6	12	18	24	30	36	42	48...
0	7	14	21	28	35	42	49	56...
0	9	18	27	36	45	54	63	72...

Try colouring in these steps on your own 100-square.

You can count in steps of any number. You need to learn to do this with 25s and 1000s.

0	25	50	75	100	125	150
0	1000	2000	3000	4000	5000	

Can you see any patterns?

Can you keep these sequences going?

✓ Tips

- 6 + 6 + 6 is 'three lots of 6', or 3 × 6. They all equal 18.
- 7 + 7 + 7 + 7 + 7 + 7 + 7 + 7 + 7 is 'nine lots of 7', or 9 × 7. They all equal 63.
- 9 + 9 + 9 + 9 + 9 is 'five lots of 9', or 5 × 9. They all equal 45.

Remember that counting in steps and times tables facts have lots in common.

Talk maths

- The textbook provides an oral challenge to count accurately in various steps, racing against the clock. Challenge small groups of children to practise doing this for fun, either with the entire group chanting the numbers together, or with each member taking it in turn to say the next number in the count – the latter is particularly challenging.

Activities

- The sequences in the textbook can be extended by having children count on to 100 or 1000, and back to zero.
- The *Year 4 Practice Book* activities include those that involve counting from numbers other than zero.

Problems

- The children's work should provide an indication of those who can use their skills in context.

Talk maths

Try racing against the clock. What is the fastest you can count aloud in 6s, 7s and 9s up to 100 without making a mistake?

What about counting in 25s up to 300?

Or counting in 1000s up to 10,000?

Activities

1. Complete these sequences: count on four more steps for each.
   a. Count on in steps of 6.   **36…**
   b. Count on in steps of 7.   **56…**
   c. Count on in steps of 9.   **45…**
   d. Count on in steps of 25.   **350…**
   e. Count on in steps of 1000.   **2000…**

2. Complete these sequences: count back four more steps for each.
   a. Count back in steps of 6.   **90, 84…**
   b. Count back in steps of 7.   **77, 70…**
   c. Count back in steps of 9.   **81, 72…**
   d. Count back in steps of 25.   **875…**
   e. Count back in steps of 1000. **9000…**

Problems

Brain-teaser
Joe saves £6 a week for eight weeks. Kate saves £9 a week for five weeks.
Who has the most money, and how much more do they have?

Brain-buster
Kate's older sister wants to save £800 for a holiday abroad. If she can save £25 a week, how long will she have to save for?

Number and place value   11

100 Maths Lessons Year 4 links:

- Autumn 1, Week 1 (pages 8–12): count in multiples of 25 and 1000
- Summer 1, Week 1 (pages 172–177): count in multiples of 6, 7 and 9

Year 4 Practice Book links:

- (pages 6–7): Counting in 6s, 7s and 9s
- (page 8): Counting in 25s and 50s
- (page 9): Counting in 1000s
- (page 24): Number patterns
- (page 25): Place-value test (choose appropriate questions)

Negative numbers

Prior learning

- Can count forwards and backwards from any number.
- Can identify and represent numbers on a number line.

Learn

- Using a drawn or digital number line from 0 to 20, remind the children that when they count on/forwards, they move to the right along the number line, and when they count back, they move to the left along the number line.
- Using both a number line and a thermometer, demonstrate and practise counting on and back across zero. Ensure that the children have plenty of time to appreciate how the number line below zero is constructed. The links to *100 Maths Lessons Year 4* provide focused lessons to support this work.
- If space permits, arrange children in groups of seven and give each group cards showing the numbers −3 to +3, including zero. Can they arrange themselves in order? Ask them to demonstrate counting on and back through zero, by saying each number as they pass an object along the line.

Curriculum objectives

- To count backwards through zero to include negative numbers.
- To solve number and practical problems that involve all of the above and with increasingly large positive numbers.

Success criteria

- I can count backwards through zero to include negative numbers.

Negative numbers

Learn

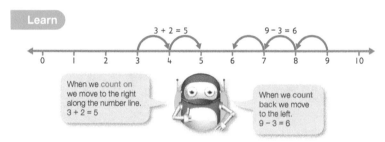

Numbers can be negative as well as positive.

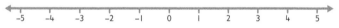

Look at the numbers on each side of zero.
On the right, the more you move away from zero, the bigger the numbers get (5 is bigger than 2).
On the left, the more you move away from zero, the smaller the numbers get (−2 is bigger than −5).

We can count back through zero. Use the number line to count back in steps of 1.

Start at 1 and count back 2. You should stop at −1.
Start at 2 and count back 4. You should stop at −2.
Start at 4 and count back 7. You should stop at −3.
Start at 1 and count back 5. You should stop at −4.
Start at 3 and count back 8. You should stop at −5.

Did you know?

°C means degrees Celsius. Zero degrees Celsius is the temperature at which water freezes.

✓ Tips

- Temperature is a great way to practise counting back through zero.

12   Number and place value

Talk maths

- If possible, give small groups of children a large picture of a thermometer. (This could be A3 and laminated.) Ask the children to practise counting on and back from different temperatures. Counters may be useful for supporting this work. More confident learners could progress to writing down each count as a calculation (for example, $2 - 3 = -1$).

Activities

- The questions in the textbook can be supplemented with activities from the resources in *100 Maths Lessons Year 4* and from the *Year 4 Practice Book*. More confident learners might work on calculations without the support of a number line, as well as counting across zero in larger steps, such as in 2s or 3s.

Problems

- When the children have completed the problems, provide them with lists of minimum and maximum temperatures for a range of places around the world. The children can then be challenged to find temperature variation in specific locations, as well as between locations.

Talk maths

Draw a thermometer, as large as you can, and mark its scale from −10°C to 10°C. Ask someone to check that you have written the scale correctly.

Working with a partner, place a small object or counter somewhere on the scale of the thermometer. Challenge your partner to count on or back.

If you want to make this harder, don't mention the temperature and just present your challenges as subtractions.

> Count back 7 from 3°C.

> 3°C, count back 7, stops at −4°C.

Activities

1. **Use the number line to help you solve these problems.**

   a. 6 count back 5
   b. 3 count back 4
   c. 1 count back 4
   d. 2 count back 7
   e. 0 count back 5
   f. 5 count back 10
   g. 8 count back 9
   h. 10 count back 16

2. **Say how many steps have been counted back on each number line.**

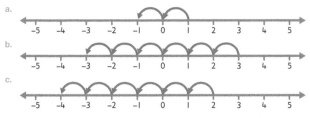

Problems

Brain-teaser
The temperature starts at 2°C, and then goes down 3°C. What is the new temperature?

Brain-buster
The temperature drops from 9°C to −6°C. How many degrees has it dropped by?

Number and place value 13

100 Maths Lessons Year 4 links:

- Summer 1, Week 1 (pages 172–177): read and understand negative numbers

Year 4 Practice Book links:

- (page 10): Counting with negative numbers

Roman numerals

- Can recognise and read the Roman numerals for 1 to 12 on an analogue clock.

Learn

- Review our number system, revising place value and the use of the digits 0–9 for representing any number. Follow this by comparing a clock face with Roman numerals to one that uses the numerals 1–12. Draw a chart to show what each Roman numeral stands for. Elicit the rules for creating each number (especially 4 and 9) and establish that there is no Roman equivalent for zero. (The CD-ROM accompanying *100 Maths Lessons Year 4* has an interactive clock with Roman numerals.)

- Separately, display the numbers 1–100 with their Roman numeral equivalents. Discuss the rules for writing Roman numerals for numbers greater than 10.

In particular, consider the unusual cases of 40 (XL) and 90 (XC). If possible, keep this chart displayed and return to it repeatedly for short practice sessions.

- *100 Maths Lessons Year 4, Spring 1, Week 1, Lesson 4* provides further support.

Curriculum objectives

- To read Roman numerals to 100 (I to C) and know that over time, the numeral system changed to include the concept of zero and place value.

Success criteria

- I can read and use Roman numerals up to 100 (I to C).

Roman numerals

Learn

In our number system, all of our numbers are made using ten different digits.

0 1 2 3 4 5 6 7 8 9

Using place value (100s, 10s and 1s), we can use these ten digits to represent any number we wish.

There are many different number systems. One other that we still use is Roman numerals.
The Romans used letters to represent some numbers.
There are five Roman numerals that you need to know.

I (1)   V (5)   X (10)   L (50)   C (100)

By using these numbers together, they could make any number, but it isn't always easy!
The chart below can help you to learn Roman numerals to 100.

Number	1	2	3	4	5	6	7	8	9	10
Roman numeral	I	II	III	IV	V	VI	VII	VIII	IX	X
Number	11	12	13	14	15	16	17	18	19	20
Roman numeral	XI	XII	XIII	XIV	XV	XVI	XVII	XVIII	XIX	XX
Number	30	40	50	60	70	80	90	100		
Roman numeral	XXX	XL	L	LX	LXX	LXXX	XC	C		

✓ Tips

XCIV plus LIX equals...

- It all seems very complicated, but if you learn some important numbers it can be okay.
- Learn the Roman numerals 1 to 10 by heart. It will make other numbers easier to understand.
- Also, pay close attention to how they make 4 (IV), 9 (IX), 40 (XL) and 90 (CX).

14   Number and place value

- Create sets of Roman numeral cards and have children work in pairs to make numbers with them. They must be sure that each combination is valid, and then write it, using digits.

- To help embed the children's knowledge of each Roman numeral, they could play 'Pelmanism', trying to match a number shown in Roman numerals to its equivalent shown using digits.

Activities

- The *Year 4 Practice Book* provides further challenge by introducing Roman numerals for 500 (D) and 1000 (M). As well as completing this activity, more confident learners might be challenged to write the Roman numerals for a range of numbers up to 1000 (or even 2000), using the information and rules they have already encountered.

Problems

- As an extension, provide the children with other calculations written in Roman numerals (for example, XII + XIX = ☐ , and challenge them to complete them in any way they can.

- Note: although Roman numerals form only a small part of the curriculum, working with them can help to build the children's general confidence with number.

Talk maths

Make a set of Roman numeral cards. It is important to have three 'one' cards, and three 'ten' cards. These can make any number between 1 and 100.

Next, challenge a partner to make numbers. You can either call out a number, such as seventy-three, or arrange some Roman numerals.

Whenever anyone gives an answer, they must explain their working out.

> Challenge each other to write your ages in Roman numerals.

Activities

1. Change these numbers to Roman numerals.
   a. 4   b. 11   c. 25   d. 19
   e. 52   f. 45   g. 90   h. 87

2. Change these Roman numerals to numbers.
   a. VI   b. IX   c. XVII   d. XXII
   e. LV   f. XL   g. LXXXVIII   h. XC

3. Which digit can't be shown with Roman numerals?

Problems

Change these Roman numerals into numbers, and then complete the calculations.

Brain-teaser
XIV plus XXIII

Brain-buster
XCI minus LXV

Number and place value   15

100 Maths Lessons Year 4 links:

- Spring 1, Week 1 (pages 90–95): read Roman numerals to 100

Year 4 Practice Book links:

- (pages 16–17): Roman numerals

Mental methods for addition and subtraction

Prior learning

- Can add and subtract numbers mentally, including:
  - a 3-digit number and 1s
  - a 3-digit number and 10s
  - a 3-digit number and 100s.

- Spend time revising the children's knowledge of number facts to 20. For each number fact, list all the other addition and subtraction facts that can be derived. For example, $5 + 6 = 11$ leads to $6 + 5 = 11$, $11 - 5 = 6$ and $11 - 6 = 5$.
- Move on to considering how to derive number facts that involve multiples of 10. For example, $50 + 60 = 110$, and so on.

- Using appropriate number lines in separate sessions, demonstrate partitioning and bridging techniques, and revise each method regularly to consolidate the skills involved. Model how to decide whether a calculation lends itself to a mental method.
- The links to *100 Maths Lessons Year 4* provide a range of lessons and resources to support this work.

Curriculum objectives

- To continue to practise mental methods for addition and subtraction.

Success criteria

- I can use mental methods for addition and subtraction.

Mental methods for addition and subtraction

Learn

You will probably know how to do some calculations in your head, and also how to do them by writing on paper. You must know your number bonds. Each number bond gives you four different facts.

Look at these.

$7 + 8 = 15$ $8 + 7 = 15$ $15 - 8 = 7$ $15 - 7 = 8$

And, you can use these facts to do harder mental calculations.
$70 + 80 = 150$
$700 + 800 = 1500$

Here are two very useful mental methods.

Partitioning a number into 10s and 1s is useful:
$25 + 12 = 25 + 10 + 2 = 35 + 2 = 37$

And this means that
$12 + 25 = 37$
$37 - 25 = 12$ and
$37 - 12 = 25$.

Bridging is used when one number is close to a 10. For example, for $75 + 98$, instead of adding 98, add 100 and then subtract 2.

So, $75 + 98 = 75 + 100 - 2 = 173$.

You can use both of these methods for subtraction too.

$38 - 13 = 38 - 10 - 3 = 25$ $46 - 9 = 46 - 10 + 1 = 37$

$57 - 24 = 57 - 20 - 4 = 33$ $246 - 97 = 246 - 100 + 3 = 149$

✓ Tips

- Look carefully at calculations before you try to solve them in your head – you might prefer to solve them with a written calculation.
- Look at the calculations below, which ones would you solve mentally?

  $25 + 96$ $645 + 377$ $89 - 30$ $204 - 157$

  Remember, if in doubt, write it out!

16   Calculations

Talk maths

- Using the activity in the textbook as a starting point, arrange the children in pairs or small groups and provide them with a selection of additions and subtractions on cards. Ask them to work together to separate the cards into two piles – those calculations that the group agree can be solved mentally (and the method they would use), and those they are unsure about. Bring all the groups together and discuss findings, working through mental methods where appropriate.

Activities

- While they work through the questions in the textbook, ask children to identify the method they are using for each calculation. A wide range of support and extension is available in the *Year 4 Practice Book*.

- To consolidate their understanding, children might be challenged to use inverse calculations to check their answers.

Problems

- The Brain-buster extends mental methods to 1000s. This may not be appropriate for all children. Role-play activities involving money can be used to good effect for sustained mental practice in real-life contexts.

Talk maths

Demonstrate to a partner how to use different mental methods for addition and subtraction. Remind them that the first thing to decide is whether a mental method is appropriate or not.

Use the calculations in the box to get you started.

Calculation	OK for mental methods?
23 + 11	yes
47 + 98	yes
645 + 123	yes
472 + 687	maybe not!
35 – 9	yes
642 – 102	yes
743 – 510	yes
403 – 187	maybe not!

Activities

1. Add these numbers, using mental methods.
   - a. 36 + 14
   - b. 64 + 25
   - c. 95 + 13
   - d. 343 + 51
   - e. 12 + 11
   - f. 67 + 19
   - g. 67 + 28
   - h. 467 + 97

2. Subtract these numbers, using mental methods.
   - a. 27 – 13
   - b. 64 – 22
   - c. 90 – 46
   - d. 357 – 206
   - e. 45 – 9
   - f. 72 – 11
   - g. 65 – 19
   - h. 436 – 198

3. Solve these calculations using mental methods.
   - a. 43 + 34
   - b. 67 + 32
   - c. 335 + 150
   - d. 2231 + 3607
   - e. 86 – 24
   - f. 54 – 33
   - g. 276 – 143
   - h. 5493 – 3170

Problems

Brain-teaser
a. Tina has £47 in her bank account, and she receives another £52 for her birthday. How much does she have altogether?

b. James is travelling from London to Newcastle. The distance is 295 miles. So far he has travelled 190 miles. How far does he have to go?

Brain-buster
Joe's mum buys a new car. The car costs £4500 and she pays a deposit of £2200. How much does she still have to pay?

Calculations 17

---

100 Maths Lessons Year 4 links:

- Autumn 1, Week 2 (pages 13–18): mental addition and subtraction of 2-digit numbers and multiples of 10, 100 and 1000

- Spring 2, Week 1 (pages 131–136): mental addition and subtraction

- Summer 2, Week 1 (pages 213–218): using mental addition and subtraction

Year 4 Practice Book links:

- (page 26): Adding and subtracting mentally (1)

- (page 27): Adding and subtracting mentally (2)

- (page 28): Adding and subtracting 2-digit numbers mentally

- (page 29): Adding and subtracting multiples of 10 and 100

- (page 30): Adding and subtracting multiples of 10, 100 and 1000

- (page 31): Choose the best strategy to add and subtract

Written methods for addition

Prior learning

- Can add numbers with up to three digits, using formal written methods of columnar addition.

Learn

- Using 2-digit numbers, review the formal written methods that children are familiar with. Progress to additions involving 3-digit numbers and, if appropriate, adding three or four numbers. Eventually, introduce adding 1000s, ensuring that numbers including zeros are included.

- To develop and consolidate learning, review how partitioning and inverse calculations can both be used to check work. *100 Maths Lessons Year 4, Autumn 2, Week 1* provides lessons and resources for this.

Curriculum objectives

- To add and subtract numbers with up to four digits using the formal written methods of columnar addition and subtraction where appropriate.
- To solve addition and subtraction two-step problems in contexts, deciding which operations and methods to use and why.

Success criteria

- I can use written methods for addition.

Written methods for addition

Learn

There are formal written methods for adding numbers. You may have been taught methods a bit different from this one. You should use whichever method you are comfortable with.

We arrange the numbers so that the place value of their digits line up.

Did you know?

Addition is the *inverse* of subtraction. You can use subtraction to check if your additions are correct.
$143 + 228 = 371$ checking...
$371 - 143 = 228$ correct! ☺

```
  1  4  5
+ 3  2  7
---------
  4  7  2
     1
```

That's why some people call it column addition. The secret is to add the digits in each column like 1s. Remember to add on any numbers that have been carried.

The biggest digit we can write in a column is 9. If the digits in the 1s column add up to more than 10, we must carry the 10 to the next column, and leave the 1s behind. You can do the same when adding digits in the other columns.

```
  2  4  6  1            3  2  7  4
+ 1  5  7  8          + 2  8  1  6
------------          ------------
  4  0  3  9            6  0  9  0
     1  1              1     1
```

Sometimes the digits add up exactly to 10. In the calculation on the right, we carry one 10, and leave no 1s behind. In the 100s column, we carry one 1000 and leave no 100s behind.

✓ Tips

- Remember to carry 10s, 100s or 1000s to the next column.

```
    1  3  5  2
    2  8  1  5
       6  3  4
+   3  0  2  5
-------------
    7  8  2  6
    1  1  1
```

You can add as many numbers as you want using column addition.

- Provide children with a range of completed columnar additions, differentiating where appropriate, and challenge them to explain the steps of each addition to each other. Ask them to try to identify what aspects of the method they find difficult, or don't understand. Listening in on these discussions can help to show you where you need to revise methods or tackle confusion.

Activities

- Opportunities to practise using these methods should be provided regularly throughout the year. The *Year 4 Practice Book* has a wide selection of resources for practising written methods for addition. Also, the units on measurement have activities for using addition in context.

- Ask children to estimate answers before adding, and also use inverse calculations to check their work.

Problems

- The problems are easy to extend by altering the numbers in the tables.

Talk maths

Look at this addition and explain it aloud. Say what is happening at each stage. Make sure you work in the correct order, right to left.

Try some column additions using three or four numbers, explaining each stage to a partner.

Now try explaining the method with some of your own numbers.

Activities

1. Copy and complete each of these additions.

a.
```
    2 3 7
  + 4 8 1
  _____
```

b.
```
    7 4 6
  + 2 5 7
  _____
```

c.
```
    2 4 2 6
  + 1 4 8 5
  _____
```

d.
```
    1 3 2 7
    2 4 5 1
  + 3 8 0 6
  _____
```

2. Copy and complete these additions. Use a written method on squared paper.
   a. 365 + 237   b. 467 + 259   c. 4459 + 3557   d. 2406 + 2205 + 3670 + 1338

Problems

Brain-teaser
This chart shows the number of people attending three village fetes.

Village	Plink	Plank	Plonk
Number of visitors	825	936	89

What is the total number of visitors to the three fetes?

Brain-buster
This chart shows the number of fans at three rock concerts.

Band	Crush	Push	Mush
Fans	6455	7106	3453

What is the total number of fans at the three concerts?

Calculations 19

100 Maths Lessons Year 4 links:

- Autumn 2, Week 1 (pages 49–54): add 4-digit numbers using columnar addition
- Spring 1, Week 2 (pages 96–101): use written methods for addition
- Spring 2, Week 2 (pages 137–141): add numbers with up to four digits, using columnar addition
- Summer 1, Week 3 (pages 183–188): add numbers with up to four digits, using columnar addition

Year 4 Practice Book links:

- (page 32): Written strategies for adding
- (page 33): Column skills: addition
- (page 36): Adding larger numbers
- (page 38): Addition and subtraction practice (1) (choose appropriate questions)
- (page 39): Addition and subtraction practice (2) (choose appropriate questions)
- (page 49): Addition and subtraction challenge (choose appropriate questions)

Written methods for subtraction

Prior learning

- Can subtract numbers with up to three digits, using formal written methods of columnar subtraction.

Learn

- Using 2-digit numbers, review the formal written methods for subtraction that children are familiar with. Progress to 3-digit numbers, and eventually, over repeated sessions, introduce subtraction of 4-digit numbers. Ensure that numbers including zeros are included. Model and encourage the use of estimation before calculating to aid children's thinking.
- To develop and consolidate learning, review how partitioning and inverse calculations can both be used to check work. *100 Maths Lessons Year 4, Spring 1, Week 2* provides further support.

Talk maths

- Provide children with a range of completed columnar subtractions, differentiating where appropriate, and challenge them to explain the steps of each subtraction to each other. Ask them to try to identify what aspects of the method they find difficult, or don't understand.

Curriculum objectives

- To add and subtract numbers with up to four digits using the formal written methods of columnar addition and subtraction where appropriate.
- To solve addition and subtraction two-step problems in contexts, deciding which operations and methods to use and why.

Success criteria

- I can use written methods for subtraction.

Written methods for subtraction

Learn

There are formal written methods for subtracting numbers. You may have been taught methods a bit different from this one. You should use whichever method you are comfortable with.

$$
\begin{array}{r}
{}^5\cancel{6}\ {}^{13}\cancel{4}\ {}^15 \\
-\ 2\ 7\ 8 \\
\hline
3\ 6\ 7
\end{array}
$$

Did you know?

Subtraction is the *inverse* of addition. You can use addition to check your subtractions.
73 – 48 = 25   checking...
25 + 48 = 73   correct! ☺

Notice how we exchange 100s for 10s and 10s for 1s.

Just like with addition, we can use the place-value columns to subtract larger numbers.

$$
\begin{array}{r}
{}^5\cancel{6}\ {}^12\ {}^4\cancel{5}\ {}^14 \\
-\ 1\ 7\ 3\ 8 \\
\hline
4\ 5\ 1\ 6
\end{array}
$$

You need to be very careful at each stage of a written subtraction. Look at this one.

$$
\begin{array}{r}
{}^5\cancel{6}\ {}^9\cancel{0}\ {}^14\ 5 \\
-\ 3\ 1\ 7\ 2 \\
\hline
2\ 8\ 7\ 3
\end{array}
$$

Look carefully at what you must do if you want to borrow a number when the next column has a zero.

You have to borrow from the 1000s to get ten 100s, then borrow one 100 to get ten 10s.

✓ Tips

- Check your subtractions by adding your answer to the number you subtracted.
- Try to estimate your answer before you start. It will help you to know if your answer is 'about right'.
- You can't have lots of subtractions in a list the way you can with additions. If you have to subtract two or three numbers, you must subtract one number and then subtract the next number from the answer.

Here are some top tips for accurate subtraction work!

Listening in on these discussions can help to show you where you need to revise methods or tackle confusion.

• If appropriate, challenge children to discuss estimates and inverse calculations too.

Activities

• Opportunities to practise using these methods should be provided regularly throughout the year. The *Year 4 Practice Book* has a wide selection of resources for practising written methods for subtraction. Also, the units on measurement have activities for using subtraction in context.

• Children's learning can be extended by asking them to estimate answers before subtracting, and also using inverse calculations to check their work.

Problems

• Once the children have completed the problems, ask them to create their own using the information in the textbook.

100 Maths Lessons Year 4 links:

• Autumn 2, Week 1 (pages 49–54): subtract 4-digit numbers using columnar subtraction

• Spring 1, Week 2 (pages 96–101): use written methods for subtraction

• Spring 2, Week 2 (pages 137–141): subtract numbers with up to four digits, using columnar subtraction

• Summer 1, Week 3 (pages 183–188): subtract numbers with up to four digits, using columnar subtracting

Year 4 Practice Book links:

• (page 34): Written strategies for subtracting

• (page 35): Column skills: subtraction

• (page 37): Subtracting larger numbers

• (page 38): Addition and subtraction practice (1) (choose appropriate questions)

• (page 39): Addition and subtraction practice (2) (choose appropriate questions)

• (page 49): Addition and subtraction challenge (choose appropriate questions)

Talk maths

Look at this subtraction and explain it aloud. Say what is happening at each stage. Make sure you work in the correct order, right to left.

```
  ¹2̸ ¹¹2̸ ¹3  8
-  1  3  5  6
   ─────────
      8  8  2
```

Activities

1. Copy and complete each of these subtractions.

a.
```
  3 6 5
- 1 4 7
───────
```
b.
```
  6 5 3
- 2 2 8
───────
```
c.
```
  3 2 7
- 1 6 5
───────
```
d.
```
  4 7 2 5
- 1 9 0 7
─────────
```

2. Complete each of these subtractions using a written method on squared paper.

a. 415 – 236   b. 824 – 375   c. 3542 – 937   d. 6042 – 3555

Problems

Brain-teaser
This chart shows the number of people attending three village fetes.

Village	Plink	Plank	Plonk
Number of visitors	825	936	89

a. How many more people went to Plink than Plonk?
b. How many more people went to Plank than Plink?

Brain-buster
This chart shows the number of fans at three rock concerts.

Band	Crush	Push	Mush
Fans	6455	7106	3453

If the fans of Push and Mush are combined, how many more people are there than fans of Crush?

Times tables facts

Prior learning

- Can recall and use multiplication and division facts for the 2-, 3-, 4-, 5-, 8- and 10-times tables.

Learn

- Display a large multiplication square (there is an interactive one on the CD-ROM accompanying *100 Maths Lessons Year 4*), and hide some of the numbers in the grid. Work with the children to use their existing times tables knowledge to find the missing the numbers. Remind the children that numbers can be multiplied in any order (for example, 4 × 5 has the same answer as 5 × 4).

- Practise reciting times tables and counting in steps, to help demonstrate multiplication as repeated addition.

- Over repeated sessions introduce times tables that the children are unfamiliar with until all times tables up to 12 × 12 have been covered. *100 Maths Lessons Year 4, Autumn 1, Week 3* provides a structured sequence of such lessons for this, with further support in the other links to *100 Maths Lessons Year 4* shown.

Times tables facts

Learn

You need to learn and to understand your tables.

You should already know your 2-, 3-, 4-, 5-, 8- and 10-times tables. Use the times tables grid to check your knowledge.

We can also check divisions on the grid, because division is the inverse of multiplication.

×	1	2	3	4	5	6	7	8	9	10	11	12
1	1	2	3	4	5	6	7	8	9	10	11	12
2	2	4	6	8	10	12	14	16	18	20	22	24
3	3	6	9	12	15	18	21	24	27	30	33	36
4	4	8	12	16	20	24	28	32	36	40	44	48
5	5	10	15	20	25	30	35	40	45	50	55	60
6	6	12	18	24	30	36	42	48	54	60	66	72
7	7	14	21	28	35	42	49	56	63	70	77	84
8	8	16	24	32	40	48	56	64	72	80	88	96
9	9	18	27	36	45	54	63	72	81	90	99	108
10	10	20	30	40	50	60	70	80	90	100	110	120
11	11	22	33	44	55	66	77	88	99	110	121	132
12	12	24	36	48	60	72	84	96	108	120	132	144

Remember: to use the times tables grid, you find a number on the side and a number on the top, like 3 × 4, and where the row and the column meet you get your answer. So 3 × 4 = 12, easy!

5 × 4 = 20, so 4 × 5 = 20
20 ÷ 5 = 4, and 20 ÷ 4 = 5. Three numbers, four different facts.

You should now be ready to learn your 6-, 7-, 9-, 11- and 12-times tables.
Times tables are like counting in steps. Can you see these on the grid above?

6-times table:	0	6	12	18	24	30	36	42	48	54	60	66	72
7-times table:	0	7	14	21	28	35	42	49	56	63	70	77	84
9-times table:	0	9	18	27	36	45	54	63	72	81	90	99	108
11-times table:	0	11	22	33	44	55	66	77	88	99	110	121	132
12-times table:	0	12	24	36	48	60	72	84	96	108	120	132	144

✓ Tips

- Often by looking at the 1s you can spot patterns. Look at the 9- and the 12-times tables above.
- And remember, multiplication works both ways, so if you know 6 × 7 you also know 7 × 6.

Some tables are easier to learn than others. Most people find the 2, 5, 10 and 11 tables the easiest.

Curriculum objectives

- To recall multiplication and division facts for multiplication tables up to 12 × 12.

Success criteria

- I can recall and use multiplication facts for times tables to 12 × 12.

Talk maths

- Allow short amounts of time (five minutes two or three times a week is fine) for children to regularly work in pairs to test each others' times tables knowledge, preferably providing a relatively narrow focus for each session. This can easily be extended by challenging children to focus only on division facts.

Activities

- When the children have completed the questions in the textbook, challenge them to write down all related facts for each calculation in questions 1 and 2.
- Provide further times table practice by using the resources in *100 Maths Lessons Year 4* or the *Year 4 Practice Book*.

Problems

- Once the children have tackled the problems in the textbook, provide them with work on factors, such as in *100 Maths Lessons Year 4, Autumn 2, Week 2, Lesson 1*.

Talk maths

Play *In a minute*. You will need the times tables grid and a clock or watch.

Work with a partner. Take turns asking and answering times tables questions as fast as possible.

The questioner can use a hidden times tables grid to help them check answers quickly. How many questions can players answer in one minute?

If you prefer, you can set limits, such as the 6-times table only.

What is 4 × 6?

What is 63 ÷ 7?

What is 8 × 11?

What is 81 ÷ 9?

What is 96 ÷ 12?

Did you know?

The times table grid only contains 78 different facts. (That's because many of the facts are repeated, such as 7 × 8 = 8 × 7). You already know thousands of facts, surely another 78 can't be that hard...

Activities

1. Answer these times tables questions.
   - a. 3 × 7
   - b. 5 × 9
   - c. 8 × 4
   - d. 7 × 6
   - e. 9 × 9

2. Answer these times tables questions.
   - a. 20 ÷ 5
   - b. 24 ÷ 2
   - c. 42 ÷ 7
   - d. 64 ÷ 8
   - e. 44 ÷ 4

3. Write down all the numbers in the 6-times table.

4. Write down all the numbers in the 12-times table.

5. Which numbers are in both the 6- and 12-times tables?

Problems

Brain-teaser
Josie is thinking of a number.
She says it is in the 6-times table and the 7-times table. What is the number?

Brain-buster
Jim buys nine bags of crisps for 60p each. Explain how he can use his times tables to find the total cost of the crisps, and then give the answer.

Calculations **23**

---

100 Maths Lessons Year 4 links:

- Autumn 1, Week 3 (pages 19–24): recall facts from the 7-, 9-, 11- and 12-times tables
- Autumn 1, Week 4 (pages 25–29): recall facts from the multiplication tables up to 12 × 12
- Autumn 2, Week 2 (pages 55–60): recall facts from the multiplication tables up to 12 × 12

Year 4 Practice Book links:

- (page 50): Quick recall ×2 to ×10
- (page 51): Multiplication facts ×2 to ×10
- (page 52): The 7- and 9-times tables
- (page 53): Times-table quiz
- (page 54): Times-table problems
- (page 55): Mental recall up to 12 × 12

Mental methods for multiplication and division

Prior learning

- Can use multiplication and division facts for times tables up to 12 × 12.

Learn

- Review times tables facts, demonstrating that multiplication can be done in any order, and that multiplication is equivalent to repeated addition. Move on to demonstrating division as the inverse of multiplication, and division as equal sharing or repeated subtraction.

- Over repeated sessions throughout the year, demonstrate that further facts can be derived from times tables facts (for example, 4 × 50 = 200). Also,

discuss doubling and halving, multiplying and dividing by 10, 100 and 1000, as well as strategies for multiplying three small numbers together.

- Separately, if appropriate, introduce the concept of factors and multiples, and look at times tables facts as factor pairs and multiples.

Talk maths

- Write a selection of multiplication and division calculations on cards, for example 270 ÷ 9, 60 × 8, 75 × 4. Challenge the children to choose the mental method they would use to complete each one. Ask them to try to identify what aspects of the method they find difficult, or don't understand. Listening in on these

Curriculum objectives

- To use place value, known and derived facts to multiply and divide mentally, including: multiplying by 0 and 1; dividing by 1; multiplying together three numbers.
- To recognise and use factor pairs and commutativity in mental calculations.
- To solve problems involving multiplying and adding, including using the distributive law to multiply 2-digit numbers by 1-digit, integer scaling problems and harder correspondence problems such as *n* objects are connected to *m* objects.

Success criteria

- I can use mental methods for multiplication and division.

Mental methods for multiplication and division

Learn

Multiplication is like repeated addition.
5×3 is 'five lots of 3' or $3 + 3 + 3 + 3 + 3$.

Multiplication can be done in any order.
$5 \times 3 = 3 \times 5$ (answer = 15)

Division is equal sharing.
$15 \div 3$ is 15 shared into three equal lots.

Division is the inverse of multiplication.
$2 \times 9 = 18$ so $18 \div 9 = 2$ (and $18 \div 2 = 9$)

> **Did you know?**
> You cannot divide a number by zero. The answer is infinity!

> And multiplication is the *inverse* of division!

Some calculations can be done mentally, without writing anything down. You should know any calculation that is in the times tables.
$3 \times 5 = 15$ $4 \times 9 = 36$ $15 \div 5 = 3$ $36 \div 4 = 9$

And if you know these facts you can do other calculations.
$30 \times 5 = 150$ $4 \times 90 = 360$ $150 \div 5 = 30$ $360 \div 4 = 90$

Multiplying by 2 is just doubling; dividing by 2 is halving.
$39 \times 2 = 30 + 30 + 9 + 9 = 60 + 18 = 78$ $220 \div 2 = \frac{1}{2}$ of $200 + \frac{1}{2}$ of $20 = 100 + 10 = 110$

When you multiply or divide by 10 or 100, all the digits move one or two places in the place value table.
$23 \times 10 = 230$ $4 \times 100 = 400$ $320 \div 10 = 32$ $600 \div 100 = 6$

When you multiply three numbers, they can be done in any order. It's easiest to multiply by the smallest number last.
$2 \times 6 \times 8 = 2 \times 48 = 96$

> Don't forget: anything multiplied by 1 remains the same, and anything multiplied by zero will equal zero.

✓ Tips

- 50×30 is the same as $\underline{5 \times 10} \times \underline{3 \times 10}$.
  Swap the order = $\underline{5 \times 3} \times \underline{10 \times 10} = 15 \times 100 = 1500$.
- $6200 \div 20$ is done in two stages. $6200 \div 10 = 620$, and then divide by 2 to give $620 \div 2 = 310$.

> If you are feeling confident, you can mix and match the mental methods shown above. Look at these.

discussions can help to show you where you need to revise methods or tackle confusion.

- If appropriate, challenge children to discuss inverse calculations related facts as well.

Activities

- The *Year 4 Practice Book* has lots of resources for supporting and extending children's skills, including multiplying and dividing by 1 and 0.

Problems

- Once children have completed the problems, challenge them to create their own problems using the numbers in the textbook. Problems must be solvable mentally, and cover both multiplication and division.

100 Maths Lessons Year 4 links:

- Autumn 1, Week 3 (pages 19–24): multiply mentally: 1-digit numbers by 1 and 0; multiples of 10 and 100; three numbers together
- Autumn 1, Week 4 (pages 25–29): divide mentally, including: numbers by 1; by multiples of 10 and 100; using remainders
- Autumn 2, Week 3 (pages 61–65): divide 2-digit numbers by 1-digit numbers mentally (within and beyond times tables facts)

Year 4 Practice Book links:

- (page 56): Doubling and halving
- (page 57): Know one fact, know them all
- (page 58): Use what you know!
- (page 60): Partitioning when multiplying (1)
- (page 61): Partitioning when multiplying (2)
- (pages 62–63): Partitioning when multiplying (3)
- (page 64): Using related multiplication and division facts
- (page 65): How close can you get?
- (page 66): Multiplying 3 small numbers mentally
- (page 67): Choosing the best order
- (pages 68–69): Multiplying and dividing by 10 or 100
- (page 70): Multiplying by 1 and 0
- (page 71): Dividing by 1

Talk maths

Look at the different mental methods shown on the page opposite. Using a pencil and paper, secretly write down a few multiplications and divisions using the methods, or use the ones in this box.

Read each calculation aloud to a partner and challenge them solve it. If they make errors, explain where they went wrong.

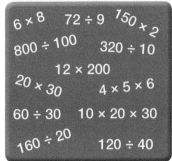

6×8 $72 \div 9$ 150×2
$800 \div 100$ $320 \div 10$
12×200
20×30 $4 \times 5 \times 6$
$60 \div 30$ $10 \times 20 \times 30$
$160 \div 20$ $120 \div 40$

Activities

1. Solve these multiplications mentally.
   - a. 36×2
   - b. $2 \times 2 \times 6$
   - c. 95×10
   - d. 3×100
   - e. 36×20
   - f. 3×400
   - g. $2 \times 4 \times 300$
   - h. $50 \times 90 \times 2$

2. Solve these divisions mentally.
   - a. $26 \div 2$
   - b. $64 \div 8$
   - c. $150 \div 10$
   - d. $3000 \div 100$
   - e. $120 \div 10$
   - f. $60 \div 20$
   - g. $300 \div 15$
   - h. $640 \div 80$

Problems

Brain-teaser

There are 120 children in a school.

- a. If they each spend 20p at the tuck shop, how much money is collected altogether?
- b. If the children are divided equally into 10 groups, how many will be in each group?

Brain-buster

There are 120 children in a school.

- a. If each child spends 20p at the tuck shop every day for three days, how much money will be collected altogether?
- b. If the children are divided equally into 30 groups, how many will be in each group?

Calculations   25

Written methods for short multiplication

Prior learning

- Can use multiplication and division facts for times tables up to 12 × 12.
- Can use mental methods for multiplying 2-digit numbers by 1-digit numbers.

Learn

- Review children's knowledge of multiplication facts and strategies for mental calculation. Spend time recapping multiplication as repeated addition, and consider division as multiplication's inverse.
- Also remind the children of our number system, demonstrating how the digits 0–9 can be used in place-value columns of 1000s, 100s, 10s and 1s to represent any number.

- In repeated, short sessions demonstrate the formal written method for multiplication. You may wish to model estimation and other methods (grid, Egyptian, chunking) that may help children in checking their work.

Talk maths

- Provide children with a range of completed handwritten short multiplication calculations, differentiating them for difficulty where appropriate. Challenge the children to explain the steps of each calculation to each other. Ask them to try to identify what aspects of the method they find difficult, or don't understand. Listening in on these discussions can help to show you where you need to revise methods or tackle confusion.

Written methods for short multiplication

Learn

We know that multiplication is repeated addition.
$4 \times 7 = 7 + 7 + 7 + 7 = 28$

We have also looked at some mental methods for doing multiplications in your head.
$12 \times 20 = 12 \times 10 \times 2 = 120 \times 2 = 240$

Sometimes calculations are just too hard to do in your head.
1247×6

That's when it's time to use a **formal written method**.

We know that our number system uses these place-value columns:
1000s, 100s, 10s and 1s.

To make multiplication easier, we can use formal written methods using these columns.

When multiplying a larger number by a number less than 10, you must multiply each digit at the top by the single digit. If necessary, carry 1s, 10s or 100s, and then add them.

```
    2  3  5
×         4
---------------
    9  4  0
    1  2
```

We call this short multiplication.

Notice how $4 \times 5 = 20$. We carry the two 10s and leave zero 1s in the 1s column. Also $4 \times 3 = 12$. We carry the one 100, then in the 10s column we add the two carried 10s to the two 10s and write 4 in this column. $4 \times 2 = 8$ but we need to add the carried 100 which makes 9, so we write 9 in the 100s column. So the answer is 940.

✓ Tips

- To carry out short multiplication, you still need to know your multiplication facts.
- And don't forget, you can estimate your answer. Use this to check that your formal written method gives you the size of answer you expect.
  For example, 124×6 will be a more than 720 but less than 780. ($6 \times 120 = 720$, $6 \times 130 = 780$)

Make sure you know your times tables facts!

Curriculum objectives

- To multiply 2-digit and 3-digit numbers by a 1-digit number using formal written layout.

Success criteria

- I can use written methods for short multiplication.

- If appropriate, challenge the children to discuss estimates and apply other methods to check the calculations.

Activities

- Opportunities to practise using these methods should be provided regularly throughout the year, remembering to differentiate as appropriate. Less confident learners could focus on multiplying 2-digit numbers by 1-digit numbers for as long as they need to.

- The links to *100 Maths Lessons Year 4* and the *Year 4 Practice Book* provide a range of ideas and resources.

Problems

- Further 'tuck shop' problems are easy to generate using money and low-cost items. Try to give children as much practice as possible, progressing to two-step problems as in the Brain-buster.

Talk maths

Look at the short multiplications below and explain them aloud. Say how each stage was done.

Remember: you still have to multiply zeros, and anything times zero is... zero!

a.
```
      3  4
   ×     4
   ─────────
   1  3  6
         1
```

b.
```
      4  6  2
   ×        6
   ─────────────
   2  7  7  2
      3  1
```

Activities

1. Copy and complete each of these short multiplications.

a.
```
   3 8
 × 3
 ─────
```
b.
```
   4 5 7
 ×   2
 ─────
```
c.
```
   3 4 2
 ×   4
 ─────
```
d.
```
   8 0 6
 ×   5
 ─────
```

2. Multiply. Use a written method for short multiplication.
   a. 153 × 3   b. 267 × 2   c. 538 × 4   d. 1273 × 6

Problems

Brain-teaser
A school's tuck shop sells muesli bars for 7p each.
143 bars are sold. How much money is collected?

Brain-buster
The school tuck shop also sells cartons of juice for 20p each.
125 children buy a muesli bar and a carton of juice.
How much money is collected altogether?

---

100 Maths Lessons Year 4 links:

- Autumn 2, Week 2 (pages 55–60): multiply 2- and 3-digit numbers by a 1-digit number using written methods

- Spring 1, Week 3 (pages 102–106): multiply 2-digit and 3-digit numbers by a 1-digit number, using written methods

- Spring 2, Week 4 (pages 147–152): use short multiplication

- Summer 1, Week 4 (pages 189–193): use short multiplication

- Summer 2, Week 4 (pages 230–235): use short multiplication for multiplying by 7

Year 4 Practice Book links:

- (pages 72–73): Short multiplication

- (page 74): Short multiplication with larger numbers

Written methods for short division

Prior learning

- Can use multiplication and division facts for times tables up to 12 × 12.
- Can use mental methods for dividing 2-digit numbers by 1-digit numbers.

Learn

- Recap the links between multiplication and division, discussing how related facts can be easily obtained. Practise using known division facts to find hidden numbers on a multiplication square.
- Using 2- or 3-digit numbers divided by 1-digit numbers, demonstrate the formal written method for short division. Start by using numbers that divide exactly progressing to carrying 10s to the next column, as on page 28 of the textbook.
- *100 Maths Lessons Year 4, Spring 1, Week 4* provides guidance and resources, with further ideas in the other links to *100 Maths Lessons Year 4* – these might be used at separate times through the year.

Curriculum objectives

- To use written methods for short division.

Success criteria

- I can use written methods for short division.

Written methods for short division

Learn

Dividing means sharing something equally. If we share six biscuits between three people, they will get two biscuits each.

We know that division is the **inverse** of multiplication, so your times tables give you lots of division facts.

3 × 5 = 15, so 15 ÷ 3 = 5 and 15 ÷ 5 = 3

6 × 8 = 48, so 48 ÷ 6 = 8 and 48 ÷ 8 = 6

10 × 12 = 120, so 120 ÷ 12 = 10 and 120 ÷ 10 = 12

Sometimes we have to divide larger numbers, such as 348 ÷ 3. If this is too difficult to do mentally, we can use a written method. Look at how we write this down.

Remember what 'divide' means. It tells you how many times one number 'goes into' another number.

$$\begin{array}{r} 1 \ \ 1 \ \ 6 \\ 3 \overline{\smash{)}3 \ \ 4 \ \ {}^1 8} \end{array}$$

- To begin, we divide 3 into the 3. This goes once so we write 1 above the 3.

- Then we look at the 4. 3 goes into 4 once with one remaining. So we put 1 above the 4 and carry the remaining 1 to the 8 to make 18.

- 3 goes into 18 six times, so we write 6 above 18.

- So, 348 divided by 3 equals 116.

Check it with a multiplication!
3 × 116 = 348

✓ Tips

- Sometimes you might not be able to divide into the first number, so you need to carry it to the next number.

$$\begin{array}{r} 0 \ \ 4 \ \ 2 \\ 3 \overline{\smash{)}1 \ \ {}^1 2 \ \ 6} \end{array}$$

- Provide children with a range of completed handwritten short division calculations, differentiating them for difficulty where appropriate. Challenge the children to explain the steps of each calculation to each other. Ask them to try to identify what aspects of the method they find difficult, or don't understand. Listening in on these discussions can help to show you where you need to revise methods or tackle confusion.

- If appropriate, challenge the children to discuss estimates and apply other methods to check the calculations.

Activities

- Opportunities to practise using these methods should be provided regularly throughout the year. Examine children's work to check for any misunderstanding of the method, and correct this early on.

Problems

- Present the children with additional problems, choosing numbers of items that have many factors (for example, 96 sweets), and ask the children to investigate how they might be shared between two, three, four, six or eight people, for example.

Talk maths

Look at the short division below and explain it aloud, saying how each stage was done.

$$
5 \overline{\smash{\big)}\, 6 \; {}^{1}7 \; {}^{2}5} \quad = \quad 1 \; 3 \; 5
$$

Activities

1. Copy and complete each of these short divisions.

   a. $5 \overline{\smash{\big)}\, 1 \; 2 \; 5}$ b. $3 \overline{\smash{\big)}\, 7 \; 2}$ c. $5 \overline{\smash{\big)}\, 9 \; 0}$

   d. $4 \overline{\smash{\big)}\, 5 \; 3 \; 2}$ e. $2 \overline{\smash{\big)}\, 2 \; 3 \; 3 \; 4}$ f. $7 \overline{\smash{\big)}\, 7 \; 4 \; 9}$

2. Copy and complete these divisions. Use a written method for short division.

   a. $116 \div 2$ b. $215 \div 5$ c. $426 \div 3$
   d. $616 \div 4$ e. $372 \div 6$ f. $927 \div 9$

Problems

Brain-teaser
There are 628 children in Pigwarts School. They are divided equally into four different House Teams. How many children are there in each House?

Brain-buster
Jen and her mum are going on a Swimathon. They have to swim 2760 metres in 5 hours. How many metres will they swim each hour if they swim at a steady pace?

100 Maths Lessons Year 4 links:

- Spring 1, Week 4 (pages 107–112): use short division when dividing by a 1-digit number (no remainders)

- Spring 2, Week 4 (pages 147–152): use short division when dividing by a 1-digit number (no remainders)

- Summer 1, Week 4 (pages 189–193): use short division when dividing by a 1-digit number (no remainders)

- Summer 2, Week 4 (pages 230–235): use short division when dividing by a 1-digit number (no remainders)

Year 4 Practice Book links:

- (page 75): Short division

Equivalent fractions

Prior learning

- Can recognise and show, using diagrams, equivalent fractions with small denominators.

Learn

- Using real objects (such as chocolate bars and fruit) or using paper or drawn circles, work with the children to consider various ways in which one whole can be divided into equal parts. Model how these are represented as fractions, with the denominator representing the number of equal parts.

- Displaying two equal wholes side by side, with one divided in halves and the other in quarters, consider the equivalence of two quarters to one half. Repeat this with thirds and sixths, fifths and tenths. Also, create a fraction wall showing the equivalence between different fractions. If possible, keep this on permanent display.

- If appropriate, point out the links between the numerators and denominators of equivalent fractions. For example, for ½ = ¼, the numerator and denominator of ¾ are each double those of ½. *100 Maths Lessons Year 4, Autumn 2, Week 4, Lesson 4* focuses on this.

Curriculum objectives

- To recognise and show, using diagrams, families of common equivalent fractions.

Success criteria

- I can recognise and use equivalent fractions.

Equivalent fractions

Learn

A fraction of a whole is an amount less than 1. It shows the whole divided into equal parts.

Two halves make a whole.

Four quarters make a whole.

Three thirds make a whole.

Six sixths make a whole.

Two quarters is equivalent to one half. We say that $\frac{2}{4}$ and $\frac{1}{2}$ are **equivalent fractions**. They represent the same amount.

Two sixths is equivalent to one third. We say that $\frac{2}{6}$ and $\frac{1}{3}$ are **equivalent fractions**. They represent the same amount.

We can use diagrams to show equivalent fractions, such as fraction walls.

1 whole									
$\frac{1}{5}$		$\frac{1}{5}$		$\frac{1}{5}$		$\frac{1}{5}$		$\frac{1}{5}$	
$\frac{1}{10}$	$\frac{1}{10}$	$\frac{1}{10}$	$\frac{1}{10}$	$\frac{1}{10}$	$\frac{1}{10}$	$\frac{1}{10}$	$\frac{1}{10}$	$\frac{1}{10}$	$\frac{1}{10}$

Five fifths make a whole.
Ten tenths make a whole.

The wall shows us that two tenths is equivalent to one fifth, four tenths are equivalent to two fifths, and so on.

✓ Tips

- Remember: when you divide a shape into fractions, every part must be the same size.

This makes it much easier to spot equivalent fractions!

Talk maths

- The activity on page 31 of the textbook shows a fraction wall of a whole, halves, quarters and eighths. In groups, the children take it in turns to cover up sections (for example, two quarters) and test each other as to what is covered, using the parts that show to help them deduce what is missing. This can be repeated using fraction walls for different multiples: thirds, sixths, ninths and twelfths; or fifths, tenths and twentieths, and so on.

Activities

- The questions in the textbook use children's basic understanding of equivalence. Use lessons and resources from the links to *100 Maths Lessons Year 4* and the *Year 4 Practice Book* to extend this work.

Problems

- Both problems are tricky as they require children to find an equivalent fraction of one of the fractions in each problem. Further support and practice can be provided with activities in the *Year 4 Practice Book*.

Talk maths

Working with a partner, use counters or paper to cover up fractions in the fraction wall. Then say what fraction has been covered and what its equivalents are.

1			
$\frac{1}{2}$		$\frac{1}{2}$	
$\frac{1}{4}$	$\frac{1}{4}$	$\frac{1}{4}$	$\frac{1}{4}$
$\frac{1}{8}$ $\frac{1}{8}$	$\frac{1}{8}$ $\frac{1}{8}$	$\frac{1}{8}$ $\frac{1}{8}$	$\frac{1}{8}$ $\frac{1}{8}$

Two quarters is equivalent to one half.

Six eighths is equivalent to three quarters.

Try making your own fraction wall, with one whole, thirds, sixths and ninths.

Activities

1. Copy these circles. Shade each one to show the fraction.

   a. $\frac{1}{3}$ b. $\frac{3}{4}$ c. $\frac{2}{5}$ d. $\frac{3}{4}$

2. Find the pairs of equivalent fractions.

   $\frac{1}{2}$ $\frac{1}{3}$ $\frac{1}{4}$ $\frac{1}{6}$

   $\frac{3}{12}$ $\frac{2}{12}$ $\frac{4}{12}$ $\frac{6}{12}$

3. Identify and write down the equivalent fraction to the first fraction.

   a. $\frac{3}{4}$: $\frac{5}{8}$ $\frac{6}{8}$ $\frac{7}{8}$ $\frac{8}{8}$ b. $\frac{2}{3}$: $\frac{8}{9}$ $\frac{7}{9}$ $\frac{6}{9}$ $\frac{5}{9}$

   c. $\frac{5}{8}$: $\frac{8}{16}$ $\frac{9}{16}$ $\frac{10}{16}$ $\frac{11}{16}$ d. $\frac{3}{5}$: $\frac{8}{20}$ $\frac{10}{20}$ $\frac{12}{20}$ $\frac{14}{20}$

Problems

Brain-teaser
Jane is racing against Paul. Jane has finished $\frac{3}{4}$ of the race and Paul has finished $\frac{5}{8}$.
Who is nearer to the finish?

Brain-buster
Tina is racing against Joe. Tina has finished $\frac{7}{10}$ of the race and Joe has finished $\frac{4}{5}$.
Who is nearer to the finish?

Fractions and decimals   31

---

100 Maths Lessons Year 4 links:

- Autumn 2, Week 4 (pages 66–70): identify and find equivalent fractions
- Spring 1, Week 5 (pages 113–117): identify equivalent fractions
- Summer 1, Week 5 (pages 194–199): identify equivalent fractions

Year 4 Practice Book links:

- (page 76): Focus on fractions
- (page 77): Fraction shapes
- (page 80): Match equivalent fractions
- (page 81): Fraction equivalents

Adding and subtracting fractions

Prior learning

- Can add and subtract fractions with the same denominator within one whole.

Learn

- Using simple circles and strips, demonstrate how fractions with the same denominator can be added to make one whole. Focus on how the numerators change and the denominators, which represent the how many parts the whole has been split into, do not. Eventually move on to considering subtraction, keeping work within the scope of one whole.

- If appropriate, move on to improper fractions, allowing more confident learners to work with mixed numbers.

Adding and subtracting fractions

Learn

| $\frac{1}{10}$ | $\frac{1}{10}$ | $\frac{1}{10}$ | $\frac{1}{10}$ | $\frac{1}{10}$ | $\frac{1}{10}$ | $\frac{1}{10}$ | $\frac{1}{10}$ | $\frac{1}{10}$ | $\frac{1}{10}$ |

$\frac{7}{10} + \frac{3}{10} = \frac{10}{10}$

| $\frac{1}{7}$ | $\frac{1}{7}$ | $\frac{1}{7}$ | $\frac{1}{7}$ | | |

$\frac{1}{7} + \frac{3}{7} = \frac{4}{7}$

| $\frac{1}{5}$ | $\frac{1}{5}$ | $\frac{1}{5}$ | $\frac{1}{5}$ | $\frac{1}{5}$ |

$\frac{5}{5} - \frac{4}{5} = \frac{1}{5}$

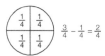

$\frac{3}{4} - \frac{1}{4} = \frac{2}{4}$

You can add and subtract fractions that have the same denominator. Just add the numerator.

Improper fractions have a numerator bigger than their denominator.

We can still add and subtract improper fractions, but you must still only add and subtract the numerators.

$\frac{5}{2} + \frac{6}{2} = \frac{11}{2}$ Five halves plus six halves equals eleven halves.

$\frac{3}{4} + \frac{5}{4} = \frac{8}{4}$ Three quarters plus five quarters equals eight quarters.

$\frac{7}{3} - \frac{5}{3} = \frac{2}{3}$ Seven thirds minus five thirds equals two thirds.

$\frac{9}{6} - \frac{4}{6} = \frac{5}{6}$ Nine sixths minus four sixths equals five sixths.

✓ Tips

- You can add three or more fractions, just like you can add three or more whole numbers. $\frac{2}{3} + \frac{4}{3} + \frac{5}{3} + \frac{3}{3} = \frac{14}{3}$

Remember:
A whole always has the same denominator and numerator.

$\frac{7}{7} = 1$ whole $\frac{3}{3} = 1$ whole $\frac{625}{625} = 1$ whole

Curriculum objectives

- To add and subtract fractions with the same denominator.

Success criteria

- I can add and subtract simple fractions.

- The activity in the textbook focuses on finding pairs of fractions that total one whole, such as four sevenths plus three sevenths. Arrange children in ability groups or pairs for this work and allow them to increase the complexity of their fractions as much as they are able to.

- Note that question 3 includes some answers that are greater than 1.
- The *Year 4 Practice Book* includes activities that can be used as further reinforcement by those who need it.

- The textbook problems are quite straightforward. These can be extended by using different fractions.

You can practise subtraction too: 'one whole minus three quarters'.

Talk maths

Challenge a partner to find the rest of the whole.

For example, if you say 'six eighths', they must reply 'plus two eighths makes a whole'. If you say 'seven twelfths', your partner must say 'plus five twelfths makes a whole'.

Try it with larger fractions. 'Nine twentieths…'
'…plus eleven twentieths makes a whole'.

Activities

1. Copy and complete these additions.

   a. $\frac{1}{2} + ? = 1$ b. $\frac{3}{4} + ? = 1$ c. $\frac{1}{3} + ? = 1$ d. $\frac{3}{7} + ? = 1$

2. Complete these subtractions from one whole.

   a. $1 - \frac{1}{2}$ b. $1 - \frac{2}{5}$ c. $1 - \frac{7}{8}$ d. $1 - \frac{13}{20}$

3. Add these fractions.

   a. $\frac{3}{4} + \frac{2}{4}$ b. $\frac{4}{5} + \frac{3}{5}$ c. $\frac{6}{10} + \frac{3}{10}$

   d. $\frac{5}{8} + \frac{6}{8}$ e. $\frac{2}{7} + \frac{4}{7} + \frac{5}{7}$ f. $\frac{5}{6} + \frac{4}{6} + \frac{3}{6}$

4. Subtract these fractions.

   a. $\frac{5}{3} - \frac{1}{3}$ b. $\frac{5}{6} - \frac{2}{6}$ c. $\frac{13}{8} - \frac{7}{8}$

   d. $\frac{7}{4} - \frac{1}{4}$ e. $\frac{4}{5} - \frac{1}{5}$ f. $\frac{21}{20} - \frac{8}{20}$

Problems

Brain-teaser

A pizza is cut into 12 equal slices.
Tina eats half of it, Josie eats $\frac{1}{12}$ and Dan eats $\frac{3}{12}$.
What fraction of the pizza is left?

Brain-buster

Some children share a bucket of popcorn. Tom takes $\frac{3}{20}$ and Amanda takes $\frac{6}{20}$.
What fraction of the popcorn is left?

---

100 Maths Lessons Year 4 links:

- Summer 1, Week 5 (pages 194–199): add and subtract fractions with the same denominators

Year 4 Practice Book links:

- (page 82): Adding fractions to make 1
- (page 83): Adding and subtracting fractions

Tenths and hundredths

Prior learning

- Can count up and down in tenths.
- Can recognise that tenths arise from dividing an object into ten equal parts and in dividing 1-digit numbers or quantities by 10.

Learn

- Recap the fractions work done to date, ensuring that the children understand the terms 'numerator', 'denominator' and 'equivalence'.
- Draw a large square on the whiteboard and divide it into ten equal horizontal rectangles. Point out that each rectangle is one tenth of the whole square.

Divide the top rectangle into ten equal sections, and mark each one as one hundredth. Draw vertical lines so that the whole of the large square is now divided into 100 hundredths.

- Keeping the grid displayed, use colours to show that one tenth equals ten hundredths and that ten tenths and 100

hundredths are both equivalent to one whole. *100 Maths Lessons Year 4, Spring 1, Week 5, Lesson 4* provides suggestions for showing this using a metre ruler.

- Provide the children with regular, short practice in counting in tenths and hundredths.

Curriculum objectives

- To count up and down in hundredths; recognise that hundredths arise when dividing an object by 100 and dividing tenths by 10.

Success criteria

- I can count up or down in tenths and hundredths.
- I can write tenths and hundredths in fraction form.

Tenths and hundredths

Learn

There are ten tenths in a whole.

$\frac{1}{10}$	$\frac{1}{10}$	$\frac{1}{10}$	$\frac{1}{10}$	$\frac{1}{10}$	$\frac{1}{10}$	$\frac{1}{10}$	$\frac{1}{10}$	$\frac{1}{10}$	$\frac{1}{10}$

We get tenths when we divide an object or number by 10.

One pizza is divided between 10 people. Each person will receive $\frac{1}{10}$ of a pizza.

Now imagine if $\frac{1}{10}$ of the pizza was shared between 10 other people.

$\frac{1}{10}$ divided by 10 will give each person $\frac{1}{100}$ of the pizza. Not much!

And there are 100 hundredths in a whole!

What would you rather have: one tenth of a pizza or one hundredth of a pizza?

We can count in tenths and hundredths.

				$\frac{1}{10}$					
$\frac{1}{100}$	$\frac{1}{100}$	$\frac{1}{100}$	$\frac{1}{100}$	$\frac{1}{100}$	$\frac{1}{100}$	$\frac{1}{100}$	$\frac{1}{100}$	$\frac{1}{100}$	$\frac{1}{100}$

$\frac{10}{100} = \frac{1}{10}$ $\frac{20}{100} = \frac{2}{10}$ $\frac{30}{100} = \frac{3}{10}$ $\frac{40}{100} = \frac{4}{10}$ $\frac{50}{100} = \frac{5}{10}$

$\frac{60}{100} = \frac{6}{10}$ $\frac{70}{100} = \frac{7}{10}$ $\frac{80}{100} = \frac{8}{10}$ $\frac{90}{100} = \frac{9}{10}$ $\frac{100}{100} = \frac{10}{10}$

✓ Tips

- Remember that $\frac{50}{100}$ is equivalent to $\frac{5}{10}$, and both are the same amount as $\frac{1}{2}$.
- $1 \div 10 = \frac{1}{10} =$ one tenth

  $1 \div 100 = \frac{1}{100} =$ one hundredth

Talk maths

- The textbook activity can be extended by challenging children to count backwards in tenths and hundredths. Ask more confident learners to count forwards and backwards in multiples of hundredths, which provides a link with counting in multiples of whole numbers.

Activities

- The textbook work can be extended by providing fractions with other denominators and asking the children to find their tenths or hundredths equivalents, and vice versa.

Problems

- The problems aim to get children thinking more about the equivalence between tenths and hundredths in preparation for decimal work. The more secure children can become in perceiving that ten hundredths is equivalent to one tenth, the easier they will find working with decimals.

Seven tenths.

Talk maths

Play *Beat the clock*.

Working with a partner, take turns to say any fraction in tenths or hundredths, such as two tenths or seventeen hundredths. Your partner then has to count on 10 more tenths or hundredths in less than 30 seconds.

Eight tenths, nine tenths, ten tenths, eleven tenths...

Activities

1. Add these tenths and hundredths.
   a. $\frac{1}{10} + \frac{6}{10}$ b. $\frac{7}{10} + \frac{5}{10}$ c. $\frac{13}{10} + \frac{9}{10}$
   d. $\frac{31}{100} + \frac{7}{100}$ e. $\frac{78}{100} + \frac{3}{100}$ f. $\frac{120}{100} + \frac{60}{100}$

2. Subtract these tenths and hundredths.
   a. $\frac{9}{10} - \frac{4}{10}$ b. $\frac{7}{10} - \frac{5}{10}$ c. $\frac{23}{10} - \frac{9}{10}$
   d. $\frac{21}{100} - \frac{11}{100}$ e. $\frac{58}{100} - \frac{6}{100}$ f. $\frac{125}{100} - \frac{80}{100}$

3. Write these fractions in words.
   a. $\frac{6}{10}$ b. $\frac{9}{10}$ c. $\frac{14}{100}$ d. $\frac{91}{100}$

4. Write these as fractions.
   a. seven tenths b. thirteen tenths
   c. thirty five hundredths d. two hundredths

Problems

Brain-teaser
Copy and complete this sentence. Three tenths = ? hundredths

Brain-buster
Copy and complete this sentence. Sixty-three hundredths = ? tenths and ? hundredths

Fractions and decimals 35

100 Maths Lessons Year 4 links:

- Autumn 2, Week 4 (pages 66–70): understand and use tenths and hundredths
- Spring 1, Week 5 (pages 113–117): understand and use tenths and hundredths
- Summer 1, Week 5 (pages 194–199): count, add and subtract with tenths and hundredths

Year 4 Practice Book links:

- (page 86): Hundredths
- (page 87): Counting in hundredths

Fractions and decimal equivalents

Prior learning

- Can count up and down in tenths and hundredths.
- Can write tenths and hundredths in fraction form.

Learn

- Recap children's basic knowledge of fractions, comparing halves with quarters and so on, and considering how these represent less than one whole. Move on to reviewing our number system and discussing the place value of 100s, 10s and 1s, and then introducing tenths and hundredths. Refer to the place-value table on page 36 of the textbook or draw a large one on the board.
- In presenting decimal equivalents to children, it may be beneficial to convert each fraction into fractional tenths and hundredths first. This can help the children to see the connections more clearly. For example: ¾ = ⁷⁵/₁₀₀ = 0.75. These tricky concepts should be visited repeatedly by spending short sessions on them.
- When appropriate, move on to converting decimals into fractions, as shown in the Tips on page 36 of the textbook.
- You are encouraged to work though *100 Maths Lessons Year 4, Spring 1, Week 6, Lessons 1, 2 and 3* to consolidate this work.

Curriculum objectives

- To recognise and write decimal equivalents of any number of tenths or hundredths.
- To recognise and write decimal equivalents to ¼, ½, ¾.

Success criteria

- I can convert between fractions and decimals.

Fraction and decimal equivalents

Learn

A fraction is a proportion of one whole.

$\frac{1}{100}$ $\frac{1}{10}$ $\frac{1}{4}$ $\frac{1}{2}$ $\frac{3}{4}$ are all fractions.

Numbers less than one can also be represented by decimals.

To show tenths and hundredths using our number system, we use a decimal point and two new columns.

- We write three tenths as 0.3 and five hundredths as 0.05.
- We can say that the number 0.47 has four tenths and seven hundredths.
- We read decimals aloud, using digits zero to nine.
- Any fraction can be written as a decimal.

100s	10s	1s	0.1s	0.01s
		.		

Fraction	$\frac{1}{2}$	$\frac{1}{4}$	$\frac{3}{4}$	$\frac{1}{10}$	$\frac{4}{10}$	$\frac{61}{100}$	$\frac{73}{100}$
Decimal	0.5	0.25	0.75	0.1	0.4	0.61	0.73

We can also have whole numbers and decimals.

For 23.62 we would say twenty-three, six tenths and two hundredths.

We say 0.5 is 'zero point five'.

We say 0.75 is 'zero point seven five'.

Or twenty-three point six two.

✓ Tips

- Decimals with one decimal place are equivalent to a fraction with a denominator of 10.
  $0.6 = \frac{6}{10}$
- Decimals with two decimal places are equivalent to a fraction with a denominator of 100.
  $0.37 = \frac{37}{100}$

  0.1 is one tenth $(\frac{1}{10})$

  0.2 is two tenths $(\frac{2}{10})$

  0.3 is three tenths $(\frac{3}{10})$

Any decimal can be written as a fraction!

Can you keep going?

36   Fractions and decimals

Talk maths

- The activity in the textbook can be easily extended by representing the decimals in the book as fractions (tenths and hundredths). Provide decimals and their equivalent fractions on cards and ask the children to use them to play 'Pelmanism' or 'Snap'.

Activities

- Children should find the questions in the textbook straightforward. The *Year 4 Practice Book* has activities that involve decimal numbers and quantities greater than 1, for example 1.5kg.

Problems

- The problems in the textbook can be used to assess children's conceptual knowledge. The children will also need practice in using decimals in practical contexts. The activities in the *Year 4 Practice Book* will provide ample opportunities for this.

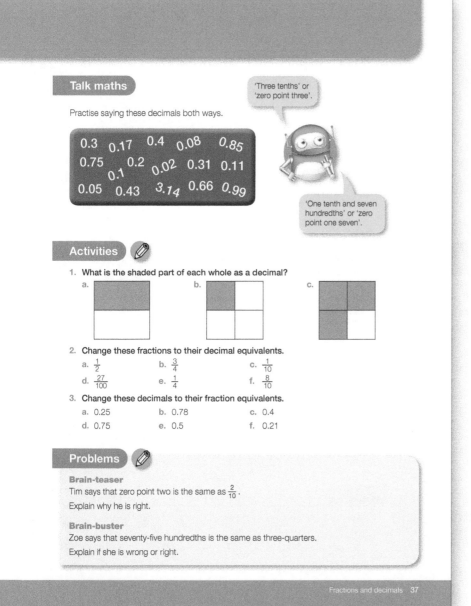

Talk maths

Practise saying these decimals both ways.

0.3 0.17 0.4 0.08 0.85
0.75 0.2 0.1 0.02 0.31 0.11
0.05 0.43 3.14 0.66 0.99

'Three tenths' or 'zero point three'.

'One tenth and seven hundredths' or 'zero point one seven'.

Activities

1. What is the shaded part of each whole as a decimal?

   a.   b.   c.

2. Change these fractions to their decimal equivalents.

   a. $\frac{1}{2}$ b. $\frac{3}{4}$ c. $\frac{1}{10}$
   d. $\frac{27}{100}$ e. $\frac{1}{4}$ f. $\frac{8}{10}$

3. Change these decimals to their fraction equivalents.

   a. 0.25   b. 0.78   c. 0.4
   d. 0.75   e. 0.5   f. 0.21

Problems

Brain-teaser
Tim says that zero point two is the same as $\frac{2}{10}$.
Explain why he is right.

Brain-buster
Zoe says that seventy-five hundredths is the same as three-quarters.
Explain if she is wrong or right.

100 Maths Lessons Year 4 links:

- Spring 1, Week 6 (pages 118–123): recognise decimals and fraction equivalents; recognise the place value of digits in decimals
- Summer 1, Week 5 (pages 194–199): use the equivalence of decimals and fractions
- Summer 2, Week 2 (pages 219–224): use decimals and fractions in measurement

Year 4 Practice Book links:

- (page 79): Less than or more than ½?
- (page 84): Fraction and decimal equivalents (1)
- (page 85): Fraction and decimal equivalents (2)

Working with decimals

Prior learning

- Can recognise and use decimal notation for tenths and hundredths.
- Can convert between decimals and their fractional equivalents.
- Can round and order whole numbers.

Learn

- It is advised that the work covered in this unit should be presented and developed several times over the course of the school year. In particular, working with decimals has many links with the different units of measure and money, which is reflected in the links provided to *100 Maths Lessons Year 4* and the *Year 4 Practice Book*.

- Referring to the place-value table at the top of page 36 in the textbook, recap the concepts of place value for numbers greater and less than 1. Focus on the use of tenths and hundredths for representing fractions of one whole. Over several sessions, work with the children to review the links between tenths and hundredths in decimal and fraction form, moving on to rounding, ordering and comparing decimals.

Curriculum objectives

- To find the effect of dividing a 1- or 2-digit number by 10 and 100, identifying the value of the digits in the answer as ones, tenths and hundredths.
- To round decimals with one decimal place to the nearest whole number.
- To compare numbers with the same number of decimal places up to two decimal places.

Success criteria

- I can compare, round and use numbers with up to two decimal places.

Working with decimals

Learn

Our number system uses **place value**.

We sometimes call this 100s, 10s and 1s.

346 is three hundred and forty-six.

Between zero and one we use decimal fractions.

.12 is point one two.

Decimals show tenths and hundredths of a whole. These are sometimes called **decimal fractions**.

Did you know?

When you solve money problems with pounds and pence, you often use decimals.

There are lots of ways we can work with decimals.

Dividing whole numbers by 10 or 100

We move the place value one column to the right when dividing by 10.

$\frac{3}{10} = 3 \div 10 = 0.3$

We move the place value two columns to the right when dividing by 100.

$\frac{45}{100} = 45 \div 100 = 0.45$

Look at these examples:

$\frac{7}{10} = 0.7$ and $\frac{7}{100} = 0.07$ $\qquad$ $\frac{23}{10} = 2.3$ and $\frac{23}{100} = 0.23$

Rounding decimals just like other numbers

Rounding to the nearest whole number: $0.7 \rightarrow 1$ $\quad$ $4.2 \rightarrow 4$ $\quad$ $6.8 \rightarrow 7$ $\quad$ $3.5 \rightarrow 4$

If it is .5 or higher, round up. If it is lower than .5, round down.

Ordering and comparing decimals

0.8 is bigger than 0.5 (eight tenths is bigger than five tenths).

0.25 is smaller than 0.32 (thirty-two hundredths is bigger than twenty-five hundredths).

We can draw number lines for decimals too!

✓ Tips

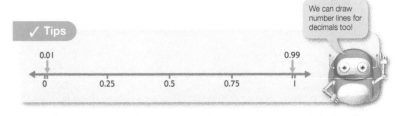

- The textbook activity can be taken further by asking children to write all of the numbers shown (and others if desired) in a table, in order of size. They should then show the effect of dividing each number by 10 and by 100. Encourage lots of talk about this, modelling correct explanations of the process, stating that the digits change their place value as the numbers are divided by 10 or 100. (It is not simply that the decimal point moves along the number.)

Activities

- The textbook questions should provide an assessment of the children's understanding of the key concepts. You can use the *Year 4 Practice Book* for further practice.

Problems

- The two problems require reasoning to complete them, but are not in any context. The links to *100 Maths Lessons Year 4* provide many problems involving decimals.

Talk maths

Choose ten numbers between 10 and 100, like the ones in the box below.
Take any two of the numbers and divide each one by 100.
Next, make a true statement about your numbers.

```
12   19   23   37   42   69
   53    84   95   75
```

> You can extend this activity by writing each decimal on a number line from 0 to 1.

For example: 23 and 75
$23 \div 100 = 0.23$ $75 \div 100 = 0.75$
0.23 is less than 0.75. 0.75 is greater than 0.23.

Activities

1. Complete these divisions.
   a. $7 \div 10$ b. $31 \div 100$ c. $3 \div 10$ d. $94 \div 100$

2. Round these decimals to the nearest whole number.
   a. 4.8   b. 3.1   c. 5.5   d. 7.4

3. Copy and insert the correct signs. Use <, > or =.
   a. 0.7 ___ 0.75   b. 0.31 ___ 0.42   c. 0.6 ___ 0.60   d. 0.25 ___ 0.23

4. Carefully copy the number line and then position these decimals on it.
   0.5   0.9   0.05   0.75   0.65   0.25   0.35

Problems

Brain-teaser
Brenda knows that 65 divided by 100 = 0.65.
What would 65 divided by 10 be?

Brain-buster
Thomas says that 0.55 rounded to the nearest whole number is 1.
What would 0.55 rounded to the nearest tenth be?

Fractions and decimals   39

---

100 Maths Lessons Year 4 links:

- Spring 1, Week 6 (pages 118–124): compare and rounding decimals; divide numbers by 10 and 100 to form decimals
- Summer 2, Week 2 (pages 219–224): divide by 10 and 100 to convert between different units of measure

Year 4 Practice Book links:

- (pages 88–89): Dividing by 10 and 100
- (page 90): Rounding decimals
- (page 91): Ordering decimal numbers

Units of measurement

Prior learning

- Can recognise and compare everyday measures and their units, including those for capacity, length, mass, money and time.

Learn

- This section provides an overview of different measures and units that the children are expected to become increasingly familiar with. Because the children can easily muddle up units for different measures, plan carefully whether to discuss units for different measures at the same time or on separate occasions.

- Whether presenting measures and units together or separately, spend time thinking of examples of when the units are used and why – it is essential that children perceive the benefit of these systems.

- Ideally, a permanent interactive display should be available to allow the children to measure different quantities over a long period of time. Estimation before measuring should always be encouraged, and links to other curriculum areas such as data handling should be exploited if possible.

- *100 Maths Lessons Year 4, Autumn 1, Week 6, Lesson 1* provides a clear foundation for this topic. Other activities in *100 Maths Lessons Year 4* provide lots of opportunities for the children to use units of measure within different contexts.

Curriculum objectives

- To identify and use different units of measure.

Success criteria

- I can identify which unit I should use to measure different items.

Units of measurement

Learn

Different quantities are measured in different ways.

Quantity	Units of measurement	Abbreviations	
Time (years)	1 year = 12 months 1 week = 7 days	years = y weeks = w	months = m days = d
Time (days)	1 day = 24 hours 1 hour = 60 minutes 1 minute = 60 seconds	hours = h minutes = m seconds = s	
Money	1 pound = 100 pence	pounds = £	pence = p
Mass	1 kilogram = 1000 grams	kilograms = kg	grams = g
Capacity	1 litre = 1000 millilitres	litre = l	millilitre = ml
Length	1 kilometre = 1000 metres 1 metre = 100 centimetres 1 centimetre = 10 millimetres	kilometres = km centimetres = cm millimetres = mm	metres = m

Think about where you see the different units above, and what they are used for.

Quantity	How to measure	Why	Examples
Time (years)	calendars, clocks	planning years, days	holidays, timetables
Money	notes and coins	buying and selling	school meals
Mass	scales and weights	to know correct amounts	making cakes
Capacity	containers	to know correct amounts	mixing drinks
Length	rulers, tape measures, maps	making things, planning journeys	making a box, going on a trip

You will learn all about converting units in the next sections.

Try to develop your understanding of different units wherever you are.

✓ Tips

- How far do you walk to school?
- How many days have you been alive?
- Do you have a water bottle? What is its capacity?
- Guess the weight of your dinner. How can you check?
- How much pocket money do you receive each year?

- Perhaps organised as a carousel activity, provide a wide selection of objects (or cue cards where this is not feasible), and allow the children time to consider and discuss how they would measure each item, and with what units. This should be done alongside practical measuring activities using appropriate equipment.

- The activities in the textbook should provide a quick overview of which children need more practical experience. In addition, provide further practice in identifying units and equipment for each area of measurement. (Note that subsequent units address converting between units.)

- If the children are finding the problems difficult, refer them to the table of units at the top of page 40 of the textbook. Some children may still find the problems demanding if they're tackling them before working on conversion between units. If they are, provide further practical tasks where they can use equipment to measure and compare different items.

Can you think of more challenging clues?

Example clue	Answer
a cup of tea	millilitres
a long journey	kilometres
a finger	centimetres
a snail	grams
a new car	pounds
a maths lesson	minutes
a cricket match	hours
a lifetime	years

Talk maths

Play *Read my mind*.

Take turns with a partner to give clues about the units you are thinking about. Try thinking of different clues for all the units on the opposite page.

Activities

1. **What units would you measure these things in?**
   a. The length of a pencil.
   b. The height of a house.
   c. The cost of a pencil.
   d. The cost of a car.
   e. The capacity of a cup.
   f. The capacity of a bath.
   g. The weight of a computer.
   h. The weight of a pencil.
   i. The duration of pop song.
   j. The duration of a holiday.

2. **What is the name of each piece of measuring equipment?**

   a.   b.   c.

3. **What equipment would you use to measure these items?**
   a. The length of a pencil.
   b. The height of your teacher.
   c. The capacity of a cup.
   d. The weight of an apple.
   e. A running race.
   f. The time until Christmas.

Problems

Brain-teaser
1 millilitre of water weighs 1 gram.
How much does 5 litres of water weigh, in grams?

Brain-buster
Tyler's dad is one metre seventy-three centimetres tall.
Tyler is exactly half the height of his dad. How tall is Tyler in millimetres?

Measurement   41

100 Maths Lessons Year 4 links:

- Autumn 1, Week 6 (pages 36–41): identify units of measure

Units of time

- Know the number of seconds in a minute and the number of days in each month, year and leap year.
- Can compare durations of events.

Learn

- Recap the different units of time used, discussing why it might be that these are not all multiples of 10, unlike other measures we regularly use.
- Discuss the calculations that the children could use to convert between different units by referring to the table on page 42 of the textbook. In particular, strategies for multiplying by 60 (that is ×6 and then ×10) should be revised and modelled regularly.

100 Maths Lessons Year 4, Autumn 2, Week 6, Lesson 2 provides additional advice.

- In short bursts over several sessions, challenge the children with quick-fire questions that involve converting between units of time. (Although the mental maths skills involved are quite tricky, you may well observe that children seem to handle these more easily in such an everyday context.)

Curriculum objectives

- To solve problems involving converting from hours to minutes; minutes to seconds; years to months; weeks to days.

Success criteria

- I can convert between units of time to solve problems.

Units of time

Learn

These are all units of time: seconds, minutes, hours, days, weeks and years.

60 seconds = 1 minute
60 minutes = 1 hour
24 hours = 1 day
7 days = 1 week
365 days = 1 year

Remember that months are not all the same length.
30 days hath September, April, June and November. All the rest have 31, except for February all alone.
(February has 28 days, and 29 days in a leap year.)

To convert between times is tricky!

Convert	Calculation	Example
years to months	× 12	3 years = 3 × 12 = 36 months
years to days	× 365	2 years = 2 × 365 = 730 days
weeks to days	× 7	6 weeks = 6 × 7 = 42 days
days to hours	× 24	3 days = 3 × 24 = 72 hours
hours to minutes	× 60	5 hours = 5 × 60 = 300 minutes
minutes to seconds	× 60	10 minutes = 10 × 60 = 600 seconds

Did you know?

The Earth actually takes 365 and a quarter days to travel around the sun.

That's why we have a leap year every four years, to catch up with the extra quarters.

Also, we say that there are 52 weeks in a year, but this is not exactly true, it is an approximation. Look:
7 × 52 = 364 days

✓ Tips

- 1 year = 365 days × 24 hours × 60 minutes × 60 seconds!

If you want to convert from a large unit, such as years, to a small unit such as seconds, you have to do one stage at a time.

Talk maths

- Challenge the children to work at school and at home to list everyday activities and the length of time they take, writing each in minutes as well as seconds. This can be extended to tasks that take hours, noting the two-step calculation to convert a time in hours to seconds.

Activities

- The children could learn their answers to question 1 and also build up their own sets of relationships, for example three years, three weeks and so on. Questions 2 and 3 are easily adaptable by changing the given times.

Problems

- The problems are multi-step and so increase the difficulty level encountered so far (for example, to convert days to minutes). This can be developed further with the suggested *Year 4 Practice Book* activity, as well by posing more complex challenges such as asking children to calculate how many seconds they have been alive for.

Talk maths

Work with a partner and think about how long different things take to do in seconds.

Task	Time	In seconds
putting on shoes	2 minutes	120 seconds
walking to school	$5\frac{1}{2}$ minutes	330 seconds

How about a football match, lunch break, eating a biscuit, watching your favourite TV programme…

Activities

1. Copy both rows then match each time in the top row to its equivalent on the bottom row.

   2 years   2 weeks   2 days   2 hours   2 minutes

   120 minutes   730 days   120 seconds   48 hours   14 days

2. Copy and convert each of these times.
   a. 2 minutes = ? seconds
   b. 3 hours = ? minutes
   c. 4 days = ? hours
   d. 5 weeks = ? days
   e. 6 years = ? months
   f. 2 years (not leap years) = ? days

3. Copy and convert each of these times.
   a. $3\frac{1}{2}$ minutes = ? seconds
   b. $2\frac{1}{2}$ hours = ? minutes
   c. $5\frac{1}{2}$ days = ? hours
   d. $7\frac{1}{2}$ years = ? months

Problems

Brain-teaser
Poppy knows that on her tenth birthday she will have lived for three leap years and seven ordinary years.

How many days has she lived altogether?

Brain-buster
a. How many hours are there in a non-leap year?
b. How many minutes are there in one day?

---

100 Maths Lessons Year 4 links:

- Autumn 2, Week 6 (pages 77–82): convert between different units of time
- Spring 2, Week 3 (pages 142–146): solve problems involving converting between units of time

Year 4 Practice Book links:

- (page 100): Time problems

Analogue and digital clocks

Prior learning

- Can tell and write the time from an analogue clock, including using Roman numerals from I to XII, and 12-hour and 24-hour clocks.
- Can estimate, measure and compare time in terms of seconds, minutes and hours.
- Can use vocabulary such as 'o'clock', 'am'/'pm', 'morning', 'afternoon', 'noon' and 'midnight'.

Learn

- Using teaching clocks or digital resources (there is an interactive clock resource on the CD-ROM accompanying *100 Maths Lessons Year 4*), spend time revising children's existing knowledge of clocks, covering Roman numerals as well as

12- and 24-hour analogue and digital clocks. Revise the use of the terms 'am', 'pm', 'morning', 'noon', 'afternoon', 'evening', 'midnight' and 'night-time'.

- Over several sessions, work with both analogue and digital clocks to give the children practise at reading the time on both, as well as converting between the two forms. Remember that for 12-hour times, we must always state am or pm, whereas this is not required for 24-hour times.

- *100 Maths Lessons Year 4, Autumn 2, Week 6, Lesson 1* provides structured activities that use the interactive clock resource on the accompanying CD-ROM. *100 Maths Lessons Year 4, Spring 2, Week 3* provides a wide range of lessons and resources for using 12- and 24-hour time.

Curriculum objectives

- To read, write and convert time between analogue and digital 12- and 24-hour clocks.

Success criteria

- I can tell and write the time to five minutes, including quarter past or to the hour.
- I can convert between 12-hour and 24-hour times.

Analogue and digital clocks

Learn

When we use the 12-hour clock, we divide the day into two halves of 12 hours each, from midnight to noon, and then back to midnight.

For 12-hour clock time, we have to say am or pm.

24-hour clocks are different – they do just what they say. They start at midnight and count 24 hours through the day.

am and pm are 'before noon' and 'after noon' to you and me!

This is an analogue clock. It uses hands to show the time. It is a 12-hour clock. It shows twenty-three minutes past ten, but is it am or pm?

You have to look out the window and see if it is day or night!

Digital clocks use digits to show hours and minutes.

11:35pm = 23:35
6:42pm = 18:42

13:25 = 1:25pm
22:45 = 10:45pm

For 12-hour digital times, we have to use am and pm. This shows that the time is before noon or after noon.

Converting between 12-hour and 24-hour digital times isn't so hard.

For pm times, we add 12 to get the 24-hour time for example 10.15pm = 22:15.

For 24-hour times past 12 noon, just subtract 12 to get the 12-hour time for example 16:47 = 4:47pm.

Learn how to convert between analogue and digital.

✓ Tips

- 'Past' times are easy. We just write the hours and the number of minutes. For example, 10:05 is five minutes past 10.
- 'To' times are harder. Learn that 30 is half past, 40 is twenty to, 45 is quarter to and 50 is ten to.

- Working in pairs or small groups, children should work with paper or plastic clocks to investigate and develop their time-telling skills. They should challenge each other to show given 12- and 24-hour times. Also, ask the children to create, develop and ultimately present a 'time story', where the time on the clock is integral to the story. When narrating the story to others, they should show the time on their clocks at every occasion that an actual time is mentioned.

- Question 1 can be extended by providing more detailed analogue statements, such as *eight thirty in the evening*, *quarter past four in the morning*, and so on. Support can be provided using resources from *100 Maths Lessons Year 4*, such as 'Time Pelmanism' and 'Time Dominoes'.

- Problems that span hours, and then days, should be gradually introduced to the children.
- A great deal of extended real-life work can be obtained relatively easily by providing children with simple shopping or holiday itineraries. More confident learners might work with online resources to plan journeys and trips. (Be careful with global trips as time-zone work is not required and can be confusing.)

Talk maths

Work with a partner to become an expert time-teller.

Draw an analogue clock like this. Put hands on the clock, using a long pencil and a short pencil, and say am or pm. Then challenge your partner to say this in 12-hour or 24-hour time.

Then write digital clock times, such as 17:35. Ask your partner to show you the time on the analogue clock.

Activities

1. Copy and complete this chart for 12-hour analogue and digital times.

Analogue	twelve noon		ten past eleven	five to four	
Digital		8:45			3:15

2. Write these analogue times as 24-hour digital times.

   a. am   b. pm   c. am   d. pm

3. Write these 24-hour digital times as 12-hour analogue times. Remember to use am and pm.

   a. 11:30   b. 15:15   c. 03:25   d. 12:45

Problems

Brain-teaser
A train departs at quarter to eleven in the morning and arrives at 12:05pm.
How long does the journey take?

Brain-buster
An aeroplane takes off from London at 21:45 and flies directly to South Africa. The aeroplane lands at 9:25am London time.
How long was the flight?

Measurement   45

100 Maths Lessons Year 4 links:

- Autumn 2, Week 6 (pages 77–82): read, write and convert time between analogue and digital 12-hour clocks
- Spring 2, Week 3 (pages 142–146): read, write and convert time between analogue and digital 12- and 24-hour times

Year 4 Practice Book links:

- (page 99): Analogue and digital times

Money

- Can add and subtract amounts of money to give change, using both £ and p in practical contexts.

Learn

- Discuss the money system and the notes we used, and spend time reviewing the notation for money. Examine the differences in writing down amounts in pounds or in pence.

- Recap that 100 pence make one pound. (*100 Maths Lessons Year 4, Autumn 1, Week 6, Lesson 3* covers this.) Work with the children to understand how to convert between pounds and pence, revising multiplication and division by 100.

- Move on to reviewing column addition and subtraction, using amounts of mixed pounds and pence. (See *Year 4 Practice Book* pages 42 and 43.)

Curriculum objectives

- To estimate, compare and calculate different measures, including money in pounds and pence.

Success criteria

- I can calculate money in pounds and pence.
- I can convert between money shown in pounds and pence.

Money

Learn

These are the coins we use in England and Wales. We also use £5, £10, £20 and £50 notes.

Money shows us the cost of things.
We use pounds and pence.
£1 = 100 pence

We show pence using two decimal places.
7 pounds and 25 pence = £7.25
That's *seven pounds twenty-five*.

Unlike other decimals, if the last digit is a zero, we still write it in.

16 pounds and 50 pence = £16.50
That's *sixteen pounds fifty*.

Look at this amount: £0.59 is zero pounds and fifty-nine pence, or 59p.

To convert pounds to pence, multiply by 100:
£6.50 = 6.50 × 100 = 650p

To convert pence to pounds divide by 100:
3265p = 3265 ÷ 100 = £32.65

> Notice that if you use the £ sign and decimals, you don't add a p at the end.

Did you know?

Before the year 1970 we used pounds, shillings and pence.

A shilling was the same as 5p, but there were 240 old pennies in a pound in those days!

> 1p is one hundredth of one pound.

✓ Tips

Operation	Example
Addition	£3.50 + £2.15 = £5.65
Subtraction	£5.00 − £1.25 = £3.75
Multiplication	£2.10 × 3 = £6.30
Division	£7.00 ÷ 2 = £3.50
Fractions	$\frac{1}{2}$ of £25.00 = £12.50

> You can use all your number skills to solve money problems.

- We can use written methods with money just like any other numbers.
- Remember to be careful with the decimal point.

Talk maths

- Bring a selection of shopping lists into class, real or invented, and allow the children time to investigate them and create their own problems from them. Role play can allow them to practise mental skills. Provide paper or plastic money to support learners where necessary.

Activities

- In addition to the questions in the textbook, the activities in the *Year 4 Practice Book* provide a range of problems involving addition and subtraction of money.

Problems

- The main thing to watch out for with the problems is the children's ability to identify the correct operations. Both problems are split into two parts, each part being a step in a two-step problem. Providing lots of practice in solving money problems will naturally consolidate children's arithmetic skills.

- *100 Maths Lessons Year 4, Spring 1, Week 2, Lesson 5* and *Summer 1, Week 2* have problems involving money.

100 Maths Lessons Year 4 links:

- Autumn 1, Week 6 (pages 36–41): convert between pounds and pence
- Spring 1, Week 2 (pages 96–101): solve two-step money problems involving addition and subtraction of money
- Summer 1, Week 2 (pages 178–182): solve money problems involving mental addition and subtraction

Year 4 Practice Book links:

- (page 42): Adding money using columns
- (page 43): Subtracting money using columns
- (page 44): Addition and subtraction money problems (1)
- (page 45): Addition and subtraction money problems (2)
- (page 48): Money and measures problems (+ and −)
- (page 101): Magical money problems

Talk maths

Find an old shopping receipt or a price list from a catalogue or website, and work with a partner to compare costs.

Next, challenge each other by asking for items on the list and paying for them.

If you feel confident, put the money away and solve problems just using the maths.

I'd like a tin of beans for 32p. Here is £1.

Here is your change: 68p.

Activities

1. Copy this chart and convert these pence to pounds.

Pence	500p	150p	3300p	59p	1000p
Pounds					

2. Copy this chart and convert these pounds to pence.

Pounds	£1	£4.25	£0.62	£20	£12.06
Pence					

3. Complete these calculations.

   a. £2.50 + £3.30   b. £4.90 + £3.20   c. £10.00 − £6.50
   d. £20.00 − £12.99   e. 8 × 50p   f. £2.50 × 4
   g. £20 ÷ 4   h. £15 ÷ 3

Problems

Brain-teaser
Ice creams cost £1.25 each. Alfie's mum buys five.

a. What is the total cost?
b. How much change will she get from a £10 note?

Brain-buster
Ice creams cost £1.25 each and ice lollies cost £1.50 each.

a. How much would three ice creams and seven lollies cost altogether?
b. How much change would there be from a £20 note?

Mass and capacity

Prior learning

- Can measure, compare, add and subtract mass (kg/g) and volume/capacity (l/ml).

Learn

- Although these two concepts are presented together in one section, you may prefer to introduce them separately.
- Review the units of mass and capacity. Using a selection of objects and equipment, ask the children to estimate and then measure their mass or capacity.
- Spend time discussing how conversion between units is performed, modelling good practice in multiplying and dividing by 1000 for simple amounts.
- Note that there are interactive scales and an interactive measuring jug on the CD-ROM that accompanies *100 Maths Lessons Year 4*.

Curriculum objectives

- To convert between different units of measure.
- To estimate, compare and calculate different measures, including money in pounds and pence.

Success criteria

- I can carry out calculations involving mass and capacity.
- I can convert between units of mass.
- I can convert between units of capacity.

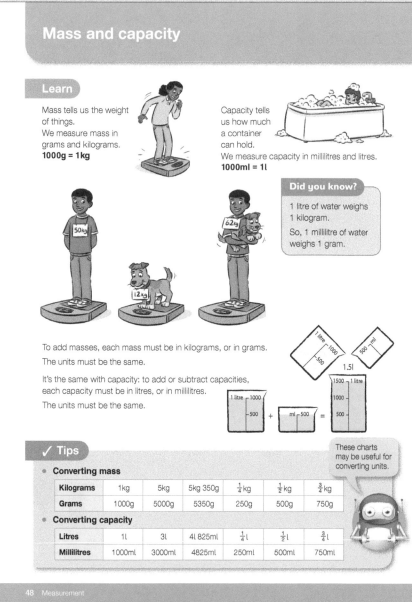

Mass and capacity

Learn

Mass tells us the weight of things.
We measure mass in grams and kilograms.
1000g = 1kg

Capacity tells us how much a container can hold.
We measure capacity in millilitres and litres.
1000ml = 1l

Did you know?

1 litre of water weighs 1 kilogram.

So, 1 millilitre of water weighs 1 gram.

To add masses, each mass must be in kilograms, or in grams.
The units must be the same.

It's the same with capacity: to add or subtract capacities, each capacity must be in litres, or in millilitres.
The units must be the same.

✓ Tips

These charts may be useful for converting units.

Converting mass

Kilograms	1kg	5kg	5kg 350g	$\frac{1}{4}$kg	$\frac{1}{2}$kg	$\frac{3}{4}$kg
Grams	1000g	5000g	5350g	250g	500g	750g

Converting capacity

Litres	1l	3l	4l 825ml	$\frac{1}{4}$l	$\frac{1}{2}$l	$\frac{3}{4}$l
Millilitres	1000ml	3000ml	4825ml	250ml	500ml	750ml

48   Measurement

- If possible, bring a selection of non-perishable groceries and drinks in to the classroom. Perhaps as a carousel activity, have the children estimate and then read the mass and/or capacity shown on each item. This can progress to the children measuring each item with appropriate equipment. Challenge more confident learners to create problems based on their measurements, such as: *How many juice cartons would fill a 1-litre jug?*

Activities

- Note that the calculations in question 5 are tricky. Some children may require easier work – and they could try the activities in the *Year 4 Practice Book* first. Also, *100 Maths Lessons Year 4, Spring 2, Week 6* provides mass and capacity activities linked to data handling.

Problems

- Some of the problems involve multiplication or division. Children who are struggling should be advised to use repeated addition of the smaller quantities until they total the larger mass/capacity.
- *100 Maths Lessons Year 4, Summer 1, Week 2, Lesson 2* focuses on weighing problems.
- *100 Maths Lessons Year 4, Summer 1, Week 6, Lessons 1 and 2* focus on capacity problems.

Talk maths

Working with a partner, look at a selection of different food and drink containers. Challenge each other to predict the capacity of different bottles, the mass of different bags of vegetables, and so on.

If you can, extend this work using scales and measuring jugs. Try to investigate the mass or capacity of as many different items as you can.

Activities

1. Write each object and write the correct capacity next to it.
   thimble   mug   bathtub
   200l   200ml   20ml

2. Write each object and write the correct capacity next to it.
   mouse   child   elephant
   5000kg   50g   50kg

3. Convert these masses.
   a. 5kg = ?g   b. 6000g = ?kg   c. $\frac{1}{2}$kg = ?g   d. 4500g = ?kg

4. Convert these capacities.
   a. 3000ml = ?l   b. $7\frac{1}{2}$l = ?ml   c. 3500ml = ?l   d. $\frac{1}{2}$l = ?ml

5. Solve these calculations.
   a. $3\frac{1}{4}$kg + 500g = ?kg   b. 450g + 700g = ?g   c. $\frac{1}{10}$kg + 320g = ?g
   d. $3\frac{1}{4}$l + 450ml = ?ml   e. 230ml + 140ml = ?l   f. $3\frac{1}{4}$l + $1\frac{3}{4}$l = ?ml

Problems

Brain-teaser
a. A carton of juice contains 50ml. How many cartons would make 1 litre?
b. A pencil weighs 27g. How much would 100 pencils weigh?

Brain-buster
a. Paper cups have a capacity of 100ml. How many cups will a $2\frac{1}{2}$l bottle fill?
b. Onions weigh 125g each. How many onions would make 1 kilogram?

---

100 Maths Lessons Year 4 links:

- Spring 2, Week 6 (pages 159–164): estimate, measure and convert masses in kilograms and grams
- Summer 1, Week 2 (pages 178–182): solve problems involving mass
- Summer 1, Week 6 (pages 200–205): estimate, measure and convert capacities in litres and millilitres

Year 4 Practice Book links:

- (page 46): Magical measures problems
- (page 47): Measures problems (+ and −) (choose appropriate questions)
- (page 97): Ordering and converting mass
- (page 98): Estimating and measuring capacity

Length and distance

Prior learning

- Can measure, compare, add and subtract lengths in metres, centimetres and millimetres.

Learn

- Recap the units of measurement and come up with three categories of objects that would be estimated or measured in millimetres, centimetres and metres.
- Progress to introducing kilometres and consider conversion between these and metres. Stress the difference between length and distance as discussed on page 50 of the textbook.
- Over several short sessions, discuss how to convert between units of length. Revisit decimals: tenths (millimetres to centimetres) and multiplying or dividing by 10; and hundredths (centimetres to metres) and multiplying or dividing by 100. When appropriate, move on to thousandths (millimetres to metres and metres to kilometres) and multiplying or dividing by 1000.

Curriculum objectives

- To convert between different units of measure.
- To estimate, compare and calculate different measures, including money in pounds and pence.

Success criteria

- I can carry out calculations involving length and distance.
- I can convert between units of length.

Length and distance

Learn

We measure short lengths in centimetres and millimetres, and some longer lengths and distances in metres.

125cm

12mm

100m

We measure even longer distances in kilometres.
You should know these. 10mm = 1cm
100cm = 1m (and 1000mm = 1m)
1000m = 1km

10km

A

B

Length is the measure of an object or line from end to end.
For example, a football pitch is 100m long; a finger is 1cm wide.

Distance is the measure of the space between two points or two objects.
For example, the distance between two towns is 10km; the gap between two parked cars is 1m.

Remember tenths and hundredths?
A millimetre is one tenth of a centimetre, a centimetre is one hundredth of a metre.

Look at a ruler and a metre rule.

✓ Tips

These charts may be useful to help you convert units. Remember, when you add lengths together, they must have the same units!

Millimetres	1	5	10
Centimetres	0.1	0.5	1

Centimetres	1	10	25	50	75	100
Metres	0.01	0.1	0.25	0.5	0.75	1

Metres	10	100	250	500	750	1000
Kilometres	$\frac{1}{100}$	$\frac{1}{10}$	$\frac{1}{4}$	$\frac{1}{2}$	$\frac{3}{4}$	1

- As well as providing measuring practice, the activity in the textbook will reinforce the children's understanding of the relative size and relationship between millimetres and centimetres. It can be easily extended to work on centimetres and metres.

- To challenge the children, introduce them to large-scale maps and ask them to estimate distances in kilometres and metres.

Activities

- The questions in the textbook focus on measuring and converting between units. The *Year 4 Practice Book* provides activities to support and extend this learning, using length and distance in calculations in meaningful contexts.

Problems

- The problems in the textbook should be straightforward for most children. To extend learning, *100 Maths Lessons Year 4, Summer 1, Week 2, Lesson 5* involves the children measuring a wide range of items and using their measurements to create their own problems. *100 Maths Lessons Year 4, Summer 2, Week 2, Lesson 5* builds on this.

Talk maths

Working with a partner, challenge each other, without using a ruler, to draw a line of a particular length, or make two dots a certain distance apart.

(Never go above 12cm, but try mixtures of centimetres and millimetres, such as 5.7cm.)

Next measure the length or distance and see how accurate your partner is.

Keep trying this until each of you get some correct.

Activities

1. Measure the length of these lines. Give your answers in millimetres.

   a. _____   b. _____

   c. _____   d. _____

2. Measure the distances between these dots. Give your answers in centimetres.

   a. A •   • B

   b. A •   • B

   c. A •   • B

   d. A •   • B

3. Copy and complete these conversion charts.

a.
mm	cm
10	
100	
	2
	35
	100

b.
cm	m
100	
1000	
	0.25
	0.5
	10

c.
m	km
500	
2000	
	$\frac{1}{4}$
	1
	9

Problems

Brain-teaser

Ahmed is 1.52m tall. He wears shoes with a 2cm heel. What height will he be with his shoes on? Give your answer in metres and in centimetres.

Brain-buster

The distance between two towns is 19km. Isobel is going to ride her bike between the towns, and wants to stop halfway. How far will she ride for each half of the journey? Give your answer in kilometres and in metres.

100 Maths Lessons Year 4 links:

- Autumn 1, Week 6 (pages 36–41): compare lengths; convert between units of length

- Summer 1, Week 2 (pages 178–182): measure and solve problems involving measurements

- Summer 2, Week 2 (pages 219–224): solve problems involving measures given as whole numbers, fractions and decimals

Year 4 Practice Book links:

- (page 47): Measures problems (+ and −) (choose appropriate questions)

- (page 92): Converting lengths

- (page 93): Comparing distances

- (page 96): Reading rulers

- (page 102): Measures problems

Perimeter

Prior learning

- Can measure the perimeter of simple 2D shapes.

Learn

- Recap the method for finding the perimeter of simple rectangles and squares by measuring. Remind children that the perimeter is the distance a person, a mouse or an ant, for example, would cover if they went for a walk around the whole edge of a shape.

- Move on to introducing quicker ways to calculate perimeter, demonstrating that a square is *4 times length of a side*, and a rectangle is *2 times length plus 2 times height*. Note that page 52 of the textbook introduces this using simple algebra – you may need to consider if this is appropriate for all children.

- In further sessions, you could look at irregular shapes, reminding the children that the perimeter is the distance around the edges, not the perimeters of each of the two rectilinear shapes combined. *100 Maths Lessons Year 4, Autumn 1, Week 6, Lesson 4* has ideas to help consolidate this work.

Perimeter

Learn

Perimeter is the distance around the sides of a shape.

This rectangle has a perimeter of 3 + 3 + 2 + 2 = 10cm.

This square has a perimeter of 4 + 4 + 4 + 4 = 16cm.

Don't forget to always show the units!

If we say that all rectangles have a length l and a width w, then the perimeter can be calculated with a formula.

We can say $P = l + w + l + w$

Or, changing the order that we add in: $P = l + l + w + w$
We can make this simpler too: $P = 2l + 2w$

The perimeter of this rectangle is

$P = 2 \times 4 + 2 \times 2 = 12$cm

What do you think the perimeter of a rectangle 6m long and 3m wide would be?

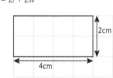

Here's a quick way to find the perimeter of a square.

✓ Tips

- The formula for a square is easier, because all the sides are the same length.

  $P = 4s$

- $P = 4 \times 3 = 12$cm

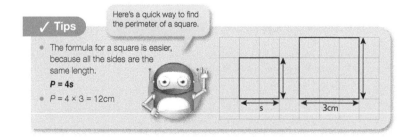

Curriculum objectives

- To measure and calculate the perimeter of a rectilinear figure (including squares) in centimetres and metres.

Success criteria

- I can measure and calculate the perimeters of rectangles and squares.

Talk maths

- The aim of the activity in the textbook is to develop children's competence in estimating and calculating the perimeter of rectilinear shapes. This can be extended in many ways, including irregular shapes, other polygons, and even measuring larger perimeters, such as the school playground, with appropriate equipment.

Activities

- The questions in the textbook focus on simple shapes, encouraging children to calculate rather than count their way to the answers. Note that question 2 requires children to measure the sides of each shape.
- *100 Maths Lessons Year 4, Summer 1, Week 6, Lesson 3* provides ideas and resources for further practice and extension.

Problems

- Solving both problems will be straightforward providing children approach the work methodically. Encourage them to sketch each problem and indicate the size of each side (drawing to scale may be difficult). The activities in the *Year 4 Practice Book* provide further problems and practice.

Talk maths

Use a pencil and a ruler to draw a selection of rectangles and squares, each with different measurements. Label your shapes A, B ,C and so on, and write the lengths of the sides separately. Next, challenge a partner you know to estimate the perimeter of each shape. Use a ruler to check their estimates. How many can they get right?

Activities

1. Draw each of these shapes and then write their perimeter inside them.
   a. A rectangle, length 4cm, width 2cm.
   b. A square, side length 3cm.

2. Measure and calculate the perimeter of each of these shapes.
   a.   b.   c.

3. Complete this chart.

Shape	Length	Width	Perimeter
rectangle	5cm	2cm	
rectangle	12mm	5mm	
rectangle	6km	2km	
square	8mm	8mm	
square	5m	5m	
square	4.5cm	4.5cm	

Problems

Brain-teaser

A square field is $3\frac{1}{2}$km long on each side. How long is the fence that goes around it?

Brain-buster

A sheet of A4 paper is 21cm wide and 29.7cm long. Calculate the perimeter of a single sheet.

Measurement   53

100 Maths Lessons Year 4 links:

- Autumn 1, Week 6 (pages 36–41): calculate the perimeter of rectilinear shapes
- Summer 1, Week 6 (pages 200–205): solve problems involving perimeter

Year 4 Practice Book links:

- (page 94): Find the perimeter
- (page 95): Area and perimeter (choose appropriate questions)
- (page 103): Perimeter problems

Area

- Can measure and calculate the perimeter of rectangles and squares.

Learn

- Review the meaning of 2D shapes, focusing on rectangles and squares. For each shape, draw them on squared paper (or on grids on the board), and recap methods for finding the perimeter by counting the sides of the squares. Move on to counting the squares inside the shape (shading as you go) and explain that this shows how much space the shape covers – it is the area of the shape.

- Demonstrate how a shape with an area of 20 squares can have several different shapes.
- *100 Maths Lessons Year 4, Summer 1, Week 6, Lessons 4 and 5* have further activities that focus on this topic.

Curriculum objectives

- To find the area of rectilinear shapes by counting squares.

Success criteria

- I can count squares to find the area of shapes.

Area

Learn

A 2D shape is flat. 2D means *two-dimensional*.

We can draw 2D shapes on paper, and we can draw them accurately with a pencil and a ruler.

A square is a special type of rectangle where all sides are the same length.

Remember, a rectangle has right angles at each corner, and the opposite sides are the same length.

Area is measured in squares.

This square is 1 square long and 1 square high.

We say its area is 1 square.

We can simply count squares to calculate simple areas.

Area of rectangle = 8 squares

Area of square = 9 squares

✓ Tips

- This shape is 2 squares wide and 3 squares long. It look like an array that we use in multiplication. We could write 2 × 3 for the array. We can use this multiplication fact to work out the area.
  There are 2 lots of 3 squares. So the area is 6 squares.
- Can you say what the area of a rectangle that is 3 squares wide and 6 squares long would be?

If you're feeling confident, try using a calculation to find the area.

54 Measurement

- Use the textbook activity as a starting point for children to investigate that different rectangles can have the same area but there is only one way to draw a square with a given area.

- More confident learners might be encouraged to investigate the numeric relationships between length, width and area, progressing to estimating and calculating larger areas such as tables.

Activities

- Encourage the children to work accurately when they draw their shapes for question 2. More confident learners could use 1cm² grid paper and, if desired, you could introduce them to squared units and the use of cm² as the unit of area.

- A nice extension is to draw a range of polygons, including circles, and have children estimate their areas by counting complete and part-squares.

They use judgement to say when particular numbers of part-squares total a whole square.

Problems

- Both problems are straightforward if the shapes are drawn out.

- Page 95 of the *Year 4 Practice Book* has a tricky problem which makes a good follow-up for more confident learners as it introduces the formula for calculating area. They might also be challenged to use some of the measurements on page 94 of the *Year 4 Practice Book* to calculate areas of rectilinear shapes.

Talk maths

Work with a partner to draw each of these shapes, if possible on squared paper.
Before you start discuss what you think the lengths and heights of each shape will be.

Shape	rectangle	rectangle	rectangle	square	square	square
Area	6 squares	8 squares	12 squares	1 square	4 squares	16 squares

Can you spot a relationship between the numbers for length, height and area?

Activities

1. Count squares to find the area of each shape.

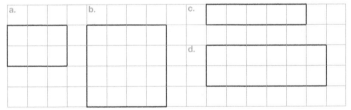

2. Find the area of these shapes. You can draw them on squared paper to help you.

   a. A rectangle that is 4 squares long and 3 squares high.

   b. A square that is 3 squares long and 3 squares high.

Problems

Brain-teaser
Sanjay draws a rectangle 12 squares long and 7 squares high, and a square with each side 8 squares long. Which shape has the greater area, and by how much?

Brain-buster
Mark makes a wall from wooden blocks. It is 3 blocks high and 4 blocks long.
It has a gap for a window that is 1 block wide and 2 blocks high.
How many blocks does Mark use for his wall?

100 Maths Lessons Year 4 links:

- Summer 1, Week 6 (pages 200–205): find area by counting

Year 4 Practice Book links:

- (page 94): Find the perimeter (choose appropriate questions ask the children to find the area of the rectilinear shapes)

- (page 95): Area and perimeter (choose appropriate questions)

Angles

Prior learning

- Can recognise angles as a property of shape or a description of a turn.
- Can identify right angles, recognise that two right angles make a half turn, three make three quarters of a turn and four a complete turn.
- Can identify whether angles are greater than or less than a right angle.

Curriculum objectives

- To identify acute and obtuse angles and compare and order angles up to two right angles by size.

Success criteria

- I can compare, order and name different angles up to two right angles.

100 Maths Lessons Year 4 links:

- Autumn 2, Week 5 (pages 71–76): identify acute and obtuse angles; compare and order angles
- Spring 2, Week 5 (pages 153–158): identify acute and obtuse angles; compare and order angles
- Summer 2, Week 5 (pages 236–241): identify right, acute and obtuse angles

Year 4 Practice Book links:

- (page 108): Angles in shapes
- (page 111): Order and compare angles

Learn

- Recap what an angle is and that a right angle is equivalent to a quarter turn. Discuss different acute and obtuse angles, and compare to right angles.

Talk maths

- Provide children with Geostrips, or another form of apparatus that connects together and can be turned to form angles. (Strips of card and paper fasteners will suffice.) Ask the children to create different types of angles, and name them and draw them. In and out of school, ask them to spot acute and obtuse angles (for example, on road signs) and list them.

Activities

- The questions in the textbook focus on naming different angles by type and comparing the sizes.

Problems

- *100 Maths Lessons Year 4, Spring 2, Week 5, Lesson 1* provides ideas for an angles game.

Angles

Learn

Angles are used to measure how much things turn.

- A quarter of a turn is called a right angle.
- A half-turn is two right angles.
- Three quarters of a turn is three right angles.
- There are four right angles in a complete turn.

Angles are also used to measure the gap where two straight lines meet.

This angle is smaller than a right angle.

Acute: less than a right angle

Right angle

Obtuse: more than a right angle, less than two right angles

Activities

1. What is each angle: an acute angle, an obtuse angle or a right angle?

   a.   b.   c.

2. Copy and number these angles a, b, c and d, going from smallest to largest.

   a.   b.   c.   d.

Problems

Brain-teaser
Draw a triangle and cut it out. Cut off each angle. Put them together so that the points are all touching. What do you notice?

56   Geometry

142   Year 4 Geometry

Triangles

Prior learning

- Can identify, describe and draw a range of 2D shapes.

Learn

- Recap children's knowledge of the key properties of triangles. Ideally, using a digital triangle on the interactive whiteboard, examine how the angles and sides change as it is manipulated, noting that the angles could all be acute or two acute and the other right-angled or obtuse.

- Show the children the four triangles on page 57 of the textbook, explaining the properties of each one. Present examples of each type – in various sizes and orientations (their orientation can make their properties more or less obvious).

Talk maths

- Create sets of cards showing different-sized triangles of all types, as well as sets of cards with written definitions of triangle types (but not the names) on them. Arranging the children in groups, ask them to turn the cards over and identify the shapes either from appearance or descriptions. They could also describe or read their cards to each other, as well as play 'Pelmanism'.

Activities

- The activity in the textbook requires the children to name given triangles.

Problems

- There are multiple answers to the problem, depending on which sides of the given triangle children use as the sides of their isosceles triangle.

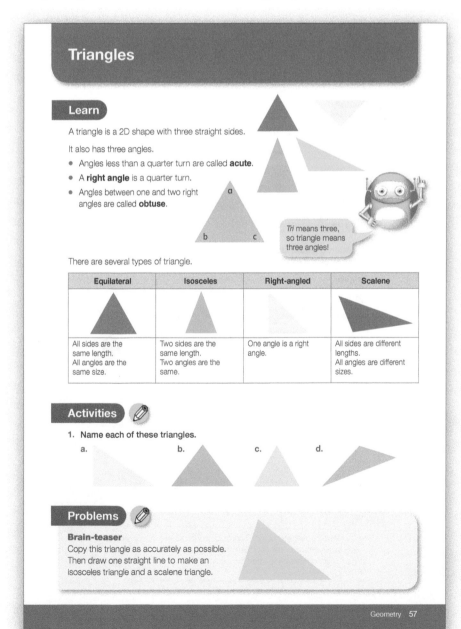

Curriculum objectives

- To compare and classify geometric shapes, including quadrilaterals and triangles, based on their properties and sizes.

Success criteria

- I can name and classify different triangles.

100 Maths Lessons Year 4 links:

- Autumn 2, Week 5 (pages 71–76): identify types of triangle
- Summer 2, Week 5 (pages 236–241): identify regular and irregular shapes

Year 4 Practice Book links:

- (page 106): Sorting triangles
- (page 107): Classifying triangles

Quadrilaterals

Prior learning

- Can identify, describe and draw a range of 2D shapes.

Learn

- List the different shapes that the children are already familiar with, including properties for each. Ideally, leave all this information on permanent display.

- In a separate session, work with the children to recognise the different quadrilaterals as shown on page 58 of the textbook. Model the vocabulary used to define the properties of the shapes.

- The links to *100 Maths Lessons Year 4* have various lessons on quadrilaterals embedded in units also covering polygons, symmetry, angles, coordinates and translation. Although these are presented separately in this book, you may wish to mix and match these areas of geometry given the way they interlink with each other.

Quadrilaterals

Learn

We say that different 2D shapes have different **properties**.

Triangle	Square	Rectangle	Pentagon	Hexagon
3 sides	4 sides	4 sides	5 sides	6 sides

A square is a **regular** quadrilateral, and an equilateral triangle is a regular triangle. All their sides and angles are the same.

Irregular shapes do not have equal sides or angles.

There are six types of quadrilateral.

Square	Rectangle	Rhombus	Parallelogram	Kite	Trapezium
All sides equal. All angles right angles.	Opposite sides equal. All angles right angles.	All sides equal. Opposite angles equal.	Opposite sides equal and parallel. Opposite angles equal	Adjacent sides equal.	Only one pair of parallel sides.

Adjacent means 'next to'.

Can you see the connection between a square and a rhombus?

✓ Tips

- Try making quadrilaterals with construction kits, straws or lolly sticks. You can see how they can be stretched and squashed to make other quadrilaterals.

Curriculum objectives

- To compare and classify geometric shapes, including quadrilaterals and triangles, based on their properties and sizes.

Success criteria

- I can name and classify different quadrilaterals.

Talk maths

- Create sets of cards showing different-sized quadrilaterals of all types, as well as sets of cards with written definitions of different quadrilaterals (but not the names) on them. Arranging the children in groups, ask them to turn the cards over and identify the shapes, either from appearance or descriptions. They could also describe or read their cards to each other, as well as play 'Pelmanism'.

Activities

- The questions in the textbook challenge the children to think carefully about the properties of quadrilaterals and to identify differences between different types. This can easily be extended by asking them to compare different pairs of quadrilaterals.

- This work can then be developed by using the sorting and classifying activities from the *Year 4 Practice Book*.

Problems

- The problems should be straightforward. To challenge children further, ask them to draw quadrilaterals with specific side lengths, or create composite pictures using only quadrilaterals. For example, a symmetrical robot that is made up of two of each type of quadrilateral.

Talk maths

Cover the names on the opposite page and practise naming each quadrilateral. Then cover the shapes and try to describe the properties for each name.

Did you know?

If you cut off the four angles of any quadrilateral, you can always fit them together to make a complete turn.

Activities

1. What is the difference between a square and a rectangle?

2. What is the difference between a rhombus and a kite?

3. What is the difference between a parallelogram and a trapezium?

4. Name each quadrilateral, and then connect it to its properties.

a.   b.   c.   d.

All sides equal. Opposite angles equal.   Adjacent sides equal.   Opposite sides Opposite angles equal. equal and parallel.   Only one pair of parallel sides.

Problems

Brain-teaser
Petra drew a quadrilateral with all sides the same length.
Which quadrilaterals could she have drawn?

Brain-buster
Roger wants to draw a kite and thinks he can do this by joining a right-angled triangle and an isosceles triangle together. Draw a sketch to show how he could do this.

Geometry 59

100 Maths Lessons Year 4 links:

- Autumn 2, Week 5 (pages 71–76): identify different types of quadrilateral

- Spring 2, Week 5 (pages 153–158): know the names and properties of quadrilaterals

- Summer 2, Week 5 (pages 236–241): identify quadrilaterals

Year 4 Practice Book links:

- (page 104): Sorting quadrilaterals

- (page 105): Classifying quadrilaterals

Symmetry of 2D shapes

Prior learning

- Can identify, describe and draw a range of 2D shapes.
- Can identify horizontal and vertical lines.
- Can identify simple symmetrical shapes and patterns.

Learn

- List shapes and objects that have a vertical line of symmetry, drawing or displaying each and indicating the line of symmetry. Extend this to more complex patterns and designs such as the butterfly shown on page 60 of the textbook.
- Introduce shapes that have a horizontal line of symmetry – either with only a horizontal line of symmetry or also with a vertical line symmetry. Progress to shapes and patterns that have three or four lines of symmetry. The Tips on page 60 of the textbook contain useful pointers to aid understanding. Read through these with the children as appropriate.
- *100 Maths Lessons Year 4, Autumn 1, Week 5* includes lessons on identifying lines of symmetry, drawing reflections and completing symmetrical figures.

Curriculum objectives

- To identify lines of symmetry in 2D shapes presented in different orientations.
- To complete a simple symmetric figure with respect to a specific line of symmetry.

Success criteria

- I can identify lines of symmetry in 2D shapes.
- I can complete shapes to make them symmetrical.

Symmetry of 2D shapes

Learn

Some objects have two identical halves.

When one half is like a mirror image of the other half, we can say the object or shape is symmetrical.

Look at the butterfly. It has a **line of symmetry**. This is a bit like a mirror. One side is an identical reflection of the other.

Some objects and shapes have their lines of symmetry in different positions and some can have more than one.

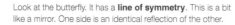

Lines of symmetry can be harder to spot. Can you see them for these two?

This diagram has two lines of symmetry.   This square has four lines of symmetry.

✓ Tips

- Remember that for patterns, colours must be symmetrical too.
- Regular shapes have the same number of lines of symmetry as they do sides.
- A circle has an infinite number of lines of symmetry.
- The letters Z and S might look symmetrical, but their halves are not mirror images.

Talk maths

- If possible, create an interactive display that contains images and objects. Children can then access the display in small groups, discussing and agreeing whether each image or object has any lines of symmetry. Provide a mirror to allow detailed examination, and be sure to include some non-symmetrical items to keep everyone on their toes.

Activities

- The children's answers to the questions in the textbook should provide a good indication of which children have grasped the concepts. Learning can be supported with the activities in the *Year 4 Practice Book*, which include the use of mirrors.

Problems

- The Brain-teaser can be made easier by providing the children with a cut-out of the shape on the grid. Rather than draw the other half of the shape, they should fold where the line of symmetry is and then carefully use scissors to cut around the shape. This can be extended or simplified to suit.

Talk maths

With a partner, discuss these shapes and identify all the lines of symmetry. Many of them only have one line, but some have more than one.

Activities

1. Carefully copy and complete these shapes to make them symmetrical.

2. Draw each number. Then show the lines of symmetry for those that have one or more.

1 2 3 4 5 6 7 8 9 0

3. Copy these regular shapes and then draw all the lines of symmetry on each one.

Problems

Brain-teaser
Copy this shape and then draw its other half to make it symmetrical.

Brain-buster
Tanya says she can think of four capital letters that each have two or more lines of symmetry. Can you show each letter with its lines of symmetry?

100 Maths Lessons Year 4 links:

- Autumn 1, Week 5 (pages 30–35): identify lines of symmetry, draw reflections and complete symmetrical figures
- Summer 2, Week 5 (pages 236–241): identify lines of symmetry in 2D shapes

Year 4 Practice Book links:

- (page 109): Sorting shapes
- (page 110): Shape sifting
- (page 112): Mirror, mirror
- (page 113): Drawing mirror images

Coordinates

Prior learning

- Can identify vertical and horizontal lines.
- Can recognise and name common 2D shapes.

Learn

- Review children's understanding of number lines. Draw simple horizontal and vertical number lines. Start each one at zero, and practise counting forwards and backwards along them in steps of 1, 2 and 5.

- Display a squared grid, and draw vertical and horizontal axes. Label each axis from 0 to 10 and point out how the axes cross at zero. Model good practice for plotting points and writing their coordinates. Always say *along, then up* so that children remember that the first number in a pair of coordinates is the horizontal distance from zero and the second is the vertical distance. Once the children are familiar with this, work together to draw different shapes on the coordinate grid, with the vertex of each labelled with a letter and its coordinates.

- *100 Maths Lessons Year 4, Autumn 2, Week 5, Lesson 3* focuses on this topic and uses the interactive coordinates resource on the accompanying CD-ROM.

Curriculum objectives

- To describe positions on a 2D grid as coordinates in the first quadrant.
- To plot specified points and draw sides to complete a given polygon.

Success criteria

- I can plot points and read coordinates on a coordinate grid.

Coordinates

Learn

Number lines are used for counting in equal amounts.

They can be drawn in any direction.

We draw graphs with a vertical *y*-axis and a horizontal *x*-axis.

Each one is like a number line. They meet at zero.

We can plot points on the grid using **coordinates**.

Points on the grid are always **plotted** with the *x*-coordinate first, and then the *y*-coordinate.

The coordinates of point G are (4, 5).

> That's 4 along the *x*-axis, and 5 up the *y*-axis.

The coordinates of point H are (6, 3).

Can you find the coordinates for points J and K?

We can join the points to form lines.

For the line AB, A = (3, 7), B = (8, 8)

We can also plot the corners of shapes.

Can you find the coordinates of the vertices of the triangle XYZ?

✓ Tips

- Remember, when you are plotting points, or reading and writing coordinates, *along first* and *then up*.
- Some people say '*along the corridor and up the stairs*'.

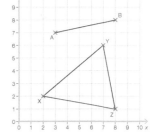

1 up

3 along

Talk maths

- The treasure map activity can be used in various ways, such as giving directions, identifying landmarks and burying treasure. Children would also enjoy playing a version of battleships: define different insects as different length lines and ask children to try to find each others' insects by identifying the coordinates on the points that the insects lie across.

Activities

- The activities in the textbook involve plotting points and drawing shapes. Ideally, children will practise these skills on several occasions. Note that the activities in the *Year 4 Practice Book* provide extended support for children who need additional practice.

Problems

- Challenge the children to plot other points that are given distances and directions from the original at (7, 2).
- *100 Maths Lessons Year 4, Spring 2, Week 5* has lessons that link coordinates with previous shape work.

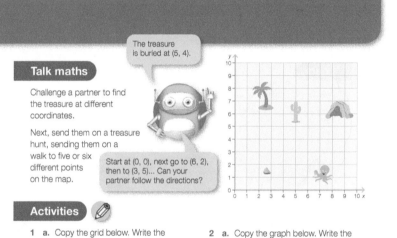

The treasure is buried at (5, 4).

Talk maths

Challenge a partner to find the treasure at different coordinates.

Next, send them on a treasure hunt, sending them on a walk to five or six different points on the map.

Start at (0, 0), next go to (6, 2), then to (3, 5)... Can your partner follow the directions?

Activities

1. **a.** Copy the grid below. Write the coordinates for points x and y.

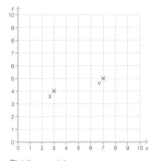

  b. Plot these points.

  A (2, 2) B (2, 8) C (8, 8) D (8, 2)

2. **a.** Copy the graph below. Write the coordinates of the triangle PQR.

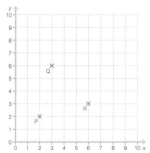

  b. Draw a new grid and plot a rectangle with vertices JKLM with these coordinates.

  J (1, 1) K (9, 1) L (9, 7) M (1, 7)

Problems

Brain-teaser
Tim plots a point (7, 2). What are the coordinates of a point three squares directly above it?

Brain-buster
John wants to draw a square ABCD. He wants to put A at (3, 0) and B at (3, 4). He draws a grid with the complete square on it. Write coordinates of C and D.

Geometry **63**

100 Maths Lessons Year 4 links:

- Autumn 2, Week 5 (pages 71–76): describe positions and plot points on a coordinate grid
- Spring 2, Week 5 (pages 153–158): describe positions and plot points on a coordinate grid
- Summer 2, Week 5 (pages 236–241): draw shapes on a coordinate grid

Year 4 Practice Book links:

- (page 114): Mystery picture coordinates
- (page 115): Mystery picture coordinates
- (page 116): Plotting shapes
- (page 117): Shapes and coordinates

Translation

Prior learning

- Can describe positions and plot points on a coordinate grid.

Learn

- Review children's knowledge of plotting points and drawing lines and shapes on coordinate axes. Model correct vocabulary and procedures, ensuring that some points sit on the axes themselves so that zero coordinates are also used.

- Next, demonstrate how to translate points by different amounts, writing out the translation as, for example, 3 left, 7 up.

- Move on to plotting two points and joining them to make a straight line, and then show how the whole line can be translated by moving each point by the same amount. In time, extend this to translating complete shapes, like the square on page 64 of the textbook.

- *100 Maths Lessons Year 4, Spring 2, Week 5, Lesson 3* provides a structured introduction to translation.

Curriculum objectives

- To describe movements between positions as translations of a given unit to the left/right and up/down.

- To plot specified points and draw sides to complete a given polygon.

Success criteria

- I can translate points and shapes on a coordinate grid.

Translation

Learn

We draw graphs with a *y*-axis and an *x*-axis.

We can join the points to form lines.

We can also plot the corners of shapes.

We write the *x*-coordinate first, then the *y*-coordinate.

A = (1, 2), X = (2, 4)   Remember: along, then up.

We can **translate** points. We can move a point on the grid, with the *x*-coordinate and the *y*-coordinate each moving a certain amount.

Translation is when all of the shape moves the same distance.

The red point A, below, has been *translated* 3 right and 4 up. The new point has the coordinates (5, 6). Can you see how the red points B, C and D have been translated?

We can also translate shapes.

The red square below has been translated 4 left and 3 down. Can you see how each corner has moved the same amount?

✓ Tips

- When translating a shape, all the *x*-coordinates change by the same amount, and all the *y*-coordinates do too.

- If possible, provide children with some kind of peg board (a laminated card with counters will do) and ask them to practise translation with each other. Using equipment will save a lot of drawing time and allow focus on the key skills and vocabulary involved.

- If children are comfortable with the questions in the textbook, ask them to create their own translation challenges for each other. Another nice activity is to challenge the children to plot points that make each letter in a word (six letters is ideal, with no letters repeated, such as *riches*). Once plotted, the letters should be able to join, in order, to each other without any line crossing another. Once the joining lines have been drawn, translate all the points equally. The new word should not cross the old one.

- The *Year 4 Practice Book* has an activity that can support children who are struggling.

Problems

- The Brain-teaser is tricky – the translation is in fact negative vertically and horizontally. Once children have grasped this, provide further points and where they have translated to, and ask the children to define the translation itself. Extend this to translating a selection of shapes.

- *100 Maths Lessons Year 4, Summer 2, Week 5, Lesson 4* provides further practice.

Talk maths

Take turns to choose different points on a graph. Say its coordinates, and then challenge someone to translate it.

- Translate (1, 1) by 2 right and 3 up.
- Translate (8, 8) by 0 left and 2 down.

Activities

1. a. Copy the coordinate grid below and translate the points W, X , Y and Z by 2 right and 3 down.

   b. Write the coordinates of the new points.

2. **Draw a 10 by 10 coordinate grid.**

   a. Plot a triangle ABC: A (2, 2), B (4, 4), C (4, 2).

   b. Translate it 3 right and 5 up.

   c. Write the coordinates of the new shape.

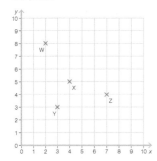

Problems

Brain-teaser

Tina draws a grid and marks point X with coordinates (5, 4).

She then translates it to (0, 0). What was the translation?

Brain-buster

Copy and translate the shape ABCD by 0 along and 3 down.

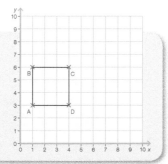

100 Maths Lessons Year 4 links:

- Spring 2, Week 5 (pages 153–158): translate shapes up/down and left/right
- Summer 2, Week 5 (pages 236–241): translate shapes up/down and left/right

Year 4 Practice Book links:

- (page 119): Describe translations

Tables and pictograms

Prior learning

- Can interpret and present data using bar charts, pictograms and tables.
- Can solve one-step and two-step questions using information presented in scaled bar charts and pictograms and tables.

Learn

- Present simple pictograms that will cover familiar territory for the children. Discuss the use of icons to represent numbers, introducing one icon to represent two, five or ten items as appropriate. Children will probably have had experience of converting these to block graphs. Again, run through this as appropriate.

- Next, display the table on page 66 of the textbook, which presents data about large animals. Work with the children to examine and interpret the information, using the data to make direct statements about each animal and to compare different animals. Some children might be able to make calculation-based statements, such as: *Rhinoceros have an average lifespan almost twice that of zebras.*

- Separately, using the interactive data handling resource on the CD-ROM for *100 Maths Lessons Year 4*, work through *100 Maths Lessons Year 4, Autumn 2, Week 6, Lesson 5* to cover frequency charts and revise pictograms further.

Curriculum objectives

- To solve comparison, sum and difference problems using information presented in bar charts, pictograms, tables and other graphs.

Success criteria

- I can interpret information in tables and pictograms.

Tables and pictograms

Learn

Pictograms provide information in an easy-to-read way. They use simple icons to represent data.

Look at this pictogram. It was created after a class survey of pets. It uses one icon for each pet counted in the survey.

- The children in this class have 17 pets altogether.
- There is the same number of budgies as hamsters.
- There are no goldfish.
- There is one more dog than cats.

Cat	☺☺☺☺☺
Dog	☺☺☺☺☺☺
Goldfish	
Budgie	☺☺☺
Hamster	☺☺☺

☺ = 1

Complicated information is often presented in tables and charts.

This table provides information about some animals in a safari park.

Animal	Height (cm)	Weight (kg)	Average lifespan (years)	Diet
Elephant	350	5000	58	herbivore
Giraffe	530	1200	24	herbivore
Lion	100	160	17	carnivore
Rhinoceros	150	1500	45	herbivore
Zebra	130	320	23	herbivore

Notice that each column has different units.

Looking down each column we can compare the information for different animals. For example, we can say about the lion:

The lion is the only carnivore. It is the shortest animal. It is the lightest animal.

We can also do calculations. For example: *The lion is 50cm shorter than rhinoceros.*

✓ Tips

- Use your fingers to help you read rows and columns of data. Or if you have a ruler available even better as it is easy to misread tables and charts.

Let your fingers do the walking.

Talk maths

- This activity requires children to partake in a mini project, collecting, collating and presenting data. You should provide as much or as little structure as required. Children should be encouraged to consider carefully the best format to present their data in.
- *100 Maths Lessons Year 4, Spring 2, Week 6, Lesson 1* provides further supportive ideas, especially on tallying.

Activities

- The activity and questions in the textbook provide initial practice in interpreting and representing data. The *Year 4 Practice Book* activities can extend this.

Problems

- Children who successfully answer both of the problems might be challenged to create their own problems based on the data in the textbook.
- To further develop children's skills, collect a bank of data based on the children themselves (sensitivity may be required). Ask the children to present this in various ways, making interpretations and deductions as they go.

Talk maths

Work with a partner to do a survey. You could do one of these.

- Create a table about your friends or families. Include information about their ages, heights, eye colour and so on.
- Create a pictogram chart of car colours.

When you have your data, discuss it, and ask each other questions about it.

Activities

1. **Copy the chart and draw a pictogram for the survey below.**

   Use one icon for every 5 days.

Sunshine					
Rain					
Cloudy					
Snow					

   Children's weather survey for a term.

Weather	Icon	Days
Sunshine	☀	10
Rain	💧	25
Cloudy	☁	30
Snow	❄	5

2. **Use the animal information table on the opposite page to answer these questions.**
   a. Which is the heaviest animal?
   b. Which animals are shorter than a rhinoceros?
   c. Which two animals have a similar lifespan?
   d. How much taller is the giraffe than the elephant?
   e. What is the difference in weight between the rhinoceros and the giraffe?
   f. How much longer on average does a zebra live than a lion?
   g. How many giraffes would weigh the same as four rhinoceros?

Problems

Brain-teaser
Tom thinks of two animals that are listed in the table opposite. He says one is twice as heavy as the other.
Which two animals is he thinking about?

Brain-buster
Zafira says that the elephant weighs more than the giraffe, the lion, the rhinoceros and the zebra combined. Is she correct? Explain your answer.

Statistics 67

---

100 Maths Lessons Year 4 links:

- Autumn 2, Week 6 (pages 77–82): solving problems using information in pictograms and tables
- Spring 2, Week 6 (pages 159–164): collecting data in a tally chart

Year 4 Practice Book links:

- (page 124): Workout pictograms
- (page 125): Presenting data

Bar charts

Prior learning

- Can interpret and present data using bar charts, pictograms and tables.
- Can solve one-step and two-step questions using information presented in scaled bar charts and pictograms and tables.

Learn

- Using simple pictograms and block graphs, revisit children's previous learning about interpreting these types of charts.
- The opening lessons of *100 Maths Lessons Year 4, Summer 2, Week 6* provide an excellent introduction to creating bar charts, including cube counting

and an interactive activity on the accompanying CD-ROM, and solving simple problems about data presented in bar charts in Lesson 3.

- Next, using bar charts and tables, like those on page 68 of the textbook, look at how different scales on the vertical axis (*y*-axis) can be used to represent large numbers. If appropriate, also discuss the

difficulties this represents, both in constructing and reading the charts. Remember that there is an interactive data handling resource on the CD-ROM for *100 Maths Lessons Year 4. 100 Maths Lessons Year 4, Autumn 2, Week 6, Lessons 3 and 4* will also support this work.

Curriculum objectives

- To interpret and present discrete and continuous data using appropriate graphical methods, including bar charts and time graphs.
- To solve comparison, sum and difference problems using information presented in bar charts, pictograms, tables and other graphs.

Success criteria

- I can create, use and interpret bar charts.

Bar charts

Learn

Bar charts are like pictograms in simpler form.

Instead of icons they use bars to represent the different quantities, with a scale on one axis to show the number of each item's bar.

This is a bar chart for pets in a class. Notice that the scale increases in 2s.

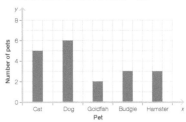

This is a bar chart for a car survey outside a school. The vertical axis is in 5s.

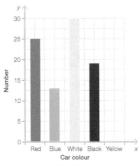

This is a bar chart for the number of pupils at four local schools. The vertical axis is in 100s.

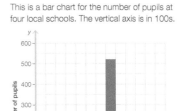

Look at the tables of data. Can you see how each number is shown on the bar chart?

Car colour	Red	Blue	White	Black	Yellow
Number	25	13	30	19	1

Now do the same for the numbers of pupils.

School	Infant	Junior	Secondary	Sixth form
Pupils	150	250	520	160

✓ Tips

- Use a ruler to mark a line to the *y*-axis. It will help you to read the scale accurately.

- This activity challenges children to discuss what bar charts might be used for. It is important that they think through the implications of any ideas: *What would be on the horizontal axis (x-axis)? What scale will you use on the y-axis? Is a bar chart the best way to represent the information?*

- The questions in the textbook require the children to interpret a given bar chart. It may be beneficial to look at the bar chart in the textbook with all the children, checking that everyone can read the correct number of books borrowed per person. *100 Maths Lessons Year 4, Spring 2, Week 6, Lessons 2 and 3* provide further work on bar charts, and the *Year 4 Practice Book* activities can also extend this learning.

- Once the bar chart has been created, ask children to consider its uses: *Is it more helpful than the table?* Try to elicit that it provides useful at-a-glance information, although specific information may be easier to gain from the table in this instance.

Talk maths

Work with a partner to try to list as many different things that you could make bar charts for. Think of surveys you might do at school or sports that you like.

Discuss what scale you might need to use.

You could draw a bar chart for favourite colours.

Activities

A group of friends count the number of books they have at home. Then they make a bar chart. Use the bar chart to answer these questions.

1. Who has the most books?

2. How many books does Karl have?

3. How many books are there altogether?

4. How many more books does Ella have than Ravi?

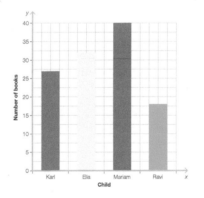

Problems

Brain-teaser
Create a bar chart for the animal lifespan information below.
Choose your scale carefully.

Animal	Average lifespan (years)
Elephant	58
Giraffe	24
Lion	17
Rhinoceros	45
Zebra	23

Brain-buster
Write two questions you could ask about the animal bar chart.

100 Maths Lessons Year 4 links:

- Autumn 2, Week 6 (pages 77–82): presenting discrete data in bar charts; solving problems using information in bar charts

- Spring 2, Week 6 (pages 159–164): creating bar charts; solving problems about data in bar charts

- Summer 2, Week 6 (pages 242–247): interpreting and creating bar charts; solving problems about data in bar charts

Year 4 Practice Book links:

- (page 120): Favourite days bar chart

- (page 121): Drawing a bar chart

- (page 125): Presenting data

Time graphs

Prior learning

- Can plot points on coordinate axes.
- Can solve one-step and two-step questions using information presented in scaled bar charts, pictograms and tables.

Curriculum objectives

- To interpret and present discrete and continuous data using appropriate graphical methods, including bar charts and time graphs.
- To solve comparison, sum and difference problems using information presented in bar charts, pictograms, tables and other graphs.

Success criteria

- I can create, use and interpret simple time graphs.

Learn

- Time graphs can be tricky for children to understand at first. Therefore, it is important that they have had plenty experience of constructing and interpreting the forms of tables and charts covered in previous sections. In preparing them for time graphs, review a range of charts and tables, as well as reviewing the construction of coordinate axes.
- Using the graphs on page 70 of the textbook, introduce simple time graphs showing temperature change per hour and height change per week, month or year. If possible, grow a plant in the classroom – French beans are good – and plot its progress on a time graph over a few weeks.
- Stress the importance of putting time on the x-axis. To clarify this concept further, ask the children to create a timeline for the day, and plot the temperature (imaginary or actually measured) at each hour.

Time graphs

Learn

We can represent information and data in different types of chart and graph.

Bar charts and pictograms are useful for presenting information from surveys.

- How do you travel to school?
- What is your favourite snack?
- Do you have any pets?

Each of these graphs has a vertical y-axis and a horizontal x-axis.

Time graphs are useful for showing how things change over time, such as temperature changing or things growing.

This graph shows how the temperature changed in the playground during a school day.

Look at how you can draw lines to find the temperature at any time of day.

Read the graph to check the table below. Can you read the temperature for 4pm?

Time	9am	10am	11am	12noon	1pm	2pm	3pm
Temperature	5°C	7°C	9°C	12°C	12°C	12°C	11°C

✓ Tips

- You can create line graphs by plotting points and then joining them.
- This chart shows the height of a tree each year for 5 years.

Time (years)	1	2	3	4	5
Height (metres)	1	3	4	5	5

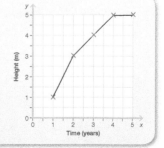

Talk maths

- The graph in this activity should focus on one aspect that changes over time, for example the growth of a person over several years. The children should work together to discuss what scale they will use for the axes. Note that many time graphs require high numbers on the y-axis, and the children will need to consider how to deal with this or how to avoid it – perhaps by choosing a topic that uses low numbers, such as temperature variation.

Activities

- The questions in the textbook focus on checking that children can interpret time graphs.
- *100 Maths Lessons Year 4, Summer 2, Week 6* has two lessons, an interactive activity and a line graph template to extend learning further.

Problems

- The Brain-teaser requires the children to think carefully about scales. (It is permissible to start the y-axis at a number other than zero when appropriate.) Once constructed, ask the children to use the graph to make further deductions, such as: *How much has the baby grown since birth? In which month did the baby grow most?*
- The *Year 4 Practice Book* activities provide further challenge.

Talk maths

Working with a partner, copy these axes and construct a time graph of your own. (It is fine to invent data rather than find real data.)

- What will the units of time be: seconds, minutes, hours, days, weeks or years?
- What will you show changing in time: a person's height, a baby's weight, the depth of water in a bath, the distance of a bike ride?
- What units will you use for the quantity that is changing: kilograms, litres, kilometres?

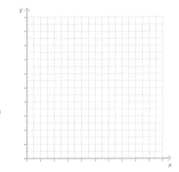

Activities

Use the graph opposite to answer these questions.

1. **At what time was the water coldest?**

2. **When was the water 4°C?**

3. **Find the difference between the warmest and coldest temperatures.**

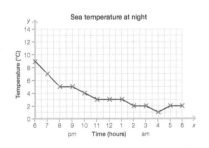

Sea temperature at night

Problems

Brain-teaser
The chart shows a baby's height for the first 6 months.
Month '0' is the day the baby was born.

Month	0	1	2	3	4	5	6
Height (cm)	37	40	42	46	47	48	50

Draw a line graph to show how the baby's height has changed.

Brain-buster
Use your graph to say how long after being born the baby was exactly 4.5cm. Give your answer in months and weeks. Assume all months are four weeks.

Statistics 71

100 Maths Lessons Year 4 links:

- Summer 2, Week 6 (pages 242–247): displaying data in a line graph

Year 4 Practice Book links:

- (page 122): Interpret information in a time graph
- (page 123): Drawing a time graph

Answers Year 3

Page 7

1   16, 24, 28, 32

2   32, 40, 48, 64

3   300, 350, 400

4   500, 600, 700, 800

5   700, 600, 500, 400

Brain-teaser: 0, 50, 100, 150, 200, 250, 300, 350, 400, 450, 500, 550, 600
Brain-buster: 16, 24, 32, 40, 48

Page 9

1   **a.** 365   **b.** 215

2   **a.** eight hundred and four   **b.** nine hundred and seventy

3   357, 537, 573, 735, 753

4   **a.** 321 > 243   **b.** 645 < 654   **c.** 720 > 702

Brain-buster: 245, 425, 524, 542

Page 11

1   567

2   576

3   856

4   300 + 70 + 9

Brain-teaser: 436
Brain-buster: 425

Page 13

1   533

2   591

3   850

4   432

5   326

6   49

Brain-teaser: £393
Brain-buster: £397

Page 15

1   **a.** 125, 165, 205

    b. 300, 350, 400

2   **a.** 11, 14, 17, **20**, 23, 26, 29

    b. 96, 90, 84, **78**, **72**, **66**

Brain-teaser: 46, 49, 52, 55, 58, 61, 64
Brain-buster: 24, 34, 44, 54, 64, 74

Page 17

1   659 − 100 = 559cm or 5m 59cm

2   650 − 100 = 550, 550 + 10 = 560 litres

3   180 + 10 = 190 seconds

Brain-teaser: 550
Brain-buster: 975

CALCULATIONS

Page 19

1   397

2   739

3   431

4   543

5   521

6   354

Brain-teaser: £702
Brain-buster: £159

Page 21

1   103

2   182

3   727

Brain-teaser: 204
Brain-buster: 751

Page 23

1   53

2   178

3   188

Brain-teaser: 368
Brain-buster: 303

Page 25

1   95

2   48

3   690

4   67

5   403

6   379

Brain-teaser: 257 metres
Brain-buster: 306

Page 27

1 71
2 111
3 34
4 138
5 95

Brain-teaser: £33
Brain-buster: £132

Page 29

1 72
2 11
3 12
4 27
5 12
6 48

Brain-teaser: 6
Brain-buster: 8

Page 31

1 69
2 17
3 32
4 24
5 92

Brain-teaser: 22cm
Brain-buster: 7p

Page 33

1 13
2 60
3 15
4 4
5 78

Brain-buster: 64 cartons juice and 128 snack packs

FRACTIONS

Page 35

1 3
2 50
3 40
4 18
5 18
6 12

Brain-teaser: 21
Brain-buster: 12 litres

Page 37

1 2
2 27
3 27
4 9
60
48

Brain-teaser: 9
Brain-buster: 6

Page 39

1 9
2 20
3 60
4 15
5 45
6 90

Brain-teaser: £27
Brain-buster: 30 litres

Page 41

1 2
2 5
3 3
4 6
5 6
6 3

Brain-teaser: 2
Brain-buster: $\frac{1}{10}$

Page 43

1 $\frac{1}{6}, \frac{1}{5}, \frac{1}{3}, \frac{1}{2}$
2 $\frac{2}{8}, \frac{3}{8}, \frac{5}{8}, \frac{7}{8}$
3 $\frac{1}{10}, \frac{5}{10}, \frac{7}{10}, \frac{9}{10}$

Brain-teaser: $\frac{1}{2}$
Brain-buster: $\frac{1}{3}$ of £15

Page 45

1 $\frac{7}{8}$
2 $\frac{6}{10}$
3 $\frac{3}{7}$
4 1 or $\frac{6}{6}$
5 $\frac{1}{5}$
6 $\frac{1}{6}$

Brain-teaser: $\frac{9}{10}$
Brain-buster: $\frac{3}{12}$

Page 47

1 $\frac{1}{7}$
2 $\frac{3}{7}$
3 $\frac{5}{9}$
4 $\frac{9}{12}$

Brain-teaser: $\frac{1}{2}$ or $\frac{5}{10}$
Brain-buster: $\frac{4}{12}$ or $\frac{1}{3}$

MEASUREMENT

Page 49

1 **a.** 8.5cm line drawn
 b. 9.6cm line drawn

2 **a.** 17cm 9mm
 b. 1mm

Brain-teaser: 6mm
Brain-buster: 9m

Page 51

1 **a.** 600g **b.** 100g
 c. 1000g **d.** 750g

2 c > d

Brain-teaser: 100g
Brain-buster: 20g

Page 53

1   1 litre or 1l

2   300ml

3   500ml

4   100ml

5   900ml

Brain-buster: Three glasses, 100ml left in the bottle

Page 55

1   **a.** Hands set at 19 minutes past 7.

   b. Hands set at 24 minutes to 8.

   c. Hands set at 17 minutes to 1.

2   **a.** 11 minutes past 8.

   b. 28 minutes to 10.

Brain-teaser: Tim
Brain-buster: 20 minutes

Page 57

1   20

2   25

3   **a.** Hands set at a quarter past 6

   b. Hands set at 27 minutes to 9

   c. Hands set at 27 minutes past 9

Brain-teaser: 10 minutes past 5
Brain-buster: 29 minutes to 9

Page 59

1   **a.** 06:30

   b. 20:45

   c. 15:33

   d. 14:50

   e. 00:07

   f. 04:15

Brain-teaser: 06:37
Brain-buster: 22:42

Page 61

1   **a.** morning

   b. afternoon

   c. noon

2   **a.** 35 seconds

   b. 23 hours and 59 minutes

Brain-teaser: 70 seconds
Brain-buster: 8 seconds

Page 63

1   **a.** 29 days

   b. 1 hour 15 minutes

   c. 180 minutes

   d. 1 minute 30 seconds

Brain-teaser: 12 seconds
Brain-buster: 53 minutes

Page 65

1   **a.** 8cm

   b. 5cm

   c. 11cm

2   **a.** 60m

   b. 28cm

Brain-teaser: 48cm
Brain-buster: 88cm

Page 67

1   **a.** £1.12

   b. 62p

   c. £8.21

   d. 67p

Brain-teaser: £4.15
Brain-buster: £3.42

Page 69

1   **a.** 29cm

   b. 403m

   c. 10cm 1mm

   d. 3cm 2mm

Brain-teaser: 8cm
Brain-buster: 12m, 12m, 33m, 33m

Page 71

1   **a.** 140g

   b. 39g

   c. 16g

   d. 47g

Brain-teaser: 111kg
Brain-buster: 468g

Page 73

1   **a.** 157ml

   b. 90ml

   c. 560ml

   d. 190ml

Brain-teaser: 48 litres
Brain-buster: 625ml

GEOMETRY

Page 75

1 **a.** Perpendicular **b.** Parallel

2 Vertical line drawn

3 Horizontal line drawn

4 **a.** One horizontal line labelled 'H', two vertical lines labelled 'V'

   b. 'P' written in two right angles

   c. One

Brain-buster: Regular octagon

Page 77

1 **a.** Square with sides of 7cm drawn.

   b. Rectangle with sides of 6cm and 10cm drawn.

   c. Irregular pentagon drawn. Check that it has an accurately drawn right angle, and that one side measures 5cm.

   d. Right-angled triangle with two sides of 6cm drawn.

Brain-teaser: Square with sides of 5cm drawn. Square.
Brain-buster: Rectangle. Rectangle with sides of 6cm and 8cm drawn.

Page 79

1 **a.** cube

   b. square-based pyramid

   c. cone

2 6

3 5

Brain-teaser: Pyramid

Page 81

1 **a.** obtuse angle

   b. acute angle

   c. right angle

2 **a.** 2

   b. 3

Brain-teaser: One acute angle labelled 'A', one obtuse angle labelled 'O', two right angles labelled 'R'.

STATISTICS

Page 83

1 **a.** 41

   b. Munchkin

   c. British shorthair

Brain-teaser: 5

Page 85

1 **a.** 27°C

   b. 2°C

   c. 6°C

Brain-buster: April

NUMBER AND PLACE VALUE

Page 7

1. **a.** seven thousand, three hundred and eighty
   b. two thousand and sixty-nine

2. **a.** 6841   **b.** 5002

3. 8 92 250 725 1612 3875 5000 9999

4.

1000 more	3350	**2243**	**5789**	**8000**	**9999**
Number	2350	1243	4789	7000	8999
1000 less	1350	**243**	**3789**	**6000**	**7999**

Brain-teaser: **a.** Dipton   **b.** Blinkton
Brain-buster: eleven thousand, two hundred

Page 9

1.

	To the nearest 10	To the nearest 100	To the nearest 1000
a. 77	**80**	100	0
b. 583	**580**	600	1000
c. 1232	**1230**	1200	1000
d. 3765	**3770**	3800	4000

2. **a.** 80   **b.** 70   **c.** 120

3. **a.** 600   **b.** 300   **c.** 1300

4. **a.** 6000   **b.** 4000   **c.** 12,000

Brain-teaser: Blinkton and Mumsford
Brain-buster: 11,000

Page 11

1. **a.** 42, 48, 54, 60   **b.** 63, 70, 77, 84   **c.** 54, 63, 72, 81

   d. 375, 400, 425, 450   **e.** 3000, 4000, 5000, 6000

2. **a.** 78, 72, 66, 60   **b.** 63, 54, 45, 36   **c.** 63, 54, 45, 36

   d. 850, 825, 800, 775   **e.** 8000, 7000, 6000, 5000

Brain-teaser: Joe has £3 more.
Brain-buster: 32 weeks

Page 13

1. **a.** 1   **b.** –1   **c.** –3   **d.** –5   **e.** –5   **f.** –5   **g.** –1   **h.** –6

2. **a.** 2   **b.** 6   **c.** 6

Brain-teaser: –1°C
Brain-buster: 15°C

Page 15

1. **a.** IV   **b.** XI   **c.** XXV   **d.** XIX   **e.** LII   **f.** XLV   **g.** XC   **h.** LXXXVII

2. **a.** 6   **b.** 9   **c.** 17   **d.** 22   **e.** 55   **f.** 40   **g.** 88   **h.** 90

3. 0

Brain-teaser: 14 + 23 = 37
Brain-buster: 91 – 65 = 26

CALCULATIONS

Page 17

1. **a.** 50   **b.** 89   **c.** 108   **d.** 394   **e.** 23   **f.** 86   **g.** 95   **h.** 564

2. **a.** 14   **b.** 42   **c.** 44   **d.** 151   **e.** 36   **f.** 61   **g.** 46   **h.** 238

3. **a.** 77   **b.** 99   **c.** 485   **d.** 5838   **e.** 62   **f.** 21   **g.** 133   **h.** 2323

Brain-teaser: **a.** £99   **b.** 105 miles
Brain-buster: £2300

Page 19

1. **a.** 718   **b.** 1003   **c.** 3911   **d.** 7584

2. **a.** 602   **b.** 726   **c.** 8016   **d.** 9619

Brain-teaser: 1850
Brain-buster: 17,014

Page 21

1. **a.** 218   **b.** 425   **c.** 162   **d.** 2818

2. **a.** 179   **b.** 449   **c.** 2605   **d.** 2487

Brain-teaser: **a.** 736   **b.** 111
Brain-buster: 4104

Page 23

1. **a.** 21   **b.** 45   **c.** 32   **d.** 42   **e.** 81

2. **a.** 4   **b.** 12   **c.** 6   **d.** 8   **e.** 11

3. 0 6 12 18 24 30 36 42 48 54 60 66 72

4. 0 12 24 36 48 60 72 84 96 108 120 132 144

5. 0 12 24 36 48 60 72

Brain-teaser: 42
Brain-buster: You can say 6 × 9 = 54, and then multiply by 10.
Answer = £5.40

Page 25

1. **a.** 72   **b.** 24   **c.** 950   **d.** 300   **e.** 720   **f.** 1200   **g.** 2400
   h. 9000

2. **a.** 13   **b.** 8   **c.** 15   **d.** 30   **e.** 12   **f.** 3   **g.** 20   **h.** 8

Brain-teaser: **a.** 2400p or £24   **b.** 12
Brain-buster: **a.** 7200p or £72   **b.** 4

Page 27

1. **a.** 114   **b.** 914   **c.** 1368   **d.** 4030

2. **a.** 459   **b.** 534   **c.** 2152   **d.** 7638

Brain-teaser: £10.01 or 1001p
Brain-buster: £33.75 or 3375p

Page 29

1. **a.** 25   **b.** 24   **c.** 18   **d.** 133   **e.** 1167   **f.** 107

2. **a.** 58   **b.** 43   **c.** 142   **d.** 154   **e.** 62   **f.** 103

Brain-teaser: 157
Brain-buster: 552 metres each hour

FRACTIONS AND DECIMALS

Page 31

1   a. $\frac{2}{6}$ shaded   b. $\frac{3}{4}$ shaded   c. $\frac{4}{10}$ shaded   d. $\frac{9}{12}$ shaded

2    $\frac{1}{2} = \frac{6}{12}$, $\frac{1}{3} = \frac{4}{12}$, $\frac{1}{4} = \frac{3}{12}$, $\frac{1}{6} = \frac{2}{12}$

3   a. $\frac{6}{8}$ b. $\frac{6}{9}$ c. $\frac{10}{16}$ d. $\frac{12}{20}$

Brain-teaser: Jane
Brain-buster: Joe

Page 33

1   a. $\frac{1}{2}$ b. $\frac{1}{4}$ c. $\frac{2}{3}$ d. $\frac{4}{7}$

2   a. $\frac{1}{2}$ b. $\frac{3}{5}$ c. $\frac{1}{8}$ d. $\frac{7}{20}$

3   a. $\frac{5}{4}$ b. $\frac{7}{5}$ c. $\frac{9}{10}$ d. $\frac{11}{8}$ e. $\frac{11}{7}$ f. $\frac{12}{6}$ or 2

4   a. $\frac{4}{3}$ b. $\frac{3}{6}$ or $\frac{1}{2}$ c. $\frac{6}{8}$ d. $\frac{6}{4}$ e. $\frac{3}{5}$ f. $\frac{13}{20}$

Brain-teaser: $\frac{2}{12}$

Brain-buster: $\frac{11}{20}$

Page 35

1   a. $\frac{7}{10}$ b. $\frac{12}{10}$ c. $\frac{22}{10}$ d. $\frac{38}{100}$ e. $\frac{81}{100}$ f. $\frac{180}{100}$

2   a. $\frac{5}{10}$ b. $\frac{2}{10}$ c. $\frac{14}{10}$ d. $\frac{10}{100}$ or $\frac{1}{10}$ e. $\frac{52}{100}$ f. $\frac{45}{100}$

3   a. six tenths   b. nine tenths   c. fourteen hundredths
d. ninety-one hundredths

4   a. $\frac{7}{10}$ b. $\frac{13}{10}$ c. $\frac{35}{100}$ d. $\frac{2}{100}$

Brain-teaser: three tenths = thirty hundredths
Brain-buster: sixty-three hundredths = six tenths and three hundredths

Page 37

1   a. 0.5   b. 0.25   c. 0.75

2   a. 0.5   b. 0.75   c. 0.1   d. 0.27   e. 0.25   f. 0.8

3   a. $\frac{1}{4}$ b. $\frac{78}{100}$ c. $\frac{4}{10}$ d. $\frac{3}{4}$ e. $\frac{1}{2}$ f. $\frac{21}{100}$

Brain-teaser: They are both two tenths.
Brain-buster: She is right, they are both equivalent to 0.75.

Page 39

1   a. 0.7   b. 0.31   c. 0.3   d. 0.94

2   a. 5   b. 3   c. 6   d. 7

3   a. 0.7 < 0.75   b. 0.31 < 0.42   c. 0.6 = 0.60   d. 0.25 > 0.23

4   Decimals should be arranged in this order: 0.05, 0.25, 0.35, 0.5, 0.65, 0.75, 0.9

Brain-teaser: 6.5
Brain-buster: 0.6

MEASUREMENT

Page 41

1   a. centimetres   b. metres   c. pence   d. pounds   e. millilitres
f. litres   g. kilograms   h. grams   i. minutes or seconds
j. days or weeks

2   a. weighing scales   b. measuring cylinder   c. stopwatch

3   a. ruler   b. tape measure   c. measuring cylinder
d. weighing scales   e. stopwatch   f. calendar

Brain-teaser: 5000g
Brain-buster: 865mm

Page 43

2 years = 730 days; 2 weeks = 14 days; 2 days = 48 hours;
2 hours = 120 minutes; 2 minutes = 120 seconds

a. 120 seconds   b. 180 minutes   c. 96 hours   d. 35 days
e. 72 months   f. 730 days

a. 210 seconds   b. 150 minutes   c. 132 hours   d. 90 months

Brain-teaser: 3653 days
Brain-buster: a. 8760   b. 1440

Page 45

1

Analogue	twelve noon	quarter to nine	ten past eleven	five to four	quarter past three
Digital	12:00	8:45	11:10	3:55	3:15

2   a. 01:50   b. 16:25   c. 06:00   d. 23:15

3   a. half past eleven am   b. quarter past three pm
c. twenty-five past three am   e. quarter to one pm

Brain-teaser: 1 hour and 20 minutes
Brain-buster: 11 hours and 40 minutes

Page 47

1

Pence	500p	150p	3300p	59p	1000p
Pounds	£5	£1.50	£33.00	£0.59	£10.00

2

Pounds	£1	£4.25	£0.62	£20	£12.06
Pence	100p	425p	62p	2000p	1206p

3   a. £5.80   b. £8.10   c. £3.50   d. £7.01   e. £4   f. £10
e. £5   h. £5

Brain-teaser: a. £6.25   b. £3.75
Brain-buster: a. £14.25   b. £5.75

Page 49

1   thimble = 20ml, mug = 200ml, bathtub = 200l

2   mouse = 50g, child = 50kg, elephant = 5000kg

3   a. 5000g   b. 6kg   c. 500g   d. $4\frac{1}{2}$kg or 4.5kg

4   a. 3l   b. 7500ml   c. $3\frac{1}{2}$l or 3.5l   d. 500ml

5   a. $3\frac{3}{4}$kg or 3.75kg   b. 1150g   c. 420g   d. 3700ml   e. 0.37l
f. 5000ml

Brain-teaser: a. 20   b. 2kg and 700g
Brain-buster: a. 25   b. 8

Page 51

1   a. 50mm   b. 30mm   c. 45mm   d. 27mm

2   a. 4cm   b. 7cm   c. 6.3cm   d. 4.1cm

3   a.

mm	cm
10	1
100	10
20	2
350	35
1000	100

b.

cm	m
100	1
1000	10
25	0.25
50	0.5
1000	10

c.

m	km
500	$\frac{1}{2}$
2000	2
250	$\frac{1}{4}$
1000	1
9000	9

Brain-teaser: 1.54m or 154cm
Brain-buster: $9\frac{1}{2}$km or 9.5km or 9500m

Page 53

1   **a.**

length 4cm, width 2cm
perimeter = 12cm

b.

side length 3cm
perimeter = 12cm

2   **a.** 8cm   **b.** 8cm   **c.** 12cm

3

Shape	Length	Height	Perimeter
Rectangle	5cm	2cm	**14cm**
Rectangle	12mm	5mm	**34mm**
Rectangle	6km	2km	**16km**
Square	8mm	8mm	**32mm**
Square	5m	5m	**20m**
Square	4.5cm	4.5cm	**18cm**

Brain-teaser: 14km
Brain-buster: 101.4cm

Page 55

1   **a.** 6 squares   **b.** 16 squares   **c.** 5 squares   **d.** 12 squares

2   **a.** 12 squares   **b.** 9 squares

Brain-teaser: The area of the rectangle is 20 squares greater than the square.
Brain-buster: 10 blocks

GEOMETRY

Page 56

1   **a.** acute   **b.** obtuse   **c.** right angle

2   **a.** 3   **b.** 4   **c.** 2   **d.** 1

Problem: They make a straight line, which is two right angles.

Page 57

1   **a.** Right-angled   **b.** Isosceles   **c.** Equilateral   **d.** Scalene

Brain-teaser:

There are various possibilities. Isosceles triangle must have two sides of the
same length; and the scalene must have sides that are all different lengths.

Page 59

1   A square has sides that are all the same length, whereas a rectangle
only has opposite sides of equal length.

2   All the sides of a rhombus are the same length, whereas only adjacent
sides are equal on a kite.

3   A parallelogram has two pairs of parallel sides, whereas a trapezium
only has one pair of parallel sides.

4

a. Trapezium	b. Parallelogram	c. Kite	d. Rhombus

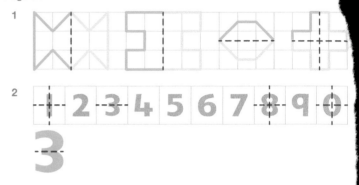

All sides equal. Opposite angles equal.	Adjacent sides equal.	Opposite sides equal. and parallel Opposite angles equal.	Only one pair of parallel sides.

Brain-teaser: A square or a rhombus
Brain-buster: It is possible. Check that the sketch shows the right angle at
the top of the kite, with equal sides in the correct places.

Page 61

1

2

2 3 4 5 6 7 8 9 0

3

3

Brain-teaser:

Brain-buster: H I O X

Page 63

1   **a.** X = (3, 4), Y = (7, 5)
     b. Check that a square has been plotted with these coordinates:
     A (2, 2), B (2, 8), C (8, 8), D (8, 2)

2   **a.** P = (2, 2), Q = (3, 6), R = (6, 3)
     b. Check that a rectangle has been plotted with these coordinates:
     J (1, 1), K (9, 1), L (9, 7), M (1, 7)

Brain-teaser: (7, 5)
Brain-buster: Check that a square has been plotted with these coordinates
A (3, 0), B (3, 4), C (7, 4), D (7, 0) (C and D could be the other way round).

Page 65

1 Check that the points have been plotted correctly:
   W = (4, 5), X = (6, 2), Y = (5, 0), Z = (9, 1)

2 **a.** Check that a triangle has been plotted correctly at these
   coordinates: A (2, 2), B (4, 4), C (4, 2)
   b. Check that a triangle has been plotted correctly at these
   coordinates: A = (5, 7), B = (7, 9), C = (7, 7)
   c. A = (5, 7), B = (7, 9), C = (7, 7)

Brain-teaser: 5 left, 4 down
Brain-buster: Check that a square has been plotted with these coordinates: A
(1, 0), B (1, 3), C (4, 3), D (4, 0).

STATISTICS

Page 67

1 Check that the pictogram has been drawn correctly.

2 **a.** elephant   **b.** lion and zebra   **c.** giraffe and zebra
   d. 180cm   **e.** 300kg   **f.** 6 years   **g.** 5 giraffes

Brain-teaser: lion and zebra
Brain-buster: Yes. The combined weight of all the other animals is 3180kg.

Page 69

1 Mariam

2 27

3 117

4 14

Brain-teaser: Check that the bar chart has been drawn correctly.
Brain-buster: Check that the questions can be answered from the animal bar
chart.

Page 71

1 4am

2 10pm

3 8°C

Brain-teaser: Check that the time graph has been drawn correctly.
Brain-buster: 2 months and 3 weeks

Notes

SCHOLASTIC

National Curriculum
MATHS

A new whole-school primary maths programme

- A complete maths toolkit for teachers: planning, assessment, textbooks, practice activities and ready-made lesson plans

- Cost-effective with no expensive subscription fees or repeat costs

- Flexible and supportive planning resources that will save teachers time

- Accessible and engaging content, fully matched to the maths curriculum for England

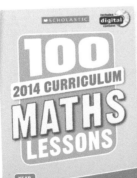

Planning   Lessons   Textbooks   Practice   Assess

scholastic.co.uk/ncmaths